Educational Linguistics/TESOL/ICC
Graduate School of Education
University of Pennsylvania
3700 Walnut Street/Cl
Philadelphia, PA   19104

WHAT ARE PHILOSOPHICAL SYSTEMS?

WHAT ARE PHILOSOPHICAL SYSTEMS?

JULES VUILLEMIN

PROFESSEUR DE PHILOSOPHIE DE LA CONNAISSANCE,
COLLÈGE DE FRANCE

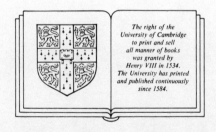

The right of the
University of Cambridge
to print and sell
all manner of books
was granted by
Henry VIII in 1534.
The University has printed
and published continuously
since 1584.

CAMBRIDGE UNIVERSITY PRESS

CAMBRIDGE

LONDON   NEW YORK   NEW ROCHELLE

MELBOURNE   SYDNEY

Published by the Press Syndicate of the University of Cambridge
The Pitt Building, Trumpington Street, Cambridge CB2 1RP
32 East 57th Street, New York, NY 10022, USA
10 Stamford Road, Oakleigh, Melbourne 3166, Australia

First published 1986

Printed in Great Britain at the University Press, Cambridge

British Library cataloguing in publication data
Vuillemin, Jules
What are philosophical systems?
1. Philosophy
I. Title
101   B53

Library of Congress cataloguing in publication data
Vuillemin, Jules.
What are philosophical systems?
Bibliography: p.
Includes index.
1. Methodology. 2. Languages – Philosophy.
3. Ontology. I. Title.
BD241.V85 1986   140′.12   85-24259

ISBN 0 521 30540 3

CONTENTS

PREFACE

In every discipline the order of exposition tends to reverse the order of inquiry.

I began my own inquiry about philosophical systems by reminding myself of what every historian of philosophy knows: namely, that philosophers are divided and that no part of the philosophical enterprise has ever been the object of common agreement. Neither Kant's critique of metaphysics nor the so-called 'scientific method in philosophy' has been successful in bringing peace, or even armistice, to the battlefield. Granting the truth of these statements, I had to seek the reason behind them by examining the nature and origin of philosophy. The systematic form of philosophy was elaborated to answer the ontological question posed by the advent of axiomatics when it jolted the unified world of myth, moulded as it was, by natural language. But all collective communication requires a formal recognition of the material that is perceived by means of the linguistic signs (what Saussure called the 'signifier'). Thus, the question 'How does language make the unity of the sensible world possible?' came to be followed immediately by a question about the structure which is already given at the level of our animal perception.

In this essay my exposition reverses the order of my inquiry. The first chapter will deal with perceptual organization, and the second with language and the sensible world. In the third chapter I shall inquire into the nature and the systematic form of philosophy or rather of philosophies by analysing the relations that ontologies bear to axiomatics. The fourth and last chapter will introduce a classification among philosophical systems whose observed plurality was the starting-point of the inquiry.

The order of exposition, then, deals with a hierarchy of successive achievements, each of which is for the following one a necessary but not a sufficient condition. The forms of perceptual organization give language its building materials, and the first use of language is to communicate perception. But the machinery of communication and publicity produces possibilities which are beyond the power of perception, and there is more in the categories of language than in the forms of perception. Next come the philosophical principles. They will be found to have to the categories of language a relation which is analogous to the relation which the categories of language have to the forms of perception. Philosophical principles are fashioned from linguistic categories and from the primitive elementary sentences by which they are expressed, but on the two conditions that these linguistic categories and sentences should be entitled to claim a universal power of explanation and that they should stand the test of logical consistency. Such great demands make an important difference. In so far as the primitive sentences, various as they are, are spontaneously used, they may be assigned truth-values independently from each other. This does not apply to the philosophical principles that immediately enter into competition with one another for the highest and exclusive prize. This explains why there have been and there are many incompatible philosophical systems. History and present experience suggest that no agreement has been or ever will be reached. But though polemic is still raging in the field, there are none the less some signs of peace, a peace obtained by resignation rather than by victory. Some philosophers have shown themselves to be fully prepared and even quick to change their systems. Others, while they preserve their faith in their proclaimed principles, are more eager to scrutinize and delimit their domain of validity than to criticize rivals. A last effort of classification thus remains to be made. Can all philosophical systems be brought under a finite number of ultimate classes or, in other words, do the philosophical principles enter into a classification as do the primitive elementary linguistic sentences? It is clear that if the latter classification works, applying the ontological and logical transformation which changes the primitive elementary linguistic sentences into philosophical principles will suffice to obtain the new classification that is put forward in this book.

The reader familiar with contemporary analytic philosophy will be surprised that, on the four issues at stake, I contradict widespread views by implication, without discussing them. I deny in the first chapter that language shapes perception, since perception precedes language. In the second chapter, despite the relative autonomy of linguistic organization with respect to perceptual organization and though its collective conceptual stability expresses and embodies, for each particular society, a determinate *Weltanschauung*, i.e., a collective code of classification, I deny that a *Weltanschauung* is a philosophy, since publicity entails neither consistency nor a wish for consistency. In the third chapter, because philosophy and science have a common origin in the discovery of antinomies and in the development of axiomatics, I deny that strong continuity between philosophy and common sense which is advocated by many philosophers of natural language. Finally, when in the last chapter I arrive at the question of philosophical truth, I give my fellow-philosophers the slip and leave them to go further than I do. While they argue for a unique scheme of philosophical truth, I am content with saying what all of these possibilities of truth are.

Nothing is worse than off-hand manners in a philosophical debate. However, I have, in a rather involved argumentation, aimed at clarity and concision. I have had therefore to limit myself to positive reasons. Where I could not escape negative justifications, I have put them in the notes. As to philosophical truth, it is clear that, if my prudence is justified, the plurality of philosophies makes the concept of philosophical truth inadequate and inappropriate, at least if the word *truth* is used in its ordinary sense. I have not, however, settled this fundamental question; I have not even explicitly brought it up. In the end I have nothing better to offer my reader than a prudence fraught with risks and further queries.

I am grateful for the assistance, especially with the English, given to me by Jasper Hopkins, Michel Blais, Thomas Morran and Gilles Granger. Their patience was sorely tried by the progress of my manuscript.

1 | PERCEPTUAL ORGANIZATION

The largest part of the present chapter deals with the question: what are the experienced relations which organize perception, and how do they expand so that in agreement with the evolution of the higher central nervous system they culminate both in simulating life-surroundings and in planning actions? The principles of organization will be shown to apply to the data so as to produce appearances of a given kind, and then to reapply to these appearances so as to yield appearances of yet another kind, until, no further innovation being yielded in this way, the process is put to an end and perceptual organization is considered complete. The diverse kinds of appearances that will be thus distinguished (qualities of position and of state, images and representations) are biologically useful only because they are given an objective interpretation. This description is then followed by two discussions. The first is about the kind of symbolic forms that span perceptual organization: have we to accept the claim of these forms to objectivity or must we rather interpret them in terms of subjective signals? The second discussion will concern what is wanting in perceptual organization for making group communication possible.

Though the following description of perceptual organization is systematic, it only aims at sketching the phenomenology of sensible appearances. It must be distinguished from psycho-physiology as well as from developmental psychology and philosophical constitution. Psycho-physiology may have to criticize as illusions some well-established appearances or even their general pretension to objectivity. Developmental psychology may show that items which are simple for phenomenological descriptions lack genetic priority altogether. Lastly the description is philosophically neutral between kinds of logical commitments or choices between 'physicalist' and 'phenomenological' bases. Phenomenology does not try to reduce qualities to sets of things, or things to sets of qualities. We perceive 'abstract' qualia and 'concrete' particulars and the same stimulus may be felt now as a pure colour, now as the colour of a thing, and the only question is to what level of organization qualities as such and properties as supported by things belong.

All we need is that the categories of appearances we shall distinguish do in fact correspond to our subjective experience and exhaust it. Since we describe the appearances, we do not have to decide the question whether a quality would be better construed as a class of things or a thing as a class of qualities, as long as both qualities and things are found among genuine appearances.

Some preliminary remarks may be useful for exhibiting the traits of the phenomenological method.

(1) We would be lost among the immense variety of the events which constitute the world if we were not able to extract from it an order and an arrangement such that all that variety entered into a manageable number of classes or types of connection. In the course of discussing the question why we conceive with more stability and vividness the idea of an effect when our perception is presented with a cause, Hume found as a general law ruling the operations of our mind that the same reinforcement of vividness occurs with the two other kinds of association: when we are presented with an impression, the idea that is associated with it by contiguity or resemblance will also be more stable and vivid.[1] In the same way, the types of connection which will be described by the phenomenological method are characterized by the vividness with which they are experienced, while in ordinary circumstances sensations as well as their integrating mechanisms escape our conscious attention.

(2) These types of connection may be divided into two principal levels. Writing on the association of ideas, Hume already recognized the same implicit division. When he defines a cause as 'an object, followed by another, and where all the objects similar to the first are followed by objects similar to the second',[2] he relies on contiguity and similarity as elements of the new association to be integrated by habit. Thus contiguity and resemblance are, for Hume, first-level associations, while causality is a higher-level association.[3] An analoguous distinction is found in the *Critique of Pure Reason*, where Kant, clearly reminiscent of Hume, opposes to the mathematical categories of quantity and quality the dynamical categories of relation and modality. The mathematical categories establish simple and direct connections of *compositio* between homogeneous elements given by intuition and do not, by themselves, lay claim to ascertaining anything beyond intuition, that is, beyond subjective determinations of our faculty to be affected. On the contrary, the dynamical categories build complex and indirect connections of *nexus* between heterogeneous elements (like substance and its accidents or cause and its effect), one of which is not given by intuition but is inferred as existent by an act of synthesis productive of the analogies of experience.[4] The two levels of perceptual organization which we shall recognize correspond to

Hume's and Kant's distinction, with, however an important reservation. Although they disagree about the necessity of causal connection and the hypothesis of a pure reason, Hume and Kant admit a common principle, according to which perception and science follow the same rules. For Hume, there is identity between the object of experience and experience; and for Kant, there is identity between the possibility of the object of experience and the possibility of experience. This principle is not a part of the present method, which therefore does not prevent science from contradicting not only the possibility of experience but also actual schemes of experience so well entrenched in our habits as to make their revision completely unexpected.[5]

(3) The phenomenological method refrains from inquiring into the causes and the mechanisms of these types of connection and their levels. However, since they describe human perceptual organization, a reasonable hypothesis is ready to hand, according to which the peculiar evolution of our species must account for this organization. Following from this hypothesis, the human types of connection and their levels could be neither *a priori* categories nor products of idiosyncrasies, but must be specific adaptations selected by evolution. It should be fruitful, then, to compare them with the corresponding perceptual organizations characteristic of other species or groups. Answering to our phenomenological description, the objective technique of comparative physiology and especially ethology would make possible experiments showing that the types and levels of connections with which we have been endowed by heredity, and which therefore seem 'the' natural way of perceiving the world, are neither universal nor necessary.[6] Though these themes will not be developed here, and though they depend on a hypothesis that is natural but foreign to phenomenology, they may be called upon to offset the feeling of obviousness and self-evidence we get from the routine business of our perception.

(4) Whenever a part of an experience is able to evoke the whole of the experience, the part is said to be a sign. The given impression which a type of connection characteristic of perception associates with a class of actual or possible impressions is such a sign, and a natural one, which will be called *a signal*, in the sense that the association works in the same way for all the members of our species without requiring the particular conventions of a social group. The question will thus arise as to the relations between the natural signals of perception and human language.

2 A DESCRIPTION OF PERCEPTUAL ORGANIZATION

The first level of organization: signals of position and qualities of state
The first and simplest classificatory level of perception is governed by two

main principles. Among appearances there are (1) an order of contiguity and (2) an arrangement of resemblance.

It is easy to show that both the order and the arrangement lack determination and depend on respects or points of view which change with the present interests of perception. Everything is contiguous to everything else. Even once we have dismissed the contiguities which we produce by remembering or by fancying, we may wonder whether we count a cloud and a roof as contiguous or not accordingly as we perceive them as patches of colour or as things. In the same way, everything resembles everything else and there is always a way in which the most disparate things may be said to be similar.

This indetermination disappears as soon as we explicitly take account of the point of view or of the *modulus* of the relations – we borrow the word from mathematics and mechanics by twisting its meaning in order to avoid speaking of modalities, a term already invested in philosophy with another sense. It is specific and always relative to a domain or a sub-domain of impressions. The question whether two contents of experience are contiguous or similar is settled when we decide that the contiguity bears on colour patches and that the resemblance deals with musical notes or, more precisely, with their loudness, their pitch or their quality.

That they are bound to a modulus is a characteristic of the relations of contiguity and resemblance and accounts for the simplicity and the homogeneity of what these relations will produce. At this first level of perceptual organization only impressions belonging to a same sense or even to the same modality of a given sense are connected, so that the emerging order or arrangement will be only partial. Now, partiality entails imperfect or deferred objectivity. The modulus means not only that determinations which would be necessary to make up an object are lacking, but that we are given determinations as floating pieces not moored to an object at all. If there is a claim of objectivity inasmuch as something is told us about a real external diversity, there is, none the less, no commitment that would call for a thing referred to.

We perceive positions and qualities as such in a pure state when we awake out of a narcosis or a deep dream. Every time a conflict arises in our perception of objects, we try to analyse them into those positions and qualities. Many psychological tests produce and study them under experimental set-ups. French impressionism in painting even aimed at training perception to dismiss objects in favour of qualities.

Finally, it is the same given diversity which is organized by contiguity and resemblance. Because of this organization the impressions are inserted into a multiplicity of orders and arrangements that make them signals for other impressions. Here it is necessary to introduce a distinction, the origin of which is logical but which will be shown to have its direct phenomenological expression. Contiguity will not go beyond signal impressions, because of the formal properties characteristic of contiguity relations: they cannot determine equivalence classes. A given impression A, by being the neighbour of an impression B or by being to the right of an impression B or by being part of an impression B, is indeed perceived as standing for the impression B. But this standing for does not go beyond signalization, since both terms of the relation must be effectively given. On the contrary, in the case of resemblance, one impression is not a mere signal of the other. Since perfect resemblance is an equivalence relation, it results in the specific appearance we call a quality of state, even when only one term of the relation is given, while the corresponding qualities of position will merely develop at the second level of perceptual organization, where they constitute the first class of images.

Either impressions associated by contiguity are actually given, or the given impression is connected with another impression which has almost disappeared and is retained as a shadowy presence. The word *contiguity* is understood in a spatial and in a temporal sense.[7] Strictly speaking, two impressions would be said to be contiguous if and only if the whole experience to which they belonged could be divided into two and only two parts. The existence of perceptual thresholds gives sense to this definition. Ordinarily we weaken the restriction to simple impressions and we mean contiguous groups of impressions – two neighbouring patches of colour, for instance. Such a relation is irreflexive, symmetric and intransitive. Such formal properties are too weak to determine the multiple orders that are offered by perceived impressions. To illustrate contiguity, Hume says that 'the mention of one apartment in a building naturally introduces an inquiry or a discourse concerning the others'.[8] Now, two apartments on the same floor, when separated by another apartment, are not contiguous, and an apartment in the attic of an apartment house is not contiguous to a first-floor apartment. Let us then imitate Hume and conceive contiguity as covering two-term relations such as neighbourhood, the relations of whole–part, left–right, and before–after, as well as three-term relations such as betweenness and alignment. Most of the contiguities where more than three terms are concerned are mixed with resemblance, a commonplace of *Gestalt*-psychology. Many among the two-term relations covered by contiguity are irreflexive, antisymmetric and transitive, and therefore generate series, a fundamental type of order.

The appearance produced by contiguity consists in signals of relative dispositions and positions of impressions. But, because of the modulus pertaining to a sensorial organ, the signals of position thus determined are endowed with an absolute character. Up and down, left and right are fixed in our visual field because of the axial symmetry common to our species. The continuous temporal extinction of vividness gives a unique and absolute orientation from before to after.

What makes this absolute determination possible is the constant though generally only partial presence of a discriminated impression of position. All other signals of position are centred around it as around their constant but changing referential point and thus make a complete and gapless but also changing picture. I shall call this distinguished impression my own position when I have localized my own position in space.

Tactile, visual, and kinaesthetic signals differ among themselves as much as their respective moduli do. Some painters have known how to express the possible distortion of these heterogeneous orders. Places – and moments – remain beyond the reach of simple contiguity. Modulated and isolated as they are, the signals of position do, however, allow us to collect, to individualize, to mark off. Marking off is facilitated when contiguous impressions contrast. The contour which delimits them is enhanced, an enhancement which enables us to recognize things in outline drawings. According to Hume, contrast or contrariety results from a mixture of causation and resemblance: 'where two objects are contrary, the one destroys the other; that is, the cause of its annihilation, and the idea of the annihilation of an object, implies the idea of its former existence'.[9] Such contrasts belong to the second, objective level of perceptual organization. Thus nightfall drives out day.[10] There are contrasts, however, that arise at the first level of perceptual organization and lack any existential inference. When a homogeneous black area faces a homogeneous white area, there is no play of causality. The impressions are rather distributed into three classes: (a) those which are impressions of black and are contiguous only with similar impressions, (b) those which are impressions of white and are contiguous only with similar impressions, and (c) those which are terms of a relation of contiguity holding between impressions not belonging to the same similarity class. Salience of contours seems thus to be reducible to a combination of contiguity and resemblance.[11]

Resemblance, though often reproached for its fuzziness, enables us to appreciate with high precision the sameness of two impressions or two groups of impressions as soon as the modulus of comparison is completely fixed. The principle of such an appreciation has been formulated by Bouguer, the founder of photometry.[12] If we want to determine what sameness of impressions is relatively to illumination, we have to give up not only the absurd question of whether two people see the same degree of illumination, but also the phenomenologically dubious question of whether the same person in front of three different degrees of illumination a, b, c, sees the distance between a and b as identical with the distance between b and c[13] in order to concentrate on the question of whether the same person sees two different illuminations as equal or as having the same degree.

This phenomenological fact has been of tremendous importance for the development of physics. The three elements to which statics had reduced the so-called 'primary' qualities, namely, number, length and weight, either immediately by counting individuals or indirectly by using measuring rods or weighting the scales of a balance, obey the laws governing magnitudes. On the other hand, no magnitude seems to correspond to 'secondary' qualities such as colours, sounds, and odours, because there is no clear convention at hand that would allow us to assign definite units and define the operation of addition. Because our sense organ knows, however, how to decide which impressions are indistinguishable, we may – on condition of weak assumptions about a functional relation between impressions and stimuli – use it as a null instrument. The stimuli responsible for the 'secondary' qualities are thus subjected to a weak order, which the ordinary routine of physical hypotheses will transform into full measurement. In this way, we need no other criterion than matching impressions for showing that 'any three different colored lights whatsoever (except if one of the three can be matched by mixing the other two) can always be mixed in the correct proportion to produce any color whatsoever'.[14]

Since a match is nothing else than a perfect modulated resemblance, each impression or group of impressions is a possible match for another impression or group of impressions. In a relation of contiguity the terms have to be actual, because contiguity requires that. In order to acquire the value of signalling another impression an impression must in that case be actually given together with what it signals. The relation of resemblance, on the contrary, makes actual impressions or groups of impressions signals for other simply virtual impressions or groups of impressions, which may be scattered over parts of experience not actually presented by any conscious act of memorization. Such signals are even referred to virtual models or norms. Pure tones and pure colours play this normative role, though it is difficult to describe with accuracy the feelings we get from them.[15]

When an impression or a group of impressions functions as a signal for absent referred-to impressions, we tend to feel the signal as such in the given impression and we interpret it as a definite quality. This specific appearance is due to the formal properties of matching or rather to the exploitation that our psychological make-up makes of them. The relation of modulated resemblance is indeed symmetrical and transitive – and therefore reflexive – and thus constitutes an equivalence relation given a sensorial modulus. Now phenomenology obeys a principle of abstraction, according to which

whenever a relation, of which there are instances, has the two properties of being symmetrical and transitive, then the relation in question [is not meant to be] primitive, [but seems to be] analysable into sameness of relation to some other term; and this common relation is such that there is only one term at most to which a given term can be so related, though many terms may be so related to a given term.[16]

When I hear a pianist and a singer producing the F sharp in the middle of the keyboard, the two impressions, though completely different in musical quality and perhaps in intensity, completely resemble one another in pitch. What I feel therefore is the same pitch quality. Then when I hear one of these impressions, I spontaneously forget in my concrete feeling the modalities of loudness and musical quality to abstract the pitch quality, which in fact refers to an equivalence class of which all the other terms are missing.

These qualities, called qualities of state, specify, repeat, and assimilate. Their striking repeatability introduces potential universals into perceptual organization. I say *potential*, because these qualities are always given in a particular group of impressions, and perception has no means of severing them from their particular context, a performance reserved for language. Now, although the qualities of state are defined relatively to a sensorial modulus and, from this point of view, do not differ from contiguous signals, whereas these signals are felt as centred around our own signals of position, there is, in accordance with the requirements of repeatability, no such felt dependence for the qualities of state. We certainly feel qualities of our own state – tactile, kinaesthetic, internal, thermic, and so on – not to speak of pleasures and pains. But when we suffer from jaundice we do not confound a real yellow with the yellowness which we project on to all the colours. Despite the uncertainties that affect the apprehensions of 'objective' qualities as such, and though we perceive the same water as warmer or colder according to whether we touch it with our cold hands or with our warm elbow, a distinction is nevertheless maintained in the world of appearances between the quality of cold and the quality of being cold.

Many elementary biological reactions may be explained by an organism's being given such signals of position and such qualities of state. There have been philosophers, like Russell, who admit as basic only such meagre propositions as 'Redness at the right upper part of the visual field'. They needlessly place too much of the burden upon language and not enough upon perception. Though their claim may be true for the universe of a frog,[17] it misses the mark with regard to animals closer to us. Still, the perceptual basis for such propositions is lacking at the first level of organization which I have just described. Signals correspond to verbs, not to nouns. We need qualities of position. More generally, we need a higher level of perceptual organization for coordinating our action.

The second level of organization: images and representations

The *compositio* to which contiguity – and resemblance – types belong was direct, homogeneous and intuitive. The signals of position and the qualities of state that they produced have not yet attained to the status of internal and stable associations. It is often the case that the simple application of an act of synthesis fails to bring to light its full potential. It can happen, however, that a second application of the same act to its original products does actualize its hidden virtue. Hence the method by which we get sensible objects as given in perception is at hand. The same relations of contiguity and resemblance are to be reapplied to the signals of position and to the qualities of state themselves. Higher-order signals will then arise, characteristic of a *nexus*, where something stands for something else which, indirectly given if at all and heterogeneous as it is, may lay claim to an autonomous existence.

When applied to signals of position, contiguity and resemblance produce *images*. They produce *representations* when applied to qualities of state. Images determine the form, and representations determine the content of the object.

Appearances of modulated places and moments only arise when we group together similar signals of position. A group x of impressions is situated at the right upper part of the visual field – the conventions concerning grouping of thresholds being agreed on – if and only if all impressions z which are contiguous to x are to the left of x or below x, a condition that we abbreviate into: 'all z have the relation T to x'. Then two groups of impressions, x and y, are resemblant relatively to the right upper part of the visual field if and only if, for all z, if zTx, then zTy. But, according to the principle of abstraction, if two groups of impressions are resemblant relatively to the right upper part of the visual field, they occupy the same right and upper part of the visual field, i.e. the same modulated place. In the same way, a modulated moment may be defined by the grouping of all impressions belonging to a given modulus such that all the impressions belonging to the same modulus which have immediately preceded them presented no relation of succession among themselves. Such 'places' and 'moments' are merely modulated qualities of position, and it may require training before they will be seen to give way to discriminate appearances. Thus, except in simplified situations, it requires attention to distinguish, with Helmholtz, the absolute field of vision (*Sehfeld*), whose qualities are simultaneously presented to the resting eye and therefore are common to every visual perception; the glancing field of vision (*Blickfeld*), whose qualities are associated with the motions of the eyes; and the looking field of vision (*Gesichtsfeld*), whose qualities vary with the motion of the head.[18] The more specific the kind of connection relative to their moduli, the more necessary it becomes to give an accurate description of these qualities of position. Different moduli indeed obey different rules, and contiguity or simultaneity may entail either diversity as when we hear as separate the notes of a chord, or sameness, as when we compose colours, the result being then a determinate and unique colour whose appearance retains nothing of the diversity of the components.[19]

Although it is possible to define some 'geometrical' qualities and some 'modulated' spaces – at least at the level of a rudimentary *Analysis situs* – by matching well-chosen signals of position, either the characteristic quality of extension as a given simultaneous diversity remains beyond the construction when visual perception is not used, or, when it is used, the appearances give only a partial space, because space requires intersensorial appearances.[20] Another type of connection is needed to get geometrical appearances and space, and qualities of position have to be subjected to a new association by contiguity.

Here the question should be discussed whether and in what sense modulated qualities of position, like modulated qualities of state, are potential universals, what relation if any they have to a distinguished referential, and finally how both the order transferred from the signals to the qualities of position and the arrangement of the qualities of position unite to produce phenomena. On all these points, however, nothing will be lost and greater clarity will be gained when the qualities of position have been freed from their moduli. The whole question can therefore be postponed until pp. 14ff.

We will be said to perceive free qualities of position once we no longer need to have recourse to a particular modulus, such as the partition of the absolute field of vision or the kinaesthetic organization of the glancing field, to condition and to fix the resemblance relation between signals of position. In other words the match between impressions relevant to a given modulus must be extended to a match between all the different moduli. However, this second matching cannot result from a comparison by resemblance, because there is no common element between signals of position belonging to different senses or to different sensorial modalities.[21] Nor can it be the product of a raw relation of contiguity, because it does not suffice that places relevant to the absolute field, to the glancing field and to the looking field of vision be co-present, or bound by togetherness for giving rise to the *sui generis* appearance of the same visual place. *A fortiori*, kinaesthetic places, tactile places, visual places and auditive places need some new type of connection in order to appear as full and simple places. The same reflection applies to moments.

An extra condition is therefore required of contiguity to do the job of de-modalizing the qualities of position. Places – and moments – are indeed freed from their moduli only when the corresponding modulated places – and moments – have been put into coincidence or superposition. Then, but only then, the overlapping of qualities of position belonging to different senses leads to what was once called 'common sense' – the *sensus communis* of the ancients[22] – and the association by contiguity of all their common qualities integrates them into a surrounding whole. Upon this particular type of connection rests the appearance of geometric qualities and of space.

Now, the nature of this connection becomes apparent as soon as we try to describe how we perceive geometrical properties. Poincaré rightly derived the most striking among them, length invariance, from our manipulation of solids. He meant that lengths and consequently sensible sizes were invariant relatively to the group of rigid motions.[23] As to the mechanism he put at the basis of congruence, it relies on a specific association by active contiguity aimed at restoring a destroyed passive contiguity. To simplify Poincaré's description, two rods are congruent or, according to the principle of abstraction, have the same length, when we can always cancel a change arising in our passive visual or tactile impressions (a motion of the rod, for instance a displacement of a given quality of position – a relatively short and narrow aligned set of points – in the absolute field of vision) by a compensating change in our kinaesthetic impressions (our own motion, or better the counter-displacement of our glancing field produced by the motion of our eyes). In short, the group theoretical properties required by the appearance of length belong to the relation of contiguity because the axiom of the inverse element is empirically realized by the distribution of passive and active impressions into compensating perceptual modalities.

From a phenomenological point of view, Poincaré's description is too narrow. Other geometrical invariants are given us. We feel some qualities of position as geometrically similar or having the same form. Since it is only Euclidian geometry which admits that the group of rigid motions may be embedded into a group of similitudes, this important appearance assures us of the Euclidian character of our perception – an assurance which conflicts neither with the possibility of a non-Euclidian partial mechanism of sensorial information nor with the possibility of non-Euclidian physical space. Besides congruence and parallelism, we are able to feel invariants of order, of incidence or of comparability between two unequal magnitudes of which the lesser, if repeatably added to itself, succeeds in exceeding the greater. The fundamental notions characteristic of a natural geometry emerge from our manipulation of solids complemented by our ability to build reduced-scale models. Sizes and forms, topological and projective relations, the Archimedean axiom itself, arise as constituent parts of our behaviour. Now, since these different geometrical qualities are all invariants relative to definite groups of transformations (whose relations constitute the real object of geometry), we may extend Poincaré's description by considering compensatory motions that regard relations of position more general than congruence. To test, for instance, whether two shapes have the same form, we have to orient our sense organs, helped by our memories, in such a way that all corresponding angles are seen in 'coincidence' (all the paired sides of the two shapes are seen as parallel), or, if the forms are symmetrical, we must fix the axis of symmetry so that one shape becomes the reflected image of the other. The compensatory motions necessary to compensate a given difference of orientation may be difficult. They may be beyond the adjustments which are at the disposition of our psycho-physiological make-up. Only a proper part of geometrical qualities is thus visualized in appearances, and the correspondence is still looser between projective and topological groups of transformation and perceived qualities. But this is to be expected if a revolution of thought is needed to pass from perception to science, and the discrepancies begin with the appreciations of length that strongly depend on the absolute orientation of our visual field.

Once compensation has been recognized as the type of contiguity connection which is required for perceiving qualities of position, two questions remain to be answered: (1) In what sense are these qualities of position repeatable universals? (2) Such qualities being the objective invariants which, as configurations of compensated passive impressions, correspond to groups of motions, does any appearance correspond to the active and compensating impressions belonging to the correlated group of motions?

(1) On a first examination of the first question, the qualities of position are, as potential universals, entirely comparable to the qualities of state. Both of them repeat. Both are abstracted from the same complete and concrete impressions from which they cannot be really separated. There is, however, an important difference between them, and it is most apparent when we perceive a receding file of geometrical equal areas. Consider a long alley of trees. Our feeling that the paired trees remain equally distant is paradoxically

given through the impression that the lines of the alley converge. Or consider the representation of a pavement in a Renaissance painting. Two receding squares are felt as equal only if, according to the law of perspective, they are figured by certain trapezoids. What is surprising here is not the felt constancy of distances or areas – a feeling which we shall find again when analysing the constancy of qualities of state – but the fact that a quality of position is given as constant, i.e. as repeatable, through the given appearance of its systematic deformations. The phenomenological 'objective' datum, namely the constancy of the quality, is given through phenomenologically 'subjective' variations, and both belong to the structure of appearances. Moreover, the law of perspective is suited to dictating the changes which are expected from constant appearances of position when they recede in space. The appearances felt as subjective signals are therefore nothing other than the correction which an objective order of qualities of position requires to *appear* as constant. Freed by contiguity from their modulus, the qualities of position may be called *images*. What indeed are images, if not a lawlike correspondence according to which through a given datum some more stable quality is intended, where we interpret the datum as a subjective signal for the absent, but objectively interpreted, quality? Qualities of position, therefore, offer a typical instance of images, since a variable datum must be compensated for in order to stand for some geometrical invariant. When the systematic division between felt and apparent constancies is better observed, two different but correlated laws of compensation are seen to cooperate, one governing the relations between the apparent trapezoids of the pavement, the other transforming them into tiles felt to be equal. The products of such complicated imagery would be better labelled *schemes* than *images*. This growing complexity, however, does not alter the identity of procedures.[24]

Here it will be asked what group of motions leaves invariant a temporal quality such as a melodic or a rhythmic *Gestalt*? In the simplest case of a childish ritournelle a simple sequence of notes is repeated, and the end of a sequence is like a compensation restoring the initial impressions. The restoration, however, conflicts with our memory that we have heard a never-erased succession of notes. A peculiar feeling accompanying temporal qualities stems from a restoration made imperfect since there is no possible superposition of different times. A second melodic or rhythmic start is only like the first, is always perceived as distinct from it, and our only sense of temporal perspective is due to our memories' growing fainter and fainter. Such a rudimentary organization prevents a full development of temporal images and schemes, which cannot, except by borrowing,[25] compete with spatial qualities.

In contradistinction to the universals we found in the qualities of state, images and schemes clearly show that and how they are always referred to a distinguished centre of coordinates, namely to our own quality of position. The scission of appearances into phenomenologically subjective signals and phenomenologically objective qualities results from this reference. This scission, however, is still relevant to two different appearances bound to my own position. A first appearance will merely sum up the subjective feelings arising from the compensatory motions whose group structure was responsible for the geometrical invariants. In this sense, we say that all qualities of motion such as slow and fast are estimated from corrections taking account of the direction of the motions relatively to my own position. Such an appearance of my own position will be simply relative to the 'objective' appearances of all other qualities of position, and its description will answer the second question concerning the kind of 'subjective' appearances bound to groups of motions. Nothing in this answer will bypass the framework of the application of a particular relation of contiguity, namely compensation, to the signals of position. The other appearance relative to the places and moments will only arise when we have reached another phenomenological level, on which the relation of resemblance applies to the qualities of position.

(2) When we look out of the window of a moving train, we normally see the landscape at rest, through subjective appearances of its running away. How is it that we are prevented from interpreting the displacements of the retinal image due to the motions of our eyes as motions of perceived things? Two complementary illusions may help us understand what our own kinaesthetic impressions contribute to perceiving motion.

On one hand, passive motions of our eyeball, when it is moved with a finger, for instance, produce the appearance of an objective motion of the external things in the opposite direction. Since the passive and therefore unnoticed rotation of the eyeball is ignored by perception, we must 'conclude' – to use Helmholtz's expression – that the noticed retinal displacement of the image is caused by a motion of the world in the opposite direction.

On the other hand, when a man suffering from paralysis of the eye muscles tries to look in the hindered direction, he sees the external things springing in the sense of the intended but uneffected rotation of the eyeball. Here perception is not conscious of paralysis, and supposes that the order issued from the brain is obeyed and that the eyeball moves in the expected direction; the external world is therefore supposed to accompany the motion, but, since the retinal image remains at the same place, the missing change which was expected in consequence of an active eye motion and was to be interpreted in terms of a subjective motion gives way to the illusion of a springing landscape.[26]

In normal cases, we anticipate a change by effecting an intended motion. The landscape is seen at rest when to the perceived change there correspond active motions of our eyes which should make us expect it. We see it in motion if no active motion of our eyes elicits in us an expectation of the change and compensates in this way for the displacement of the retinal image. Thus, in a broad sense, a motion is felt as subjective or as objective, accordingly to whether it is expected or unexpected. The distinction on which Poincaré rightly insisted between active and passive impressions is fundamental to deciding on the interpretation of appearances, be its result adequate or illusory.

Although the active motions to which the appearance of my own position is bound are very specific, the ways external qualities of position and my own position appear – as has just been described – are by no means opposed. Both are potential universals, both are relative to one other, and my own position is merely the subjective and active counterpart of the external qualities of position, a counterpart of which it makes no more sense to ask whether it can be felt as an absolute appearance than for its passive correlate. To ask such a question, a new level of analysis is necessary.

Geometers see the preceding description as exhausting the qualities of position and as sufficient to determine places and moments. Hence Poincaré wrote that we perceive bodies, not space:[27] that experiments bear on the relations of the bodies between themselves, and never on the relations of the bodies with space or on the mutual relations of the diverse parts of space.[28] Therefore, there is no particular question concerning the constituents of space, namely, places, which has not been already solved, when the question about qualities of position has been answered. Not perceived in itself, space is nothing other than a concept of a group. Indeed, nothing but groups of compensation are needed to explain all concluded properties of space, such as its homogeneity, its three-dimensionality, its infinity, etc.[29] A similar explanation could be given for symmetry, another determination sometimes advanced to show the irreducibility of spatial intuition.[30]

Now, doubts arise when we examine just what problem it is that Poincaré solved. This problem, which had been advanced and partially solved by Helmholtz and Lie, consisted in seeking for a law allowing the construction of space from punctual, i.e. non-spatial, impressions. 'None among our isolated sensations would have been able to lead us to the idea of space; we are brought to it only by studying the laws according to which these sensations follow one after the other.'[31] Perception of space thus has nothing primitive about it, since we derive it from a group law connecting successive impressions. This remarkable construction, however, explains all the geometrical qualities of space without accounting for its most striking appearance. In contradistinction to the other geometrical qualities, geometrical places are given indeed as a simultaneous unique totality containing all its parts *in actu*, and not only *in potentia*. In other words, the parts of space are situated in it and not subsumed under it, as is each instance under its corresponding potential universal. This peculiar appearance is, to use Kant's terminology, what distinguishes intuitions from concepts.[32]

Most attempts to capture what specifies intuition have failed, for they have underestimated the power of concepts. This happened when intuition was claimed to be at the base of the law that two colours could not be in the same place at the same time. The same illusion often arose when people explained differences of behaviour by different species with respect to their orientation by urging an advance of intuition depending on the substitution of a more peripheral by a more centrally 'represented space'.[33] In both cases it will be shown that a concept explains what was thought to be a prerogative of intuition.

The simplest way of seeing what is at stake in this discussion is to sketch the main arguments of both parties in a kind of antithetic of imagination. Then the two concepts of place which are thus required will be to hand and it will become possible to decide which of them plays a part in the phenomenology of perception.

Let us use signals and qualities of position to delimit and fix a certain volume. The qualities of state that are associated with it are said to fill it. Let us call a *content* such an association. A content is nothing but the reunification of the analysed elements of our impressions. Its usefulness regards the mutual variations of its constituents, since we perceive motion when different qualities of state come to fill the same volume. Now, everybody agrees on that description of the perception of motion, but some say that such a description is neither determinate nor complete. Here is the origin of the antithetic of imagination.

Antithetic of imagination

1	Places are completely independent of contents.	Places depend on contents.
2	Relations between places are invariant.	The so-called relations between places are nothing but relations between contents and vary with them.
3	The total sum of places is the absolute and simultaneous space.	The potential order making contents simultaneous is a relative space.

4 Places are in space as in their container.	Contents are subsumed under space as under a law.
5 We imagine space as an infinite given magnitude.	We imagine space by a progression repeated *in infinitum*.
6 There are absolute motions.	All motions are relative.
7 A motion is absolute when the mobile changes its place.	Motion is the dissociation between qualities of state and qualities of position.

Both parties would admit that the set of all interchangeable qualities of state within a same fixed volume defined a necessary condition for being a place if, in addition, some salient relation of position with the other former contents were preserved, while new qualities of state flowed through the fixed volume and shaped a *Gestalt* strong enough to stabilize a framework of reference.

Such a weak concept suffices to account for the law excluding two different colours from the same place. As given on the simple level of the absolute field of vision, colours indeed cannot be seen except as next to one another and separately. Exclusion by places adds nothing to exclusion in a modulated space, except the association of compensation, which is not relevant here. As to the role of the centrally represented space, the power of surveying a multiplicity of data makes a difference, since it allows noticing a greater number of relations of position and therefore anchoring more firmly the required framework of reference. However, this has nothing to do with the antithetic of imagination.

The question is whether stronger conditions must be given for defining places. Aristotle answers positively when he considers that whole contents are needed to fill places and to flow through them, a place being the same 'innermost boundary' of these contents and a boundary that is motionless.[34] Places and space are then what remains when we abstract any content from our impressions. Places are completely independent of contents. Consequently, Caius and Sextus may change their relative places, but the place where Caius stood and the place where Sextus stood remain unmovable. All the other assertions which constitute the thesis of the absolute space follow in the same way. Such absolute places contrast with the universals which fill them. (1) Their diversity does not require a corresponding diversity of impressions, since all this diversity has been emptied with the contents. (2) Though the places belong to the qualities of position, their diversity does not rely on compensation, since there would be no compensation without mutually compensating impressions.

The decision about the antithetic may be made from two different points of view.

From the point of view of truth, since places, as absolute positions, have no conceptual and therefore no universal foundation, they are mere illusions, which should melt away with what a geometer called 'the Ego extinction'.[35] This is the meaning of Poincaré's statement that experiments bear neither on the relations of bodies to space nor on the mutual relations of spaces. If we admit that space is absolute, I can stay at the same place though all my impressions have changed from a first to a second instant view. But how can I identify this place, if, when I perceive the second view and I situate myself in it, I do not keep any record of my former situation and I do not make any comparison between my past and my present impressions? The idea of an absolute change of position results from the contradictory supposition that all the contents have been dismissed but that signals of position remain anchored relatively to me.[36]

The point of view of appearance is still open. From this point of view, the relative and conceptual reconstruction which supposes the ego in the world among the other objects is only half the truth. The world is also in the ego in the sense that, for localizing contents, I resort to an act of showing. Could ego's position in the world be assigned without a prior assignment of the world's position with respect to ego? When we account for appearances, the appearance of places in an absolute space where we perceive the contents is the same as an indexed container or a 'subjective form', in Kant's sense.[37]

This interpretation, peculiar to appearances themselves, is thus bound up with a datum which no geometrical axiom and no science may express: I stay on a determinate spot, here is my present place. This place I can show, but I cannot describe it. Owing to this place the perspective order through which I am able to assert the constancy of qualities of position becomes determinate. The centrally 'represented' space is then transformed into a full image, of which my own position is the movable centre. Still this movable centre is moored on immovable contents whose apparent relations never change and authorize my changing view to refer to 'motionless boundaries'. Without such a view and without such a non-extinguishable view there would be no such thing as appearance.

Events, i.e. changes of contents, appear to be localized in the moments of absolute time in the same way as contents themselves appear localized in the places of absolute space, except for these important differences between *now* and *here*: now is never fixed, and the mutual exclusion between moments and moments on the one hand, and places and places on the other, obeys different laws which give the intuitions of space and time their specific characteristics.

While signals of position and qualities of state floated on this side of the opposition between subjectivity and objectivity, qualities of position as well as places and moments raised a first ontological claim. Images and schemes developed into the assertion of invariant qualities given through appearances felt as subjective. As to places and moments, they constitute a universal container for objects. There is thus a complete framework awaiting the appearance of objects. But that is not all: there is more. There is an association by compensation produced by the demodalization of the geometrical invariants: size, form, projective order and so on. Although these invariants, as mere qualities of position, are still not localized in space as real objects are, as soon as they are combined with qualities of state to constitute contents they are projected into places and moments. This projection brings into play a remarkable transmutation in the way the two components of a content appear to us. Inasmuch as they are localized, qualities of state as well as qualities of position are indeed transformed into properties of a content. Henceforth they are felt as its colour or its form, for example.

As changes of such contents, events go a step further. Changing qualities of state and qualities of position are associated into more or less durably and determinately connected bundles, which are given a location – and, according to their composition, a changing location – within the general order of space and time. Events themselves are loose and transitory units. But in so far as they are considered as units, they are not mere juxtapositions of qualities of state and images. They already anticipate what will be the rule at a higher and more general level of perceptual organization, where permanent objects will be represented by properties or instances localized at various places and moments.

The contrast between images and representations is a threefold one. Firstly, in the domain of images, impressions were classed as active or passive; in the domain of schemes, qualities of position were divided into 'subjective' and 'objective' qualities. Both distributions intended to present us with a simple, directly given, appearance. The correlation by which images bind impressions bypasses the power of elementary contiguity, but all impressions can still equally and homogeneously be used as signals. In representation, the appearances will all be referred to an object which they indirectly represent. This indirect way of representing does not mean that some subjective manifestations should be related to their object by means of an intellectual argument; the manifestations are rather felt as the immediate signals of their transcending things. Subordination and specialization replace correlation and assign impressions one of two roles: representing or being represented. Secondly, while places and moments were only given in the wholes we called space and time, the diversity of properties or instances will, in representations, be subsumed under the unity of a potential universal. A part is seen by intuition in its whole, but a property or an instance is conceptually connected with its principle of unity. Thirdly, qualities of state such as this purple, this white, this black, did not claim anything beyond what they gave as such, and they stood for nothing other than their classes of resemblance. On the contrary, the 'same' data, when they are perceived as properties of objects, represent a purple, a white, a black thing, and therefore refer to existents by a reference which may, if not genuine, deceive us.

Representations in general are produced when contiguity and resemblance are applied to qualities of state as given in places and moments. They may thus be expected to fall into two types. When the qualities of state are associated by contiguity, we call what is represented *substance* and call its representatives *properties*, *modes* and *accidents*. When the qualities of state are associated by resemblance, we call what is represented *natural kind*, *species* or *genus*, whose individual members are the representatives. Two kinds of contiguity and of resemblance will be seen to correspond to these two types of representation: substantial and causal ampliation on the one hand, specific resemblance on the other.

When we analyse the type of representation which is exhibited by sub- stances or things the celebrated principle 'No entity without identity' does not by itself lead to a unique criterion of identity. What makes the concept of substance intricate and classes it among the 'family concepts' is not the lack, but rather the multiplicity, of such criteria. A heap of sand, Theseus' ship, and a bird are equally recognized as substances. However, they instantiate the concept of substance with differing degrees of perfection, according to whether they do or do not meet several criteria of identity. Two main criteria may be distinguished: the unity of continuity which is relative to real analysis, and a more internal unity which is relative to modal analysis.

Primary substances obey a principle of material unity. Like events – but with more precision and stability – they are located in space and time, where they can be indicated by ostension. They constitute wholes subject to real division. This division, which is relevant to the laws governing images, may eventually lead to geometrical analysis, as will be insisted by those who reduce material substances to the *res extensa*, or who at least inquire into the possibility of geometrical physics. Or it may not, if material substance is made of indivisible and invisible bits. Some wholes seem to require specific parts that we may sometimes separate, and sometimes not. This phenomenon seems to suggest an indefinitely complex mixture of materials differing qualitatively among themselves. Perceptual analysis thus potentially contains hints of divisions which philosophy and science will reveal to be mutually incompatible. The material unity of substance is nevertheless protected against these threats by two paradoxical circumstances. Whatever sense we may give to the word *element*, the same elements are not required to be preserved by a given substance. Grains of sand, planks of Theseus' ship, may be changed. On the other hand, except for the limiting cases of metamorphoses, the whole sensible wrapping of substances must in compensation stay on a constant, self-restoring, continuous and ever-imperceptible line of development. This unity was called by Aristotle a *unity of continuity*, and its main criterion which admits of graduation is to be sought in the unity of motion. A heap of sand is made up of handfuls, and the elements of handfuls may be thrown together. A ship has a passive unity of motion. The shin-bone, we are told, has more unity than the leg, and the leg has more unity than the whole body. Finally, above this unity of continuity which determines the unity of its parts, there is, in the case of animals, a unity of articulation which allows a substance to resume its disposition as a whole.

The external permanence we lend to substance amounts therefore to a potentiality of maintaining or of restoring at different places and moments a determinate bundle of qualities of position, either because of the replacement of materially like parts in weak arrangements of position, or because of the reproduction of complex external forms having the same size. Qualities of position become properties of position when their maintenance and their restoration are connected with the same qualities of state in various places and moments. Several assemblages and arrangements of different pieces or parts will then count as so many representatives of the same material unity. It happens, however, that, because of its uncertainties, real analysis presents no unique partition of the perceptual field. This hampers the clear distribution of representation into its two complementary roles, unless the material unity melts into kinematical considerations. The appearances of two main processes, sticking and bouncing, present us with the opportunity of removing our hesitations as to whether to count two things as one or one thing as two. Both of them resort to one and the same principle governing a perceived kinematical *Gestalt*: the principle of ampliation. Since ampliation amounts to the communication of force, it is appropriate to remark that Hume's criticism concerning the possibility of objectively observing such a communication does not by itself exclude the phenomenological possibility of a specific appearance corresponding to it.[38]

A black square is projected upon a screen. It moves towards a red square and, when it has reached it, they go on moving together. We have the illusion 'that a motion is causally imparted'. When two moving squares combine in such a way that they stick together in a unique motion, the bigger square is seen as the agent, the smaller as the patient, and we perceive the bigger as dragging the smaller. Another *Gestalt* is perceived when two moving squares collide. Then, according to their relative sizes and speeds, one square is seen as giving the impact, the other as receiving it, and we perceive the first as throwing the second.[39] In both cases, a motion is ampliated either by merging or by extension.[40] Thus qualities of motion, transformed into properties of contents, adhere to them as their absolute dynamical manifestations.

The dynamical properties of contents are representative more in the sense that they segregate a content from its surroundings and allow us to perceive it as a complete unity than in the sense of a real objectification of the content into a thing. Even a growth of form, though more concerned with internal and objective properties, does not go much further, unless it is accompanied by appropriate alterations of qualities of state. Objects indeed arise when qualities of state as such are collected by contiguity. With this association we leave real and kinematical analysis for modal analysis – that is, the analysis which dissects substances into their properties, modes and accidents – an analysis which fully uses representation. Modal analysis is needed whenever a quality of state or a change in quality of state cannot be separated by a real division from another quality of state or another change in quality of state. There is a real distinction between two grains of sand or between two anatomical parts of a living body. There is a modal distinction between this wall and its colour (for when repainted, the same wall may have another colour), or between the motion and the figure of one and the same body. As objective, the modal distinction must not be confused with a merely subjective *distinctio rationis*, an instance of which would be our conceiving the duration of a substance without paying attention to the substance itself, the idea of which cannot be clear and distinct.[41]

Modal distinctions carry to the very heart of the object, of its changes and of their *causal unity*. As will be shown, causal unity is to modal analysis what unity of contiguity is to real analysis.

Similar clusters of qualities of state are found at different places and moments. When observed, these clusters show a succession of changes of state: for example, alterations, growths, and diminutions. These changes of state are sometimes reversible, sometimes not; that is, within certain limits they may produce, after a given lapse of time, a complete or a partial restoration of the previous state. When observed long enough, most clusters corrupt and dissolve. Some clusters are seen to be born from similarly determinate clusters, while others are produced by work. Consider now the changing qualities of state of such a cluster. All of them will be classed among the properties representing the substance. Every property is supplied with two indices. The first one marks the momentary modal relationship of a quality of state with the other qualities inside a cluster. It refers to a particular sense-record, and sense-records are heterogeneous. The second index marks the temporal permanence or modification of a state quality inside a film. As soon as a state quality has changed, two states of a film are incompatible. It is through these two indices that sense heterogeneities and state incompatibilities are bound together. The piece of wax, as substance, is determined and represented in its momentary state by such qualities of state as colour, consistency, and odour; moreover, it is determined and represented in its history by given changes in these states. A mere distinction of reason separates cluster and film from substance.

If properties differ at all from modes, they differ only by virtue of our insisting, *vis-à-vis* properties, upon the representation of a substance and, *vis-à-vis* modes, upon the relevance of modal analysis. As to accidents, the relative shortness of their duration is their distinguishing characteristic. From duration and stability we elicit important criteria for classifying properties. We can say – although the criterion for doing so is only necessary without also being sufficient – that to count as a substance, properties or bundles of properties have to stay unchanged within the boundaries which are assigned to substances; namely, birth and death, construction and destruction. But there are permanent qualities which are classified as representing properties: for example, the colour of an animal's fur. On the other hand, when wax is brought very near to a fire, it loses its taste and its odour; 'the colour is changed, the shape is destroyed, the size increases, it becomes liquid, it becomes hot, it can scarcely be touched, and now, if you hit it, it does not emit a sound'.[42] Certainly the melted wax is none of the things we have attained by our senses: this sweetness of honey, this fragrance of flowers, this whiteness, this shape, this sound. Rather, it is a body which a little while ago was perceptible in terms of certain modes but now is perceptible only in terms of others. Are we to conclude that the substance, i.e., the wax itself, cannot be imagined and cannot be perceived at all except by the mind? This move would withdraw from perceptual organization the very notion of substance and would entail the complete revision of the correlative notion of property. However, at the level of perception which does not make use of the criteria of clarity and distinctness, we may accommodate even the extreme case in which two states of a film are entirely exclusive of any of their cluster elements.

But if, as a matter of fact, perception finds its own means of coping with the difficulty of referring to unknown substances, it is because the sense-data must hint at hidden elements that are put into the represented sensibilia as the origin of each manifest property, mode or accident. These hidden elements account for change as they account for permanence. Indeed, films and changes of state presuppose causality. At least two substances, wax and fire, are brought together – something which results in the complete transform-ation of a cluster. If the wax is moved away from the fire, it partially reassumes its former properties. Wax *qua* substance, we could just as well conclude, is identical with a *nescio quid* which belongs to sensible qualities that bypass our coarse sense but that could perhaps be ascertained with the aid of a magnifying instrument. If someone objects that the hypothesis of a sensible but hidden structure goes beyond perception and that hidden substances are good neighbours of a supposed causality, then the appropriate answer is that representation in perception must efficiently contribute both to building a surrounding's simulation and to planning actions, but may do so even by means of illusions. Now a *nescio quid* is a powerful member of a representation, if it supports, as it does, the expectation of a possible complete change of one cluster into another. Once organized in terms of representation, perception requires a something represented to support the actually given representa-tives, even if their complete change leaves nothing given behind them. As for causality, the supposition that fire produces, although in an unintelligible way, the enumerated changes in wax is a powerful reinforcement of our previous representation if the presence or the removal of the fire suffices, as it does, to make us expect either this or that completely incompatible cluster of qualities. Ordinarily the *nescio quid* does not in this way remain undetermined, and substances are associated with some permanent and easily recognizable features. Salience and discontinuity mark outlines within boundaries past which every regular cluster is dissolved. The number of petals or of limbs, for instance, belongs to the criteria distinguishing plants or animals. A causal unity is then ascribed to these relatively well-delimited wholes according to whether they are found to present systematic changes of states in connection with the presence of another substance. Without doubt, searching for a prey or a mate, growing afraid or angry, experiencing pleasure and pain, working and transforming materials, must have been important subjective sources of our framing and projecting outside ourselves the notion of substance's causal unity, or rather, the different grades of causal unity which we are ready to attribute to nature – as much when a piece of wax is being melted by fire as when a bird is hovering over the fields and is borne by the winds.

Substance and cause arise in the world of appearances when qualities of state are transformed into properties. In contrast to the corresponding transformation of qualities of position into properties that adhere to perceived contents, the properties of state refer to an X whose existence or action they manifest, but which, far from exhausting its being, they give only by pieces and sketches. There is no *Gestalt* corresponding to the permanence of substance or to the activity of cause where changing properties are brought together under the unity of an object.[43] Since we consider both the permanence of substance and the activity of cause to be something not perceptible and $= X$, the properties that we perceive as properties of the hidden unity of the object must, in the way they are given, show us a lawlike disposition which we immediately interpret as existential reference.

Three grades of this reference may be distinguished, which constitute as many inroads of conception into perception. They correspond respectively to the perceptive constancies, to the organization of properties into contraries, and to the correlation between contraries.

As long as it is a question of appearances being received as stable realities, representation uses devices still comparable to imagination. Like the qualities of position, the qualities of state would never be transformed into properties were it not for self-corrections enhancing their constancy against the changes that the circumstances make them undergo. What perception announces, it is said for example, is 'no colour, but a property, constantly adhering to the object, to reflect preferentially light of determinate wavelengths as such'.[44] In other words, the constancy of a quality of state is nothing but its comparatively invariant property, which as such is attributed to the thing. Thus a kind of schematism develops, and qualities of state are to properties of state what deformed perspectives were to forms. Real conceptual reference arises only through a projection of compensation into reality when the double variety displayed by the contiguities constitutive of films and clusters is subsumed under the unity of a law to assure substance its permanence. Substance's unity should not appear as such – within the limits of coalescence and splitting or generation and corruption – if the main features of a cluster were not seen to restore themselves after a given development of a film. Here we deal no more with the play between changing appearances and reality. Reality itself changes, and it is its unchanging unity which is sought for. While at the level of images, changes and their compensatory motions were distributed over two different kinds of impressions respectively constitutive of passive or objective qualities and of subjective actions, now both changes, and their compensations are beyond mere local motions and they are relevant to the object itself.

The second conceptual reference is based upon the limited character of the changes within a film, failing which the unity of substance would be lost, as would happen if, for instance, the piece of wax were cut into two parts. In order that the changes of properties themselves should signal that they point to a possible permanence of substance, extreme limits are imposed on them and with respect to a given modality a film runs between such limits which are called *contraries*. The wax was solid, cold, hard; it becomes liquid, warm, soft. What we perceive at a given moment of the film is then a state of property between the contraries which themselves appear at the beginning and at the end of the process. It is because every possible state of a property lies between contraries and changes take place from a contrary towards a contrary that, when we see wax melting, the momentary state of property we notice (1) actually excludes all the other states of the same property, (2) is immediately replaced by another transient state, (3) is determined as a stage on the way leading from a contrary towards its contrary, (4) appears as a transitory stage of a progress or a becoming. The state of a property in a film thus stands for an actual but transitory manifestation of the substance, a stage in the progressive realization of other states actually excluded but potentially inscribed in the range of development recognized for this substance, and, finally, the effect of a contiguous cause. What binds together the diversity of the changing states of a property is the unity of an X which is actually what it is while being potentially other, when the internal exchange of potential and actual determination is propagated by a complementary external exchange of properties put in a contiguous Y called its cause. The concept at stake is the rule according to which experience makes us subsume under a unity the actual and the potential diversity of appearances.

This second conceptual synthesis, bearing on the development of one modality of qualities of state within a film, would not succeed were it not supported by another concerning the intersensorial connections which make a cluster. When wax is melting, we notice intersensorial analogies: when hard, substances emit sounds; when soft, they become sound-deadening. The diverse modalities of a cluster are then no longer put together by blind contiguity. Perceiving a given property, we expect another one belonging to another modality according to a rule, because experience has instructed us to connect the property A of X with its property B, and therefore to expect that a change in A cannot go without a correlated change in B. The concept at stake is nothing but the subsumption of diverse properties and their changes under natural laws.

By bringing contiguity under imagination and under concept and by applying it to qualities of state, one has obtained the material unity of substance. Both the unity of continuity and the unity of causality belong to matter. The first belongs to it because it associates images; the second, because associating qualities of state by concept makes the representative properties and the represented substance, even if it is left undetermined, actual and particular. Thus, a heap of sand has its substantial unity adequately specified. But artifacts and especially living organisms, which are the most typical substances, need some higher principle of identification and reidentification, and therefore of unity. In order to give some precision to these material unities, we have been obliged to take account of the boundaries that limit the existence of any substance. In order to mark out the causal unity, we summoned up the unity of shape which, while it certainly belonged to the level of the images, was nevertheless not strictly confined to matter, inasmuch as the resembling images were collected into geometrical forms. In both cases the final criterion of identity was borrowed from comparing similar substances themselves, i.e. from associating qualities of state by resemblance and not merely by contiguity. In other words, the representation of substances by their properties, modes and accidents happens to depend on the representation of general ideas of artifacts or natural kinds by their individual members. Here is the link between the two types of representation, and this link consists of the two different roles played by the same substance, at one point a material identity represented by a variable cluster of properties susceptible of partial restorations, at another point a numerical identity representing a generality like a species or a genus. Ultimately it is because we are able to identify the same species among the many individual subjects belonging to it that we are also able to recognize such-and-such stable individual interconnections of a cluster and a film, and to identify a substance as a subject of inherence for its properties. In order that genuine permanent substances may have given properties, it is necessary for them to be instances of forms – whether (at a lower degree of identification) forms of artifacts or (at a higher degree of identification) forms of natural kinds.

The second type of representation owes its determination to its formal character. It has always been a matter of wonder and of legitimate wonder 'how out of the same sperm the most diverse parts of an organic body (such as hair, nails, veins, arteries, sinews and bones) could develop'.[45] We ask how despite this material dissimilarity between its point of departure and its full maturity ontogeny obeys the same strict law of development in a given species and leads individual organisms to the same anatomical and physiological constitution, to the same adaptation to their surroundings, to the same behaviour-pattern of self-preservation, restoration and reparation. Indeed, it is a matter of wonder how permanent and individually fixed characters of the species are objectively kept and transmitted through the process of reproduction. The unity of the species, which supports the material unities of its individual members, is said to be formal. Firstly, the same general scheme is found among every member and cannot therefore be identified with any individual matter. Fish-bones, notwithstanding their homology, differ from human bones. Secondly, for an individual substance to represent its species it must have a potential ability to perform the activities characteristic of the species, that is, to use its bodily organs for definite and specific functions. The eye of a fly, of a frog, and of a man – despite their resemblances – have specific functions that are linked to specific systems of locomotion.

Formal and functional interpretations of representation do assuredly project subjective anthropomorphic experiences into the perceived world. Witness the kind of unity which is found with regard to artifacts. Here the possibility of accomplishing an assigned function is the ultimate criterion of unity. Since this functional unity is clearly man-dependent and happens to change with the occasion (as when we use tools in non-standard ways), the relation of representation between a substance and its species becomes uncertain or even capricious. But it is when this relation is most capricious that we are made most clearly and easily aware of the ideas of function and of form. Indeed, they then reduce to a conscious experience of purpose or of planning an action. The degree of obscurity and even unintelligibility associated with them concerns the power by which intentions are supposed to produce actions. However, as it is universally recognized that Nature can make organs that perform determinate functions, we tend to call forth this objective power in order to support and to warrant the efficiency of our subjective intentions. The external finality which rules our conscious behaviour and the internal finality according to which Nature's products are organized involve give and take. Function-as-intention is the *ratio cognoscendi* of form-as-organization; and the form is the *ratio essendi* of the function. Our immediate awareness that we can plan our actions would remain inefficient were not Nature to lend us her impenetrable power. We in turn impute to Nature our own way of doing things according to wills and intentions and we repay her assistance by reading plans into her. Simulating and planning are thus the two keys of the second type of representation[46] because we interpret Nature's products in the light of our experience with the products of our own art.

Simulating and planning are both required in order to perceive adequately a living organism, the typical product of Nature. In order that this organism should represent its species it must subsume a multiplicity of functions under the unity of a form according to a concept whose specificity will be better understood and evidenced if we analyse its most important manifestation, namely, the perception we men have of our fellow-men as compared with the perception members of other species have of the members of their own kind. While the form of a tool is merely its function or use, the relation between an organic form and its functions is all the more complex the more disparate are the functions, developing perhaps over a long period of time, connected with a unique form. A mother, for example, rears, warms, nurses, protects, cleans her baby; she attends to it, plays with it, helps it walk, speak, and so on. Now, everybody naturally expects that the same person should fulfil these diverse functions, and it seems only natural that the child associates the various uses it makes of the same object that it will call 'mother'. If we consider, however, the ways in which corresponding associations are performed by other species, the peculiar feature of the present kind of representation will appear more clearly.

It happens, indeed, in Nature that the unity of all the functions which go together to make up the form of a fellow-specimen may be experimentally separated and fixed on different objects, even on individuals belonging to different species.[47] There are birds which have been induced, for instance, to discharge an instinct on a man, another one on a bird of another species, a third one on a bird of the same species.[48] The identity of the form 'species' as represented by its individuals has therefore nothing natural and compelling with respect to the different functions which we expect to be associated with this form, though only certain species can discharge determinate functions like flying. The object corresponding to certain instinctual functions may be identified by a few salient specific signals[49] that, when presented at the right critical moment, release the appropriate behaviour.[50] The criteria which have been used to characterize, in terms of a specific 'imprint', such a releasing mechanism (exclusive occurrence in the first stage of development, irreversible behavioural effects, connection with functions still latent at that time) have all been questioned.[51] But disagreements bear upon the particular conception psychologists have of instinct and learning. They leave the experiments themselves intact and the experiments show that animals have at their disposal two different methods for solving the question of the unity between form and function.[52]

According to the first method, a 'social' function is released by an intuitively given constellation of particular stimuli.[53] Even if learning dispositions are already present at this stage, they are neither orientated towards members of the same species nor *a fortiori* towards determinate individuals. In the ordinary circumstances of life the releasing signals which determine the diverse functions relative to the complete pattern of the other, be it mother or father, brother or sister or mate, are successively and often on later occasions presented on the same recurring object, and this same object then happens to bind all these functions into a mosaic-like whole.[54] A dissociation, however, remains always possible if the successful presentation of the necessary signals is bound to different objects, especially when a complete and autonomous reaction is required by instinct.[55] In this case, the perceived unity of the species seems to rely on perceptual external resemblances between its members. The subjective integration which comes from discharging different instinctual functions on the same object is missing and the social individuality of the other depends on the chance which given signals have of uniting in the same object. What associates a function or a host of functions in a unique organic form is an objective and external association without any firm subjective foundation.

The second method proceeds in the reverse direction. Firstly, even if at a first step the functions corresponding to instincts are more or less automatically and independently released in relation to specific constellations of stimuli, they mature into mutually dependent and integrated drives, orientated towards the satisfaction expected from the same and uniquely individuated object. Secondly, the object which is expected to unite so many diverse functions can no longer be given at one stroke, as if by intuition. It slowly develops, or rather is nothing but the unity of these functions inasmuch as it supports the comparison made among the members of a species. The last comparison, founded upon recurring qualities of position and of state, would be made objectively were it not for the subjective linking of the functions that supports it and gives it its stability. A species gets its formal unity in perception not from a directly perceived class resemblance which would always remain in question, but from the subordination of this class resemblance to the concept of a subjective unity of instinctual functions. Thirdly and finally, for individuating a fellow-member of the species one among several representatives must be picked out in order that the required unity of the functions defining the fellow is exclusively referred to it. This fellow-object, X, I perceive then as the counterpart of the subjective synthesis by which I feel all these functions as 'mine'.[56]

Human beings clearly use the second method for perceiving their companions. More distinctly than does the representation of substance, the representation of species exploits an organization of signals which abandons intuition in favour of conceptual and subjective syntheses. The diverse properties of substance were referred to the unity of an object X through the concept of an efficient cause, i.e. of a law bringing permanence and change under universals such as the evolution of films within contraries, or the intersensorial connection of clusters. Now, the ultimate nature of these universals may conceal the *a priori* activity of a subjective intellectual synthesis, or it may merely result from habit. In any case, the universals themselves are then given us as objective appearances, and philosophical reflection would be needed to interpret as the trace of a transcendental or a psychological action a world-order which all of us naively experienced as the order of things. On the contrary, the various members of a species are referred to its unity through the concept of a final cause, namely, of requirement that the various functions coordinated with instinctual drives be derived from a same social object X, an object that is intended in a generic as well as in an individual sense. Such an object appears to be inseparable from the subjective synthesis of desire. Mother, father and all other social companions must then be seen as unities of functions, in consequence of which there are forms preceding and shaping all our 'objective' experience, determined as it is by substance and causality.

Representation completes the organization of perception. Applied to representations – in contradistinction to images – new associations by contiguity or by resemblance would not go beyond the classes already obtained to attain to a higher level of classification. Representations are either things or properties or natural kinds. Contiguous things, if contiguity is stable, would again generate things; resemblant things are simply natural kinds. Contiguous or resemblant properties are what we call natural laws, and contiguous or resemblant natural kinds go to make up the particular object of natural history. Such concepts, if they rise to genuine appearances, are already counted among representations. When this is not the case they cannot be fixed without language and then bypass perceptual organization.

Applied directly to impressions, the relations of contiguity and resemblance gave us signals of position and qualities of state. Then, as mediated by compensation, contiguity applied to signals of position and transformed them into qualities of position, while resemblance, in its turn, mediated by a non-compensated abstraction, turned these same qualities into absolute places and moments. Finally, representations were obtained from qualities of state by subordinating contiguity and resemblance to conceptual syntheses. Beyond these objective and subjective syntheses there remains no room for new productive applications of contiguity and resemblance.

It has often been observed that perceptual identification is facilitated and made more precise when the perceiving subject knows how to name the object of identification or at least how to associate it with a sound – even a nonsensical one – emitted by himself.[57] The importance of such man-made intentional signs for mastering perceptual organization cannot be overestimated, as Hellen Keller's celebrated case clearly shows.[58] But using signs, either institutional or conventional, lies beyond perception and already leads us into the world of language. At the present stage, appearances contain syntheses and even subjective syntheses. They do not contain the possibility of their communication.

3 THE HELMHOLTZ PRINCIPLE: THE SUBJECTIVE CHARACTER OF PERCEPTUAL SIGNALLING

Belonging to the species 'man' implies for us, as individuals, planning specific actions in surroundings in which our artifacts are to be found among natural kinds. The simulation must therefore be interpreted by the organism in terms of a real picture of things, where among those things occur the more or less developed means that the organism uses or produces for fulfilling its intentions. The inherence of properties in their substances, as well as the instantiation of the species by its individuals, presupposes that the signalling by which representation refers properties to substances and substances to natural kinds is objective, natural and devoid of all arbitrariness. Dispossessed of its objectification, the picture of the perceived things would be neither complete nor convincing. There would be possible loopholes that would have to be filled by new types of signs and there would remain a general uncertainty as to the firmness and the reliability of the whole construction. From the point of view of biological evolution such a shaky perceptual organization would be a *contradictio in terminis*.

There are hints to be found locally that perceptual signalling cannot really sustain its claim to objectivity. There are local loopholes and local doubts and hesitations. In order to become aware of sense-data we may even train our attention in such a way that the affections of our own sense replace the objectively interpreted elements of the things themselves. But according to a principle already used by Descartes in his last Meditation and first explicitly formulated by the founder of psycho-physiology, Helmholtz, 'we are extraordinarily well-trained in extracting from our sensations the objective properties of the things, without being trained at all in observing our sensations themselves; and this training itself concerning our relation to the external world prevents us from exhibiting pure sensations to the clarity of awareness'.[59]

We must, then, consider perceptual organization as it has been described as a subjective synthesis or as a phenomenology, not as an ontology. Indeed, the ultimate criterion of phenomenological signalling is not truth but survival-value. It would be a worthwhile task for a general psychological semiotics to survey and to study the several criticisms that the postulate of phenomenological objectivity has undergone. Psychophysiology and psycho-physics analysed qualities into their subjectively specific contributions. As to the images, the irreducibility of spatial extension has been questioned by Helmholtz, Lie and Poincaré. As we saw, they asked: how do we construct space with punctual sense-data, and into what specific kind of relation of order do the alleged orders of simultaneity have to be recast? Granted, then, that our different impressions are necessarily given to us in succession, and that we only assume the order of time to be indefinable, two alternatives follow: either the changes of impressions admit of compensation and annulment or they do not. If the first alternative is true, they fit into a mathematical group-structure which is nothing other than space. We classify these impressions as qualities of position; and we classify their changes as changes of position. If spatiality subjectively appears as a primitive and objective quality in perceptual organization, it is because adaptation must rely on quick decisions. It is easier to look at a television screen than to read shorthand writing. If the second alternative is true (for instance, when water has been mixed with wine), the changes of state and the impressions themselves are classified as qualities of state. Accordingly, time is the form common to both changes and is the only indefinable image.[60] The claim which appearances make about an absolute intuitive space is just illusion. Finally, at the level of representation, and whatever the mechanisms are which support conditioning, we see that arbitrary successive impressions may associate with one another, so that subjective signallings are spontaneously interpreted as natural and real representations. It is precisely this arbitrariness perceived as natural connection that Locke called an association of ideas.

Suppose we answer, as Kant did to Hume, that in order to be stable the association has to be constant and therefore founded upon a natural regularity, and that the repetition or reinforcement which selects permanent associations is simply the working of Nature's law. Even so, we would have to admit that what we consider as objective and picturesque representations arise exactly as artificial and arbitrary associations do. Hence, the objective interpretation of the representations merely expresses a subjective mechanism. While to the distinction between the processes of reinforcement and extinction there corresponds in Nature the distinction between the working of law and casual contiguity, nothing justifies our clothing substances with inhering properties and our comparing these clothes as if they were not man-made.

We are entitled to award to the described perceptual organization as little objective reality as we want. We are by no means committed to common-sense realism, and there is no conflict between a sound scientific scepticism and a phenomenological description of perceptual appearances that achieves its end by postulating an illusory, but biologically beneficial, objectivity.

The case of colours is particularly relevant. We perceive as circular their linear order, in consequence of which we distribute growing wave-lengths into 'contraries' and we create subjective colours to which no stimulus corresponds.[61]

4 WHAT IS REQUIRED TO COMMUNICATE PERCEPTUAL ORGANIZATION?

The criticism of perception just sketched originated from an external scientific examination. The list which follows of new needs which go beyond perception issues from the pressure of communication. When we observe others' behaviour, gestures, mimicry, expressions of emotions, onomatopoeias and interjections, we recognize that all the means which perception provides are notoriously too meagre to convey the perceptual organization itself and to make the subjective synthesis of one man available to his fellow-creatures.

Here a 'culturalist' objection must be briefly rebutted. The linguistic unity of the signifier and the signified prevents us from supposing that concepts are pre-existent to words. The English language has only the one word *man* for the two primitive German word-concepts *Mann* and *Mensch*. On the other hand, there are many languages having only one word, let us say *grue*, for two basic word-concepts in English: *green* and *blue*. Such facts authorize us to conclude that primitive, or basic, concepts – that is, concepts expressed by single synchronically irreducible words – are relative to given languages and cultures. But from a synchronically missing form we cannot infer a corresponding lack of the concept, which may be borrowed or composed. Thus we cannot show the truth of 'culturalism',[62] a doctrine according to which perception is framed by language and thought and has no autonomous existence outside given and particular languages. On the other hand, linguistic universalism can also never be shown to be true. For nothing can prevent a diachronic inquiry from falling upon a forgotten borrowing or composition underlying the best-authenticated synchronically basic word-concept.[63] Hence a more modest settlement is advisable. That thought, which Saussure compared to 'a nebula where nothing is necessarily delimited',[64] remains amorphous and indistinct prior to language, does not at all prevent the possibility of perceptual organization. This organization is even indispensable if languages are to be spoken and heard.[65]

The limitations of perception with respect to linguistic communication may therefore be meaningfully delineated.

The first limitation concerns the universals – that is, the classes of resemblance, i.e., of species or genera – that in the second type of representation are represented by the individual substances. We perceive only individuals, even if universals give our perception of them its structure.

In conformity with the definitions by abstraction,[66] these universals, whether they are conceived as classes or attributes, have a mere virtual or potential presence. Being immanent in their representatives, they never separate themselves from them in order to constitute higher-level (or what Aristotle calls secondary) substances, which can only be apprehended by the activity of a pure understanding. Thus, if they are communicated, they are communicated in ways that lie beyond perception.

Secondly, when we perceive other living substances, we spontaneously project into them our capacity of simulating as well as of planning. Observe a soaring buzzard suddenly falling on a mole and taking wing with its prey in its talons. Who could resist the belief that it soared in order to get the prey, even if we knew there to exist a chain of external and internal stimuli that had no relation to plans and finality and that was sufficient for explaining the observed behaviour? Now, interpreting as intentional certain bodily expressions within the limits of the perceptual organization would convey only a small part of our experience, the subjectivity of which essentially escapes observation and perception. Except for some rather stereotyped simulations and plans expressed by means of determined behaviour, the largest part of our subjective synthesis would remain lost for our fellow-men.

Thus, if group learning is to be adequate for individual learning, human language must face three tasks. Besides the task of communicating the perceptual organization, as such, it also has the task of substantiating universals and of expressing subjectivity.

Before analysing how language communicates perception, it is appropriate to recapitulate in a synoptic table just what it is in perception that language will have to communicate. (The symbols 'C' and 'R' respectively designate the operations of associations by contiguity and by resemblance; the symbols 'o x' express that an operation applies to the object x; the arrow '→' means that the combination of an operation and an object 'produces' another object. 'Objects' are here appearances.)

Level of organization	Domain of contiguity	Domain of resemblance
Simple association	C o impressions→ signal of position	R o impressions→ quality of state
Images	C o signals of position→quality of position	R o (qualities of position + qualities of state)→places and moments
Representation	C o qualities of state→properties/ thing	R o qualities of state→things/natural kinds.

How is it possible for men to communicate their perceptual organization?

Firstly, an analysis of the conditions making this communication possible will reduce the question to the classification of the linguistic categories of individuals. Next a thread for the deduction of these categories will be sought. Linguistic categories will be shown to bypass perceptual organization and to allow its communication. Finally, the deduction itself will be made.

I THE SENTENCE AS ULTIMATE CONSTITUENT OF LINGUISTIC COMMUNICATION AND HOW THE CLASSIFICATION OF INDIVIDUALS BY MEANS OF ELEMENTARY SINGULAR SENTENCES MANAGES TO COMMUNICATE THE ORGANIZATION OF PERCEPTION

The question if and how it is possible to communicate perception subdivides into two questions. There is first the general question of the possibility, answered by the general concept of a sentence. Then the particular question of finding a possible correspondence between perceptual organization and language will be shown to amount to classifying the categories of individuals through classifying the elementary singular sentences.

For individuals to be able to communicate their perceptual experiences, two conditions must be fulfilled. Their system or code of communication must be universal, and it must be open. A code is universal if no particular restriction is imposed on the content or on the nature of the messages, and it is open if nothing, in principle, limits their lengths. Natural language is such a code.

These conditions are necessary to build a complete sign, but a complete sign is not a complete message, i.e. a sentence. Therefore to reach the conditions sufficient for making the message complete, the linguistic analysis, once it has treated of universality and openness, will need a new start to lead us from signs to sentences.

First of all, language is universal. Neither the specialized dances of the bees, which refer, but refer only to sources of honey, nor the more diversified but dependent warnings of the gibbons which are emitted, or rather elicited, only in the presence of their object of reference, nor the stereotypes of the chimpanzees, which refer freely but are only about a few distinct predetermined situations, would do. The rich systems by which apes convey their feelings is also excluded, because such immediate expressions of subjective states cannot draw another's attention to the appearances that have been experienced as objects. The distinction between phonetics and phonology most clearly shows what obstacle the immediacy of expression opposes to universality. Among spoken or heard sounds, phonology retains a finite number of relevant or distinctive features, characteristic of phonemes, that, within the concrete signals employed, delimit what contributes to reference, whereas phonetics deals with the whole of these concrete signals whose irrelevant traits are mainly used to express the emotions of the speaker. Finally, for universal signals there is a harder task than referring simply as pictures and icons do: reference here must be possible not only when the object is absent, but when it is referred to as non-existent. It is only messages suited to this extreme case that are fully universal. But this amounts to saying that universal signals must be arbitrary.

Perceptual associations used natural signals. At a lower level of perceptual organization the signals were themselves members either of the group or of the class of equivalence which they signalled; or they were parts of the substance or members of the natural kind which they represented. Universality does away with this confusion. How could I convey the idea that there is not such-and-such a thing if I did not have at my disposal words, i.e., arbitrary signals that, as a rule, neither instantiate nor mimic the things they refer to? Naturally, even arbitrary signals require publicity and therefore have both to be made of some stuff taken from perception and yet to be set apart from it. Social groups must provide them with recognizable properties which, in the course of time, become a second nature. Rather than simply being called arbitrary, then, the universal signals might better be annexed to the province of social institutions.

Natural language is also open: the scene of experience which it is about is by no means confined within definite bounds, though most messages corresponding to similar circumstances inevitably repeat themselves. Messages may expand, and new circumstances call for new messages. To this end, language makes use of a recursive device, by which from a finite number of elementary messages committed to memory our most complex messages may be built according to a finite number of rules constituting the grammar of language. Any language, then, must be atomic, since some atoms are needed to start the building process. Empirically, the whole construction results in messages expressed by a linear chain of spoken sounds.

Universality and openness give the linguistic organization its characteristic framework with respect to the articulation and the perception of the messages, as well as with respect to the comprehension of what it is about. This organization reuses the two principles at play in perception, namely contiguity and resemblance, but, in accordance with the new requirements, it transforms them into syntagms and paradigms. The transformation, however, is more conspicuous in the case of contiguity and syntagms than in the case of resemblance and paradigms. In the first case, rules clearly govern the process by which the different pieces of a complex message are assembled. Natural associations of contiguity would never appear to suffice for expressing institutionalized connections, for the parts which unite in the message unite precisely *in praesentia* one of another according to grammatical rules. Thus language immediately transfigures perceptual contiguity into linguistic syntagms. On the contrary, the corresponding transfiguration of perceptual resemblance escapes notice and seems to stand for its equivalence class by exactly the same association of perfect resemblance which perception brings into play. We then forget that the atoms too are determined arbitrarily, that is, obey social, not natural, laws. An atom would indeed never be memorized or even recognized within the concrete performances which unavoidably mix it with every kind of unintentional perceptual signal, if it did not enter into systems, where it is associated with all the other atoms that compete with it either as its possible substitutes or as its negative complements – a distribution which fully exploits the relations of contrariety organizing the first level of perceptual representation. These systems of substitution and opposition, or paradigms, are then to resemblance what syntagms are to contiguity. In contradistinction to syntagms, they often remain unnoticed simply because they occur not *in praesentia*, but *in absentia* of one another. Paradigms thus obey, just as syntagms do, the same institutionalized laws which make linguistic messages universal and open. It remains to be seen how they enable signs to constitute these messages. Two stages will be distinguished: the monemes, the simplest signs organized into paradigms, then their syntagmatic association into morphemes, among which complete signs will be found.

Universal and open messages must contain some parts which are encoded and decoded according to rules, and, if they are to succeed, they must convey the idea of a distinguished feature of perception by the means of an arbitrary association. Moreover, the idea corresponding to the distinguished feature of perception must be a universal and, if the feature is regarded as simple, a simple universal.[1] Indeed, if the ordinary constituents of our linguistic messages stood for particulars, the atomicity and consequently the openness of language would be denied any possibility of regularity, for there is an indefinite number of particulars. Consequently, there are atomic parts of the message, called *elementary signs* or *monemes*, each of which is the unity of a signifier and a signified.[2] Their list constitutes the ultimate lexical basis of a language.

The signifier – if there must be different elementary signs – is itself composed of further elements that are no longer signs themselves but mere distinctive units institutionally selected among possible concrete sounds. A double articulation or duality is therefore characteristic of language. Before reaching the stage of signs there are the phonemes, and underlying the phonemes there are the discriminative features. Though arbitrary, neither of these units expresses meanings as the units of the other level will do. Monemes, within longer syntagms, constitute the characteristic units of this other level.

Potential universals in perception are unavoidably accompanied by a host of particulars, because perceptual signals are parts or members of the signalled universals. For words[3] – the ordinary formations corresponding to monemes – the situation is different. When we think of the separated universals which the monemes stand for without the aid of imaginative and particularizing associations to which they adhere in perception,[4] we recognize that we cannot express what they do without being determined by means of their paradigmatic associations with the other words that are similar in meaning or in opposition to them. Though substitutes and competitors occur only subjectively and *in absentia*, the association is objectively governed by the particular code of the language. Meaning is, so to speak, a matrix. Why, indeed, do the linguists insist on the arbitrariness of their signs? Not because *Mann* or *homme* are the German and the French correlates of the English word *man*, but because such correlations do not always exist and are not generally biunivocal, as is evidenced by our being compelled to translate the German sentence 'Elizabeth ist ein guter Mensch' by using a new expression and saying, for example, 'Elizabeth is a good person.' It is, then, the arbitrariness of the linguistic sign which seals in the sounds themselves the unity of the signifier and the signified and precludes the occurrences of casual associations between the individual instance of the word *man* and the individual instances of an alleged pre-existing concept *man*. We could not understand an instance of the word *man* without equivocation if this instance were bound up with the accessory, changing and subjective associations which are always operative in determining the perception of a man. Speakers who use the English word *man* consider as irrelevant every particular idea which would contain any precision beyond 'being a male representative of the human species or embodying the bundle of properties constitutive of a person'. At the same time, because it competes with the word *Mensch*, the German word *Mann* happens to stand only for a part of the general idea which corresponds to the English word *man*. Therefore, words stand for an actual definite and more or less restricted universal accordingly as they are strictly determined by the constellation of rival and complementary words which, within a completely arbitrary and unmotivated linguistic system, convey such-and-such selected features of perception.

De Saussure insisted on this peculiarity of the symbolic association characteristic of language. Language, he said, is a Form, not a Substance,[5] because the idea which a word stands for never expresses a natural classification that preexists the particular codes of our diverse idioms, but always depends on the specific systems of differences and oppositions to which the given word belongs through its relations with the other words. Consequently, the different instances of a word express the same Universal, or the same general idea, inasmuch as the Form of its language selects and determines what recurrent features of experience or concepts will be signified by the signifier, since these concepts are merely differential and since their meanings are fixed not by their positive content, but by their negative relations with the other terms of the system.[6]

Such universality, the determination of which merely proceeds by negation, is not yet in opposition to particulars. It remains unaffected by differences of quantity and oblivious to the distinction between generalization and instantiation. Proper linguistic codes, therefore, deal with roots or rather with themes which do not mark off 'humble' from 'humility' or 'human' from 'humanity'. We must leave paradigms for syntagms when we go on further and transform themes into complete morphemes. The transformation depends on two main procedures: either two ordinary monemes enter into composition, or grammar operates on a theme to give it a more determinate meaning in conformity with general rules. The distribution of the two procedures is extremely arbitrary and varies with every natural language.

The general or conceptual value which language realizes in monemes might be compared to an as yet unassembled tool, the head and handle of a hammer, which will acquire its working function only when put together. Morphemes are monemes thus transformed and ready for use. Among them occur complete signs, i.e., signs that completely express this or that feature of experience.

Such complete signs, however, still give us only one side of the picture. Indeed, it cannot be objected that they fall short of the distinction between singular and general pictures, or that they do not express privation and negation:

morphology and syntax provide us with the means – though perhaps not at the level of monemes – for satisfying both of these requirements. But what we are after are simplest complete messages, and the syntagms just offered, though complex, are not complete: they lack two instructions.[7] Firstly, when two monemes combine into a syntactic unit – an operation which assures language of its creativity since new syntagms may always be produced and understood – this expansion is, so to speak, left floating in the air since there is nothing to let us know where to stop the procedure. To the different signs which are parts of the syntagms a new element must therefore be added in order to notify us that the syntagm is complete, or forms a sentential syntagm. Secondly, the signs connected in this way have a meaning and make us associate with the sequence of signifiers a sequence of the signified, suitably organized into the unity of a thought. Now, a thought depicts a state of affairs as complex and as definite as desired. But it, too, is left floating in the air since sentential syntagms depict only the possibility of states of affairs and their pictures remain as empty as was the standing of a paradigm for its universal. At such a stage, sentences are mere 'considerations' (*Annahmen*) which leave us completely in the dark as to whether the depicted state of affairs is or is not the case. Here there is meaning, but there is still no reference. For a message to be complete, its semantical as well as its syntactical closure must be provided for. The assignation of a truth-value only achieves the purpose of communication by transforming sentential syntagms into asserted sentences, into those living pictures[8] which show that what is considered is taken as true.

Now, sentences are beyond the province of signs. They form an infinite list and are no longer susceptible either to paradigmatic opposition to other units of a system[9] or to syntagmatical association with other parts of a message. Discriminative features of phonemes fell short of signs because they lacked meaning. Sentences go beyond signs because signs lack reference. To mean is the internal job of structures. To refer requires an external comparison between structure and reality. And only referring communicates perception because only referring decides that what our signs mean is true.

Once we have reached the complete message, the asserted sentence, to which the following considerations are restricted, we dispose of all the elements needed to answer the question of how perceptual organization may be communicated. A sweeping simplification has already cleared our path, since all messages which do not aim at communicating knowledge have been discarded, and only messages having truth-values, namely, statements, are retained. This simplification is justified both by the intrinsic importance of these sentences and by the role they are destined to play in philosophical systems.

Eliminating, then, all the constructs beyond what is required by the simplest assertable syntagms should leave us with the elementary or 'atomic' sentences that were to be compared with the perceptual presentations. Here, however, an objection might arise. If sentences are signs and if they form an infinite list, how is a classification of elementary sentences corresponding to perceptual organization possible? To answer the question we must be more explicit about reference in relation to meaning. Let us for clarity contrast (a) a complete syntagm in the sense that it expresses a complete meaning – 'Peter's running'; (b) the sentential syntagm 'that Peter runs'; and (c) the asserted sentence 'It is the case that Peter runs.' There is no difference of content between the three expressions: (b) only says that the syntagm (a) is now complete in the sense that it is assertable, and (c) only adds that (b) is true. Now, signs not taken in the unity of a sentence, as is the case with (a), mean but do not refer. But if reference arises only with (c), that does not mean that it is the sentence (c) itself which refers. Indeed, the reference is to Peter's running, not to the corresponding state of affairs which merely specifies that all the constituents of the state have been given, or to the sentence which, if it refers at all, refers to its own truth-value in a metaphorical sense. It is the complete syntagm, then, that refers, once it has been integrated by the sentence.

So the question of how to communicate perceptual organization comes down in the first instance to the question: what in a sentence are the signs which bear the burden of referring?

Suppose the constituents of the sentence had to be the ordinary universals of the appropriate codes, or had to be built from them. Then a sentence should contain at least two signs for universals, or what Aristotle called terms, and the assertion should bear on the possible qualitative and quantitative relations among them: inclusion, exclusion, positive and negative intersection. In this way, categorical sentences, universal or particular, but always general, since they are about either all or some such-and-such..., have been considered as the elementary sentences. It is remarkable how difficult it was, in this perspective, to locate the status of singular sentences and to distinguish clearly the subordination of two universals from the subsumption of individuals under a universal. One of the principal merits of modern formal logic has been to analyse the categorical sentences into logically complex relations between two propositional functions bound by quantification. This conception of the universe of discourse does introduce new difficulties: the universality of the variable, the subalternation within the square of the categorical propositions, the compromission of classificatory predication with ontological commitment. Nevertheless, it has definitely shown that an elementary assertable syntagm is not made up of two homogeneous monemes, each of which stands for universals, but of two heterogeneous signs, a sign of a universal and a singular term. A sign which has acquired a subsumptive force is a propositional function or a predicate. The singular term which designates the subsumed individual is an argument. Then the simplest sentences aim at expressing a singular state of affairs and convey a predication, i.e., the subsumption of n-arguments under an n-place predicate. For one-place predicates, every singular elementary sentence would thus yield the pattern $f(a)$, to which the following analysis will be limited.

It is easy to characterize in such atomic sentences what a predicate is, namely, the morpheme which results from the ordinary moneme as modified in order to express its functional or predicative role. It must express its meaning, namely, a genuine property, distinctly (otherwise the message would lack clarity) but indirectly (otherwise the message would be about the predicative universal), while its reference or extension is directly but confusedly expressed.[10] On the other hand, from a formal point of view, singular terms present no difficulty. Since its reference is distinct, the singular term which designates individuals holds the stage and captures the sentence's claim to reality. The referring universal occurs, then, within the assertable syntagms as a mere virtual class or property term. Ontological commitments take refuge in the argument. Expressed in terms of our modern Indo-European languages, this means that (1) once every syncategorematic mark (the 'logical' words) has been withdrawn from a finite declarative message the analysis leaves us with an atomic sentence composed of a verb and (if the verb is intransitive) of a singular subject, (2) the verb, since it expresses a classificatory universal, is deprived of ontological bearing, (3) ontology is the business of the subject.

The whole difficulty is now seen to lie in the following question. What are and what may be genuine subjects or singular terms? Symptomatically enough, the birth-act of analytical philosophy – which arose as a by-product of contemporary logic – has often been assigned to Russell's theory of definite descriptions that eliminated 'pseudo-subjects' in terms of logical analysis.[11] From that time on no agreement has been reached in philosophy as to what singular terms must be accepted as genuine or even accepted at all. Though the discussion focused on proper names and egocentric particulars, it also affected the most general topics of philosophical analysis such as whether coordinate languages are irreducible, how verbs of action are instantiated, and what modalities and propositional attitudes are about.

Inspired by a more descriptive and tolerant attitude, linguists reached more commonly agreed upon results. Nevertheless, since the formal criteria, which are the soul of their method, depend on the particular linguistic codes they study, the same relevant feature will be encoded by one language in its syntax, by another one in its lexicon, and, despite their utility for philosophical analysis, no definitive conclusions may be expected to result from their descriptions.

Naming a problem is often a step towards its solution. Let us, then, examine just what problem is at stake and see what people mean when they give it its simplest solution by denying its reality and by proposing a regimentation of language in which all singular terms are eliminated. We may, it is said, use a common linguistic device by which such singular terms are transformed into verbs, and then replace sentences such as 'Socrates walks' or 'Pegasus flies' by their corresponding analyses, thus: '$(\exists x)$ socratizes x and walks x' or '$(\exists x)$ pegasizes x and flies x.' What precisely is the problem whose solution regimentation aims at in proposing such a complete reform of ordinary language? It is clearly delineated in the philosophy of W.V. Quine, who, in developing such a programme with exemplary rigour, writes: 'The quest of a simplest overall pattern of canonical notation is not to be distinguished from a quest of ultimate categories, a limning of the most general traits of reality.'[12] Besides its technical contribution to regulating scientific language, the elimination of singular terms in favour of variables paves the way for three accomplishments. (1) A standard method is at hand to decide ontological commitments: all that there is is and that only is which is the value of a variable. (2) All the entities that are needed in physics and which constitute the ultimate furniture of the universe may be constructed by providing the values of quadruples of variables (x, y, z, t) with values of appropriate universals. However, an extension of this basis is required if a full set theory is to be applicable to physics; abstracts of classes must nominalize universals and make them possible subjects of singular sentences. (3) Since the language of science is extensional, variables must take as values only physical individuals and sets, and modalities and propositional attitudes may in principle be reworded into a talk about physical entities and classes with the linguistic signs occurring among the physical entities.

The elimination of singular terms is thus used to build a scientific ontology, made up of Democritean atoms and Platonic classes. In other words, Quine's regimentation aims at establishing that two categories of individuals suffice to shape reality, and the problem of singular terms is nothing but the philosophical classification of categories. Once being has been defined as the value of the variable, assigning the possible kinds of values gives a complete enumeration of the categories of being. Compared with Aristotle's or Kant's,

Quine's classification, because of its extensional character, enjoys the advantage of clarity, in so far as what there is is separated both from the end towards which it tends and from the way in which it may be known to us. These differences are expressive of the philosophical tenets of classifications which aim at exhausting the categories of being by systematically locating the levels to which these categories belong.[13]

In order to propose a classification of elementary singular sentences, we must, in contradistinction to these philosophical classifications of categories, take care to maintain a complete philosophical neutrality by strictly adhering to the phenomenology of language. Extensionality is not built into natural language, nor is the limitation of individuals to concrete substances or to possible experience. Now, the most important feature of natural language as compared with philosophy is probably its eclectic and free use of sentences and categories which a philosopher will be tempted to consider as incompatible and consequently to reform. On the other hand, a classification, even if it is about the provisory individuals received in natural languages, is like the philosophical classifications inasmuch as it must result in an exhaustive system.

Nothing assures us that both requirements may be satisfied together. Considered as a whole, language has been compared to a labyrinth which has no Ariadne's thread. Is it possible to find such a thread for the limited question: what are the elementary singular sentences and the categories of individuals in natural languages? Perhaps if we know how to solve this question, we shall by the same stroke answer the question which was our starting-point and which we have never lost sight of along our way: how can perceptual presentations be communicated?

2 A LEADING THREAD FOR THE DEDUCTION OF THE CATEGORIES OF NATURAL LANGUAGE[14]

As minimal asserted syntagms, elementary singular sentences state that a given individual has such-and-such a property, that is, under what general condition it may be identified. Though they differ from proper signs in not being confined within finite systems of oppositions, they still seal the unity of a symbolic chain having a truth-value and of the identification of an individual under a general condition. We shall therefore find a leading thread for deducing the categories of singular sentences and of the individuals which they are about if we lay down as a principle of the deduction that the conditions of possibility for building the symbolic chain constitutive of the singular sentence are identical with the conditions of possibility for identifying the individuals. The principle of this identity is quite natural when we think that we have to identify individuals by using signs. There will be as many categories of individuals as there are kinds of elementary symbolic chains apt to be asserted.

These kinds will be completely determined if and only if their constituents are completely specified and all the presuppositions of communication under which the constituents form a sentence are made explicit.

(1) An elementary singular sentence is expressed by a symbolic chain made up of four elements. There are the singular term standing for the individual – whatever it may be – and the (one argument-) predicate, standing for the universal, belonging to the ordinary lexicon of the linguistic system and which syntax has made ready to be filled by the appropriate singular term. Moreover, two functions must be expressed. The first one is relevant to syntax and provides for the required unity of the two preceding elements: the sequence of the predicate and the singular term forms an assertable syntagm which expresses a possible state of affairs. The other is relevant to semantics: the sentence results from asserting the syntagm in question and means that the state of affairs in question is the case. Finally, besides the four enumerated elements belonging to the signified, the symbolic chain itself constitutes an extra element belonging to the signifier.

(2) For the time being, we still do not know what the singular terms are and may be. We only know that these terms capture reference within sentences. Let us then isolate the singular term, whatever it may be, and extract it from its elementary singular sentence. Instead of dissolving it into a variable, as the formal logicians do, to forget all that can specify and particularize it, let us apply our principle of identity to it. What are the conditions of possibility for building the chain constitutive of the sentence, given the exhaustive enumeration of its elements? They necessarily reduce to the possible determinations of any distinguished element – here the designated singular term – by the different enumerated elements. These different elements work by virtue of their particular function, and the question is to understand how these different functions make it possible to build a linguistic term having a unique referential power in the sentence. Therefore, they are necessarily distributed into five exclusive classes, since the determination of the singular term occurs in respect either (1) of the general term, or (2) of the singular term itself, or (3) of the material chain of the sentence, or (4) of its syntactical unit, or (5) of its semantic unit. It is these classes which, according to our principle of identity, will be identical with the conditions of possibility for identifying the individuals. What the corresponding five classes of individuals mean will be made determinate and explained by the deduction itself. For the time being it will suffice to name the correlated classes of elementary

sentences: (1) pure predication, (2) substantial (and accidental) predication, (3) circumstantial predication, (4) judgments of method, and (5) judgments of appearance.

The unravelling of the leading thread, according to the principle of identity, may be and will be interpreted in two different ways. There is first the formal or linguistic interpretation. Has the classification which distributes the identifications of existent individuals into several possible kinds a real counterpart in natural language? General linguistics will help us to recognize the reality of these different categories by means of its specific classes of semantic and pragmatical units. By exploiting the concepts of a system of opposition and of neutralization and applying them to the analysis of the verb, we shall even follow the general progress of the deduction. General criteria of reality, however, will only be obtained when we choose the second interpretation, which is in terms of truth, not of form. The following principle of semiotics will then be applied: for communication to succeed, the participants must be able to have access to the truth-conditions of the sentences, so that a category will be considered as effectively used when the participants agree on the way they have access to the truth conditions involved by its kinds of identification.

Now it suffices that the five kinds of identification just enumerated be traced back to their formal origin to see that they divide into two major series distinguished in terms of truth. The formal principles of identification relevant to pure predication, substantial and accidental predication and circumstantial predication will reveal themselves to depend on objective structures, institutions or pragmatical decisions: the code of the language, the conventions of the group or the relation between the speaker and his message. All the relevant elementary sentences will thus fall under the series of dogmatic sentences, where the word *dogmatic* means that such sentences refer and identify without relying on the speaker's subjectivity. On the contrary, the judgments of method and the judgments of appearances will belong to a second, *subjective* series, comprehending the speaker's possible subjective contributions to the building of the sentence. Since we have excluded all subjective associations that a speaker may use privately when universal or singular terms as well as sentences are uttered, his subjectivity is permitted to interfere by exploiting only the two remaining elements. Either the whole syntactical unity of the sentence will be used in order to express how the subject constructs identification and truth; or, through his relation to the whole semantic unity of the sentence, he will convey his own propositional attitude towards identification and truth. Such are the constituents which exhaust the subjective series.

Finally, the list of categories thus obtained must be put in correspondence with perceptual organization. It must contain all the identifications which convey a kind of perceptual presentation. But other identifications going beyond perception may be proper to linguistic communication and are even to be expected, if signs differ from natural signals. The principle of identity will be considered as adequate if it gives an eclectic and complete multiplicity of categories, without committing us to any philosophical choice.

3 SKETCH OF A DEDUCTION

We shall follow the order indicated by the leading thread and successively examine what types of identification or categories result when the singular term is determined in consideration of (1) the universal term, (2) the singular term, (3) the matter of the sentence, (4) its syntactical unit, and (5) its semantic unit.

Each stage of the deduction will conform to the same plan. Firstly, according to the principle of identity, a determinate class of identification will be deduced from the determination of the singular term by the designated term selected in the chain of the sentence. Secondly, examples illustrating the formal interpretation will be given and it will be asked whether any linguistic formal class of sentences corresponds to the class of identification. Thirdly, the interpretation in terms of access to the truth conditions will allow us to build the scheme characteristic of the class of identification in question. Finally, we shall inquire to what perceptual presentation, if any, the determined class of identification corresponds.

Pure predication

What does it mean to say that the singular term in the sentence is to be determined by the universal term? According to the nature of the linguistic terms themselves, ordinary or proper terms stand for separate universals. Moreover, to occur as a complete sign within the sentence, the universal as such is expressed by a morpheme, i.e., by a predicative moneme. Therefore a singular term will be determined by the universal term if it is constructed from the ordinary paradigms which constitute the proper linguistic code by a device complementary to the transformation of universals into predicates. The syntax of the system must be able, then, to transform a universal into a singular term. The singular term is like the predicate in so far as it belongs to the proper linguistic code and thus expresses a meaning whose referent can never be shown by ostension.

Ordinary words in the lexicon express universals. Since elementary sentences necessarily admit a universal in predicate position, the question is whether there exist genuine sentences whose singular terms may be borrowed as such from common vocabulary and, while denoting a singular state of affairs, still depend uniquely on a universal meaning for the complete determination of their extension.

Sentences such as 'Eight is a natural number' and 'Humility is a virtue' answer the question affirmatively if we accept them at their face value.

Against the first sentence, one might object that it does not qualify as elementary, since the word *eight* in the argument position abbreviates a definite description, namely, 'the class of all eightuples'. That such class-abstracts are required by set theory in argument positions may be urged, but such constructions, as well as their interpretations, do not seem to belong to the elementary vocabulary of a proper linguistic code. As for the second sentence, it will be said that its universal in argument position is a property-abstract that may always be explained away by a suitable paraphrase. It is a routine exercise – practised even by Plato's interpreters – to explain 'Humility is a virtue' and 'Redness is a sign of ripeness' away as perverse ways of saying of humble concrete persons and of red concrete fruits that they are respectively virtuous and ripe – even if more difficult cases occur, such as 'humility is rare',[15] where devious analyses may be required.

Against both examples a second kind of objection runs that a speaker refers to such abstract singular objects as 'eight' or 'humility' only after he has mastered a more concrete apparatus. No natural language, as such, contains a complete coordinate language, and everywhere bodily, spatial, temporal and social connotations of number-names are traced back which are rooted in directives for ordered motions.[16] More generally, 'concrete' concepts are historically prior to abstract concepts.

None of these objections is conclusive. The first one makes the exorbitant assumption that logicism is built into the very semantics of natural language. Doubtful as it is from the point of view of natural language, this assumption would entail one of the following consequences. The first is that classes would occur within the ultimate furniture of the world, and class-abstracts would be considered as a regular syntactical device to form a singular term from a universal, and, after all, the sentence 'The class of all eightuples is a natural number' or a sentence of this type, even if belonging to a late stage of linguistic development, would count among the irreducible, and therefore for us, elementary singular sentences. The second is that logicism would be sustained by nominalist hopes oblivious to the limitations of first-order logic.[17]

Paraphrasing the sentence 'Humility is a virtue' into the sentence: 'For every x, if x is humble, x is virtuous' commits us to considering this universal as true even if no man happens to be virtuous. Dealing with an empty universe of discourse is indeed recommended, if the truth of our sentence is not bound to depend on the chances afforded by empirical observations. Ethics, Kant said, must borrow nothing from examples and experiences. But then, at least for rigorism – and rigorism makes sense even if there is no rigorist in this world – the paraphrase in terms of humble persons loses all value and justification. Abstracts are useful in just such cases.

The last objection lodges nominalism at the base of diachronic linguistics. But even when primitive number-names mean, for instance, concrete bodily motions, if what is important in these motions is their order rather than their substance, this does not decide the case against an irreducible status of singular abstract notions in language but only shows, as against logicism, that the words expressing these notions have more affinity with the genuine and idiomatic names which arithmetic uses for designating the results of its intuitive operations than with the names of logical properties belonging to concealed concepts. Recent comparative philology has questioned the general nominalist postulate which dominated nineteenth-century philology and which states that when several meanings are associated with the same root, we must always put at the origin a concrete meaning from which the abstract meanings are derived.[18]

An inducement to admitting the proposed sentences as genuinely elementary would be afforded if we were to find in some natural language a formal class expressing identifications of the same type, a formal class being defined by the fact that it is explicitly opposable to the other classes of predicative sentence forms within a system.

In our idioms, the morphemes which we characterize as verbs contain two elements. One, the verbal form, is variable and explicit, and it expresses a meaning: a number, a tense, a person, an aspect, a mood, and so forth. The other, which is invariable and remains implicit, performs two functions relevant to reference. It unites into a complete structure the constituents of the sentence, and it asserts the content of the sentence. Since most languages foreign to Indo-European lack our class of verbal morphemes, they parcel out the variable element among the several parts of discourse which they recognize, using, for instance, tensed nominal forms. As to the invariant element, it may or may not be explicit;[19] but in any case it has to be there, since, without it, sentences would not be syntactical and semantic units.

Contrary to what the present branches of Indo-European suggest, the proper predicative function is, in most languages, dissociated from the verbal form.

Now there are languages, such as Indo-European itself, which both recognize the class of *verbal morphemes* as predicates generating the ordinary sentences and build sentences in which the predicative function is performed by nominal *morphemes*. It is just in this case, where, according to Saussure's principle, the two kinds of sentences happen to come into opposition, that we can describe with precision the corresponding states of affairs. The phrase *nominal sentence* was coined by Meillet to designate sentences of the second kind.[20] Sentences of the first kind we shall call *participation sentences*. Although English makes no formal distinction between the two sentences 'Humility is a virtue' and 'Agnes is docile', so that both of them count as two occurrences of the same form '*Fa*' (even if *a* is in one case an abstract and in the other a concrete term), primitive Indo-European languages would employ a nominal sentence for the first one (according to the pattern 'Humility virtue'),[21] a participation sentence for the second.

As Benveniste writes in his accurate analysis of this opposition:

in the nominal sentence the assertive element, being nominal, *does not* admit of the determination that the verbal form bears, viz., the modalities of tense, person, and so on. The assertion will have this specific character that it will be non-temporal, impersonal, non-modal, in short, that it will bear on a term reduced to its mere semantic content. A second consequence is that this nominal assertion cannot participate in the essential property of a verbal assertion.[22] Such a property consists in bringing the time of the event into relation with the tense of the discourse about the event. The nominal sentence in Indo-European languages asserts a certain 'quality' (in the most general sense) as peculiar to the subject of the sentence, but without any determination, including temporal determination, and without any relation to the speaker.[23]

On the contrary, when a participation sentence binds two names with the substantial verb *is*, the assertive verbal form introduces verbal determinations into the sentence, namely, spatial, temporal and modal localization, as well as a relation to the speaker.[24] In contrast to the nominal sentence 'Humilitas virtus', which only subsumes *humility* under *virtue*, the participation sentence 'Humilitas est virtus', in primitive Indo-European, would rather mean 'There is a virtue of humility', where the words 'There is' get an existential and not a mere classificatory sense.

It remains to be seen what consequences this opposition entails with respect to the nature of the arguments. Now, in nominal sentences all space–time determination is removed from the predicate as name; so all such determination must also be removed from the argument. Indeed, how could such a nominal subsumption meaningfully bear on spatio-temporal things? If the predicates of natural number and of virtue cannot sometimes suit, and sometimes not, the arguments eight and humility respectively, it is because these arguments also have no relation to space and time. They are universals in referential position, and they are irreducible to persons, to things or to events in so far as these are individuated in perception; nevertheless, they are endowed with all the logical properties of full individuation. It is surely easier to identify the number eight and to distinguish it from the number three than it is to identify the ship of Theseus and to distinguish it from the sacred ship which every year sailed from Piraeus to Delos. The reidentification which raises difficulties in the case of the ship would make no sense in the case of the number. For this same reason, identifying humility and distinguishing it from justice are, all things considered, on a par with identifying and distinguishing numbers. For they are independent of all the material conditions which burden those operations when applied to sensible particulars.

Absoluteness and independence-of-situation are criteria for determining the context in which nominal sentences occur. They do not occur in narrations that intend to inform us about persons, things and circumstances. They abound in speeches and treatises where they convey the sentences and proverbs which are used for acting and convincing.[25]

Consider a speaker *A* who pronounces a nominal sentence or its equivalent in his particular idiom. In his *Lettres à une princesse allemande*, Euler, writing as a mathematician and therefore thinking of nominal sentences, represented predication by a figure composed of a circle and a point. The circle stands for the predicate, the point for the singular term. If the point falls within the circle, the sentence is affirmative, negative if it lies outside it. Besides the circumference itself, something remains indeterminate in this image of predication. What indeed determines the exterior of the circle? If the circle represents the predicate 'being an even number', the point representing the number three will fall outside the circle, which means that 'Three is not an even number.' But neither can Socrates be subsumed under this universal. Might then the name 'Socrates' not also fall outside the circle? In order to eliminate this indetermination, it is convenient, following Venn, to close the universe of discourse, that is, to determine what the negation of the universal embraces by drawing Euler's circle within a square, and by agreeing that within the area exterior to the circle but interior to the square will fall all individuals which do not fall under the universal but of which it makes sense to ask whether they fall under it. (See figure 1.)

When *A* pronounces an affirmative nominal sentence, he puts a point in Euler's circle, and he has tacitly closed the universe of discourse, i.e., the

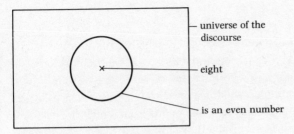

Figure 1 Scheme of the nominal sentence

category of the individuals which may meaningfully be put outside the circle. How can B who hears (or reads) A's sentence understand it? He knows that it involves only the proper code of the language with which both A and B are conversant. Having put, according to A's explicit instruction, the point within the circle, he closes the universe of discourse exactly as A had tacitly done, by excluding, in agreement with the neutralizations implied by the nominal sentence, any information which would be foreign to the proper code. Because they use the same code, the speaker A and the hearer B have the same access to the truth conditions of the message. This identity follows from the fact that, by definition, the nominal sentence conveys a purely conceptual message, since it only subsumes a universal-argument under a universal-function. Anyone who masters the proper code automatically understands such a message, in so far as the mere understanding assures, for any competent hearer, the same access to the truth conditions.

When we determine the singular term by the universal term and use pure predication, our reference cannot be found in perception. On the one hand, the identification thus allowed bears on objects foreign to ordinary space–time identification, and that excludes external perception. On the other hand, the possibility of the state of affairs is entirely encapsulated in the juxtaposition of the universal and the subject term and no place is left, in the message, for reflexivity. Internal perception and subjectivity are therefore also excluded.

To pure predication nothing in perception can correspond, and a first genuine linguistic category – the most simple and the most regular – is defined with no perceptual counterpart. This paradoxical result was, however, to be expected if the linguistic universals, in contradistinction to perceptual universals embedded in the co-presence of actual contiguities and memory resemblances, were to be 'separated' within systems of paradigmatic oppositions and syntagmatic compositions.

Substantial and accidental predications

If the proper linguistic code ignores everything which is not a universal, by using only universal functions to determine its singular term, pure predication not only works in a standard way but exhausts the linguistic standards in one go. The rest of the deduction will have to rely on irregular devices. It will divide into two main parts according to the marks from which the principle governing the determination of the singular term is borrowed. The singular term as such has until now not been accorded a linguistic status, and the material chain of the sentence taken by itself is to be counted as a perceptual event. Both determinations will be exploited for identifying particulars given in space and time. As to the two remaining marks by which the sentence is closed, they will be seen to enable the speaker to express the subjective aspects of his perception. .

This organization of the deduction is seen more clearly if we interpret it formally. Nominal sentences exclude the ontological import of the objective verbal determinations as well as of the subjective involvements of the speaker which, in our idioms, are liable to be expressed by the variable part of the verb. By recovering these verbal determinations severally, we shall achieve an exhaustive series of the dogmatic elementary sentences. Then a subjective series will account for the subjective involvement left aside up to that point.

The principle of the possibility of a first series, where sentence-forms will assume more and more distant positions from the nominal sentence, is grounded in the systematic examination of how several elementary participation sentences can be disposed of when objective verbal determinations are progressively reintroduced into assertion by modifying either the predicate or the argument. This reintroduction may occur by means of conventions extending the linguistic code, or by using the enunciation as the centre of a coordinate system. The first procedure will result in two correlated kinds of predication: substantial predication and accidental predication.

The demand that the singular term be determined by the singular term may seem to be circular, contradictory and even absurd, since the linguistic code has made no provision for singular terms. But let us spell out the requirements that such a demand contains. Firstly, singular terms are not to be found among the proper signs of language. If, therefore, the singular term is to perform the function of a singular term, it must do it while being, in principle, devoid of meaning. Secondly, the function which singular terms are expected to fulfil is their designating something unique, though without recourse to grammatical constructions since meanings have been excluded. Both requirements are satisfied only if the social group agrees by explicit conventions on a list of special terms whose role consists simply in their referring to unique existents.

The list of these special singular terms may be supposed to be such that no room is left for ambiguity of identification once the singular term is combined with a predicate. Even granting this condition, however, the extension of the code proper to include such a list will produce two different cases for possible identification. On the one hand, the meaning of the universal expressed by the predicate may define an extension which admits only such-and-such special singular terms. Even if the identity of the individual is the business of the singular term, the predicate suffices by itself to express a complete, though indeterminate, act of identification. For this kind of identification we shall reserve the term *substantial predication*. On the other hand, the meaning of the predicate may be more composite, making it impossible to tell *a priori* what kinds of special singular term will fall under its extension. In that case, until the special singular term is supplied, the predicate remains powerless to assure a determinate identification and only succeeds by engaging in an implicit subordination to substantial predication. This subordinate identification is expressed by *accidental predication*.

Nominal sentences deprive the terms which occur in argument-places of any spatio-temporal import. Instances of number and virtue are no more given in space and time than number and virtue themselves, and they must clearly be distinguished from their spatio-temporal realizations (eight men, a humble person). Now, every time a predicate admits of instantiations apart from realizations, its extension, at least in principle, may be divided into its ultimate elements according to a law. This lawlike partition allows us to reach the individuals by pure concepts or, more exactly, by concepts organized according to general rules. Plato's dialogues show the difficulties involved in the search for such rules. However, they do not question the ontological possibility of the division itself. When I define humility as the virtue that consists in the recognition that no instance of virtue can be adequately realized, my definition deserves to be criticized for its inadequacy as well as for its logical form, but it does show how concepts seize individuals. The lawlike partition of extensions is clearest when these extensions are infinite, as is the case with numbers. And it is because instantiation apart from realization is subject to laws that demonstration is possible. A case in point is the theorem which crowns Euclid's *Elements* and according to which there are five regular polyhedra. The demonstration is about instances (kinds of realizations), not about realizations.

This is why, in nominal sentences, the terms (*eight* or *humility*) that occur in argument position can both express a universal and denote an individual. Such universals might be better called *ideas*, and their names might be better called *names* of *ideas*. Two consequences directly following from the distinction between instantiation and realization concern the kind of predication at stake with ideas as well as the kind of singular terms which name them. Predicates, in that case, have only a classificatory function and, since spatio-temporal existence is left to realizations, which do not matter when it is simply a question of instantiations, they contain no verbal determination, not even the determination of existence. As to the names of ideas, there are cases, as with the natural numbers, in which, despite their indefinite number, the instances need only a finite and very low number of primitive names (as many as the elements contained in the base of numeration), from which syntax tells us how to build, according to a law, all the other possible names. This possibility, characteristic of certain coordinate languages, is strictly connected with the purely conceptual way of identifying ideas.

Ideas cannot instantiate in space and time, nor can nominal sentences identify ordinary things as given in space and time. These new functions require new types of elementary sentences in which both the predicate and the singular term undergo appropriate modifications.

Suppose predication minimally altered, just enough to make instantiations identical with realizations of the universal. A perfect identification is still expected between what fills the argument position and an instance of the universal in predicate position. As do nominal sentences, the new type of predicate will express a defining property, the instantiation of which does not admit of degrees.[26] However, since the predicate must now be realized by its instances, the purely classificatory function of the nominal predicate must be modified in order to express the required function of the 'substantive verb' *is*.[27] This is indeed the minimal verbal determination apt to project the instance into spatio-temporal reality. Even when the projection is only half-successful, as may be the case with spirits and gods, the individuals identified are at least believed to produce and to create everything in space and time which ordinary individuals do to a lesser degree and subject to more strictures. The question arises, however, as to how the individuals which are eventually precipitated into our lowly world can, without contradiction, combine with universals in such a way that the resulting state of affairs remains immune from most spatio-temporal contaminations. An answer is possible only if the universal lays hold of the individual in its totality as if, once its spatio-temporal existence has been granted, it should not, with respect to everything else, really differ from pure subsumption. The realizations involved in instantiations mean that instances that are actually now identified as being in space and time may have been already identified and may possibly be reidentified in other places and at other moments. There is, then, substantial predication only if the predicate's actual identification supports and warrants this host of pre-identifications and reidentifications. Since being an instance of humanity is bound to a contingent realization, it does not prevent Socrates, for example, from changing in other respects, but remains with him unaltered. When such a property is separated from the other properties Socrates has *qua* being this particular instance, all verbal determinations beyond pure existence must be eliminated. Consequently there is a 'definition' of Socrates as being an instance of humanity. For example, there is a law according to which a *proximum genus* will be determined by a *differentia specifica* so that it comes to cover the least extension common to all and only all individuals which invariably and permanently are its realizations. At the same time there remains a chasm between the individual and the set of its defining properties which makes the existent contingent, in so far as there is no law apt to define the individuals as such, or, if there is one, it supposes, as Leibniz puts it, an infinite conjunction of universals whose summation – corresponding to the monad's essence – escapes our knowledge and is kept in God's secret calculation. It is certainly possible to describe such an individual by an appropriate finite conjunction of universals but, as happens with extensional regimentations, each such conjunction proceeds in an *ad hoc* way and we are left ignorant of any possible essence or form of the individuals.

Such are the properties required of the substantial predicate. Its argument names an instance which, being realized in space and time, may possibly be shown. If we had a general system according to which we could express ostension in words, we might combine substantial predication with such words and thus obtain, in a regular and appropriate way, the required singular terms. But for the moment we have no such words. Moreover, they would not quite match up to their task. Suppose, indeed, I pick out an individual by ostension. The substantial predication thus obtained would belong to the type: 'This man is a man' or, at best, 'This man is mortal.' Since a substantial universal would occur both in the predicate and in the argument, substantial predications would turn into analytic truths or, at best, would subsume under a substantial predicate an individual inasmuch as it realized another substantial predicate. But we may want to refer also to such individuals in so far as they merely exist in space and time and before they are subsumed under substantial predicates, leaving to substantial predication the function it has normally to perform without already burdening the argument with that function. The last objection would also apply to a similar procedure where a non-substantial predicate would be combined with a word expressing ostension. Moreover, such singular terms would fail to encompass the whole spatio-temporal existence of the individual as required.

The appropriate singular terms then will have (a) to express adequately an identification, (b) to guarantee the host of pre-and reidentifications implied by pure spatio-temporal existence, and (c) to refrain from introducing concepts in order to name what cannot be identified by means of concepts subject to a law. Since a regular device relying on the linguistic expression of ostension is missing and moreover could not meet the second condition, language, thus forbidden to use universals, that is, proper linguistic signs, for individuation, needs additional signs which, by convention, will be intended to designate spatio-temporal individuals taken in the whole span of their existence. Such signs are called *proper names*. Since proper names, in principle, borrow nothing from conceptual identification, conventions introduce them as a supplement to the ordinary vocabulary and as a supplement which has to be maintained within narrow limits. As the pathology of age knows, they burden memory heavily, and only a limited number of substances deserve to be designated in this way.

'Jupiter is a star' and 'Socrates is a man' afford examples of substantial predication in natural language. The introduction of substantial predication, which says what a substance is, would have no sense were it not opposed, within the realm of participation sentences, to the description of the qualities and accidents a substance has independently of its defining properties. This latter type of predication deserves to be called *accidental* because it deals with the existence of the substance as it happens to be characterized not only by its defining qualities but also by the contingent and temporary states, actions and conditions which it produces and undergoes. Such identifications lay no claim to sustaining pre-identifications or reidentifications. While the subject of the change is perhaps supposed to remain the very substance that it was in substantial predication, the predicate is modified: from a nominal predicate it becomes a verbal one. Another group of the verbal determinations recovers its full employment. 'Socrates drank the hemlock', 'Socrates was white', 'Socrates was a musician' are examples of the new elementary sentence. All the verbal determinations which occur in accidental predication go beyond pure existence and come down to three indications: aspects which describe the various ways a given state adheres to its substance;[28] objective ordering of these states in a substance's lifespan;[29] and modal types of their belonging to a substance.[30]

Against treating the proposed examples as genuine cases of elementary substantial and accidental predications, two main kinds of objection are raised. Firstly, there is the question of whether there are genuine proper names in natural languages. The second kind of objection bears on the very distinction we made between substantial and accidental predications.

We have already mentioned a philosophical argument urging the general elimination of all singular terms. But that argument has to do with a reform of natural language, and this is not the place for examining it. Still, proper names have given rise to two kinds of doubt in the mind of those who aspire to describing natural languages as they really are. Some deny any difference between proper names and terms standing for universals. Some insist on their infelicities for adequately fulfilling even the strictest part of their duty: that concerning identification.

According to some ethnologists, such as Lévi-Strauss, the rule, in primitive societies, is that all 'proper names' are classificatory. The individual is never designated as such but only in so far as it belongs to such-and-such classes and enters into such-and-such relations with these classes. Even in our societies this is the case. The proper name designates not an individual but a class or patrilinear filiation. As to the Christian name, it subsumes the individual under the patronage of a Saint – representative of some important virtue – and relates him to the liturgical calendar. It may happen that instead of such an objective classification we resort to a subjective one. When we name our pets or even our children, we often class ourselves rather than the named individuals, by using terms which publicize our own social tastes and preferences. In short, no linguistic individual reference can be obtained except by relying on an intersection of universals.[31]

This whole objection results from a confusion between the origin and the use of the proper names, that is, between universals as belonging to the proper linguistic code and universals used to refer to individuals and destined to this special reference by a conventional extension of the code in conformity with the particular application of the principle governing the determination of the singular term.[32] Even if proper names happen to have a classificatory meaning, they are used independently of it, since the meaning may possibly be ignored while the proper name succeeds in fulfilling its role. For a cultivated English speaker, the three components of the name 'Theodore Taylor Jr' are universals. But he knows how to use them in the right way even if he forgets what the meaning of 'Theodore' is and that tailors are craftsmen and if he sees that this Junior has grown into an old man. Now even if there is meaning, it is the use and not the meaning which is fixed by collective convention relevant to a more or less large social group: a convention which often results from explicit rites and performatives such as baptism. Understanding a proper name, then, has nothing to do with understanding the universals which it possibly expresses. When, in primitive societies, classificatory names are assigned to individuals according to rules, these rules are a part not of the proper code of the language, but of the customs and conventions of the tribe. An ethnologist who understands the tribal idiom does not automatically know how to use these names, a use which requires the knowledge of particular customs and conventions constituting an extension of linguistic code. There was a Greek philosopher who named his daughters by the particles. It is said that they were recognized without ambiguity. This extreme example shows how a convention may arbitrarily extract from the code any word and make it play the role of a proper name. This is the reason why few substances only may be designated by proper names: all men, some animals, places, buildings, etc., that are considered as sufficiently important for the singular terms standing for them to have enough occurrences. For the other cases, circumstantial predication and definite descriptions are used, which are indeed beyond the scope of elementary substantial and accidental predication.

A second objection is drawn from proper names devoid of a unique reference, and it will receive a similar answer. Since any part of discourse may be turned into a proper name when an explicit or tacit convention attaches it, as a mark, to a particular substance, the experiences and beliefs of the group are involved in the pragmatic decision to regard a sign as a proper name or not. If a group is acquainted with a substance, the sign by which it is eventually referred to is authenticated as a proper name, even when the acquaintance itself belongs to the past and has been transmitted by tradition. The French may thus be said, in the most liberal sense of the word, to be acquainted with Napoléon. But it sometimes happens that the confidence a group puts in the existence and the uniqueness of the proper name's reference is shaken. *Zeus* and *Homer* were once good proper names. At least one of them has become a definite description. There are also proper names which were probably never intended to name existent individuals. These occur only in fictions, where sequences of words formally identical with assertable syntagms are known not to be assertable, and where the corresponding sentence forms such as 'Pegasus is winged' are indeed not genuine sentences and are deprived of truth-values. As to the change that the word *Zeus* underwent when the Greeks began doubting that there existed a god named *Zeus*, it may be analysed by examining how a sentence behaves with respect to negation. When genuine proper names occur in the negation of a sentence they occur only as a 'secondary occurrence', the negation having the whole sentence in its scope. Pseudo-proper names, on the contrary, go together with definite descriptions and may have primary as well as secondary occurrences. In the case of primary occurrence, the sentence must be analysed, and the negation then bears on the conditions of existence, or uniqueness, of the reference. In any case it is only by its being pragmatically coupled with the particular usages of speakers (including rites of baptism) that language succeeds in determining substantial individuals.[33]

The objection concerning the types of predication themselves is raised in the name of extensionality. Substantial predication is necessary, and accidental predication is not necessary. But difficulties affect the interpretation of these modalities. Must they be understood *de dicto* or *de re*? Must there be restrictions on the substitutivity of identicals and on the legitimacy of inferring from a given singular sentence its corresponding particularization? Do we mean that it is necessary that Socrates is a man or that Socrates is-necessarily-a-man? If 'This walking biped is Socrates' is a true sentence, may we accept that it is necessary that this walking biped is a man or that this walking biped is-necessarily-a-man, or both, or neither, while we are ready to accept the necessity for the husband of Xanthippe or for the master of Plato to be a man either on the *de dicto* or on the *de re* interpretation? Finally, what particular sentence are we authorized to infer from a substantial predication? That it is necessary that there exists a man? Or that there exists an x such that x is necessarily a man? Or neither or both of them?

These questions have been debated, not settled. On the one hand, there is no comparison from the point of view of clarity between the extensionality of a regimented language and natural language with its modalities. On the other hand, though the consistency of the inferences requires more complex rules when modalities are used, modalities seem to be built into natural language and nothing assures us that even devious extensional paraphrases could translate and capture the common linguistic opposition we make between substance and accident.

The examination of objections has sufficiently shown our language to recognize this opposition formally. However, before analysing how the speakers and hearers may accede to the truth conditions of a sentence, two remarks may be of use. One of them will be about accidents, the other about simplicity and composition in both substantial and accidental predication.

Accidental predication contrasts with both nominal and substantial predication. Being no longer confined within the bounds of a kind, it does not by itself indicate specific instances of the universal, and it fails to complete independently the identification of a spatio-temporal substance. Drinking or being white applies to several kinds, and nightingales and swans count as musicians among birds. Verbal universals have lost all predicative autonomy and independence because of the way they refer. While nothing is changed in their indirectly and distinctly expressing a meaning fixed by the code, they still refer, as every predicate does, directly and confusedly; but their reference is left undetermined. The predicates 'virtue' and 'man' make us expect entities like 'humility' and 'Socrates'. Predicates such as 'drank', 'was white', and 'was a musician' announce no determinate substance which they would be able to identify and to reidentify during its whole substantial existence.

The *concrete–abstract* opposition is loosely used in order to mark the difference between universals and individuals in argument-position. With better grounds it fits the contrasting roles of substantial versus verbal predication. Universals that directly identify spatio-temporal instances admit, indeed, concrete instances such as men, stars and birds. By contrast, instances that are left undetermined by their universals have no concrete existence by themselves and may be said to be abstract, since as passions, actions, or performances they have no reality apart from their substance – a substance answering to another principle of classification. A verbal universal conveys two different items of information since its reference is undetermined. Like any predicate, it announces that something will instantiate it. Besides that, its specific referential indetermination warns us that only substantial predication will fill the gap and will indicate the subject in which the verbal universal is present. It is not the substance as such which is an instance of accidental predication but the substance seized in its passion, action or performance. In Aristotelian terms,[34] what the verb adds to the general predication ('dicitur') is the notion of inherence ('inest'), understood in a sense which does not necessarily imply a spatial connotation.

Let us now come back to substantial predication. Two cases must be distinguished according to whether the individual is or is not exempt from the internal changes which are the ordinary lot of such spatio-temporal substances. Elements and deified stars have often been conceived of as belonging to the first class. The sempiternality of a subject held to be simple then complies with the eternity of the predicate. This is why this substantial predication is called *simple*. On the other hand, a substance which is thought to be composite and corruptible is fully subjected to alteration and destruction. The name of such a substance can enter into this substantial predication (which may be called *composite*) only if, as long and as far as it exists, the part of the substance that is concerned in substantial predication is permanently identical with an instance of the universal in predicate position.

A similar distinction arises within accidental predication, but on the condition that the role of the simple and the composite be exchanged.

For substances subject to simple substantial predication, there is, by

SKETCH OF A DEDUCTION | 63

definition, no possible accidental corresponding predication apt to affect their internal constitution. Only their external relations will change. On the contrary, if a substance enters into composite predication, accidentality affects not only its relations with other substances but its own core. Therefore there is first a composite *accidental* predication, where several simple substances unite to form such a temporary *compositum* or aggregate that it would be meaningless to attribute its specific properties to any or to each of its elements. Jupiter is in conjunction with Mars. In such a predication 'dicitur' applies to the relation between these planets and 'inesse' refers only indirectly to the substances themselves. It is only their relative situation which happens to change. That is why we are led to think of relations as external and to dissociate their effects from their subjects. By analogy we extend the same dissociation to substances that we consider as eternal not in themselves but with respect to some event with respect to which they behave like eternal substances. We speak of large heaps of sand, not of large grains of sand. We say that the Athenians defeated the Persians at Marathon, where individual Athenians or groups of Athenians were certainly defeated by their Persian foes. Here 'dicitur' applies to the collective subject and it is only in so far as they unite into such a temporary collective subject that 'inesse' qualifies the substances involved. Substance's modifications are in it only in so far as it is related to another one. To a relational 'dicitur' there corresponds, so to speak, a relative 'inesse'. On the contrary, 'dicitur' and 'inesse' qualify the heart of the subject, Socrates, when we say that he is sitting. The substances subject to composite substantial predication are thus alone susceptible of entering into *simple* accidental predication. The subject, in this case, never adequately expresses a universal, either because it embodies it for a life's span without capturing its eternity or because it requires for its actualization the constant and silent presence of this embodiment. Universals, therefore, are then mixed with another obscure principle which hinders their clear manifestation. In other words, individual substances are made up of form and of matter.

When the question is what the speaker does in order to fix the ways in which one has access to the truth conditions of the sentence 'Socrates is a man', the comparison with the same question raised about nominal sentences immediately shows that, in contrast to 'eight' or to 'humility', 'Socrates' designates a substance located in space and time, so that we must be able not only to identify, but to reidentify it: an operation that would be meaningless in nominal sentences. Therefore a new scheme of predication arises where the former placing of a point in the interior of a circle closed by the universe of discourse merely figures the plane instantaneous section of a solid prism. The

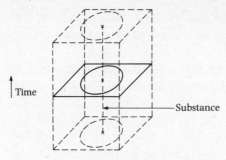

Time

Substance

Figure 2 Scheme of substantial predication

prism itself represents the extension of the universe of discourse to a continuous temporal assignability of the predication. Though the sentence 'Socrates is a man' is still poorly determined from the point of view of time, it assures us that the actual subsumption of the individual under the universal is continued in past and future. These virtual subsumptions, by which the speaker schematizes the substantival verb, mark the place for the pre-identifications and reidentifications.

Besides accounting in a simple way for the difference between nominal and substantial predication, this scheme bears in itself the reason for the peculiar mode of reference of proper names, for the distinction between substantial and accidental predication and for the opposition between simple and composite predications.

(1) The specificity of proper names, with their implicit use of substantial predication that requires their introduction by linguistic conventions, is often blurred by the fact that, because we use many proper names to designate individuals we are acquainted with, we attribute to the general use of proper names features that are peculiar to their use under the condition of acquaintance. Suppose, for instance, A knows Mr Smith by acquaintance. When he utters or hears 'Smith', he will probably associate this name with the memory of some singular feature of Mr Smith and he will easily believe that proper names refer to particulars in the same way as memories do. A person B, however, who is not acquainted with Mr Smith, will understand nothing of that sort when he hears the same name. Following the principle that proper names are related to individuals according to the conventions of the group – a principle sometimes violated by practical jokers but ordinarily obeyed – he will understand that the talk is about a man, taken in his whole temporal development and in the whole prism of his life's span, without limitation to any of its instantaneous sections.

While A's identification is supported by particular features, B's identifications are reduced to a general scheme. In B's situation – the only one which is important for the extension of the linguistic code – Mr Smith will be identified by the determinate but unknown instance of a man who is called 'Mr Smith', where B knows that every instance of a species is a substance, i.e., an individual permanent under its changes. Any material feature of Mr Smith may be used by A for his identification. On the contrary, deprived as he is of all acquaintance, B must effect identification by the form, that is, by an indefinite individuation of the species. In other words, he is only informed that, for all its duration, the referred-to individual will instantiate its relevant species, so that its representative point in the scheme must always remain in the interior of the circle, whatever section is chosen along the temporal axis. If it is possible for the speakers to agree about the kind of identification they have to expect from using proper names, their agreement seems to be essentially modal, since it requires that the whole prism be taken into account, whereas from a purely extensional point of view, any instantaneous section would do. Such a modality, however, may still be explained away by quantifying over time. The necessity inherent in substantial predication should then be paraphrased by replacing the one-argument universal by a corresponding two-argument universal where the added argument is the time variable, universally bound. Instead of 'Jupiter is-a-star' we should then read: '(t) Jupiter is-a-star-at t' – a sentence which is false, since stars are born and die, but meaningful. Where substances known to be corruptible are in question, the universal quantification takes place within a life's span. In this case, we must introduce an empirical propositional function relative to the species of which the substance is a member, such as $L(y)$, to be interpreted as: 'y is at most as long as the maximum span of a man's life', where y takes its values in the domain of durations. Instead of 'Socrates is-a-man', we should then read:

$$'(\exists t_1)\,(\exists t_2)\,[L(|t_2 - t_1|)\,.\,(t)\,(t_1 \leq t \leq t_2 \supset \text{Socrates is-a-man-at } t)].'$$

(2) In contradistinction to the scheme of substantial predication, the prism would feature in the universe of discourse of an accidental predication, were the point representative of the individual now in the interior, now in the exterior of the circle representative of the universal. Socrates is now sitting, now running. He is always a man. Conceived as transitory, the accidental predication would be modal in the same weak sense which has just been recognized for substantial predication. But here existential quantification would replace universal quantification over time.

That such a conception of modality is too weak is shown by the case of permanent accidents. Whiteness is, for Socrates, an accident. Its permanence, however, transforms it into a substantial predicate. Thus something is missing in the suggested modal characterization of the two kinds of predication. Until now the scheme of substantial predication has been examined only from the point of view of the proper name which refers to the whole prism. Considered from the point of view of the predicate, there is also a second bit of information not yet exploited. That is, the predicate is substantial because it is by itself sufficient for identifying any one of its instances. The term for a species – and the same remark applies to terms for genera and specific differences as proper parts of the species as well as for the *propria* as its consequences – conveys an autonomous and independent, though indefinite, idea of the individual which will instantiate this universal. But consider predicates such as 'is white' or 'runs'. By themselves, that is, without the presence of a determinative proper name, they do not independently determine what kind of individual will give the right instantiation. In contradistinction to 'is-a-man', they allow us to expect various disparate closures of the universe of discourse. Men, sheep, flowers, stones, armies, terror and witchcraft are said to be white; while men, horses, brooks, rumours and reputations are said to run.

This distinction between two kinds of predicative referring explains why proper names are important. They are important not in substantial predication, where their employment is redundant because of the independence of the predicate, but in accidental predication. Suppose that A – a French-speaker – spoke of Socrates or of a man, without being heard by B, who only grasps the following of A's words: 'il est blanc' or 'il court', with the anaphoric 'il' which neutralizes the English opposition between 'he' and 'it'. From these sentences B cannot infer what kind of individual is referred to. The identification of the individual announced by the accidental predicate is thus subordinated to the presupposition of a substantial identification, which alone is able to eliminate the ambiguities proper to accidental referring. In order to choose the indeterminate universe of discourse of accident, B needs the universe of discourse of substance. Such is the meaning of Aristotle's distinction between 'dicitur' and 'inest'. Identifications and reidentifications play their role in accidental predication as well as in substantial predication. But their role is independent and direct in the second case only. There they are *per se*. Thus the scheme of substantial predication is indeed complete, i.e., concrete. Terms such as 'is-white' or 'runs' cannot by themselves give a complete identification of what they refer to. Their indeterminate reference must 'be in' another determinate reference, and the accidental identification thus occurs not *per se*, but *per aliud*. It is only when the circle of the accident is intersected by the circle of the substance that the access to the truth conditions is definitively fixed.

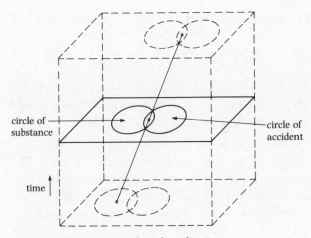

circle of
substance

circle of
accident

time

Figure 3 Scheme of accidental predication

To give a complete account of accidental predication, it is not enough to relativize the predicate to a time variable. Such a relativization cannot convey the subordination built into accidental predication. Let us consider, instead of the singular sentences themselves, the general sentences they allow us to infer by existential quantification, namely:

'$(\exists x)\ (\exists t_1)\ (\exists t_2)\ [L(|t_2 - t_1|).\ (t)\ (t_1 \leq t \leq t_2 \supset$ is-a-man-at $t, x)]$',

'$(\exists x)\ (\exists t_1)\ (\exists t_2)\ [L(|t_2 - t_1|).\ (t)\ (t_1 \leq t \leq t_2 \supset$ is-white-at $t, x)]$'

and '$(\exists x)\ (\exists t)$ (runs-at-$t, x)$.'

Not only can we not distinguish a permanent accident from a substance (though there is some hint about the distinction in the fact that the empirical propositional function $L(y)$ is related to the predicate 'is-a-man-at t, x', and not to the predicate 'is-white-at t, x'), but in the three cases we quantify in the same way over the domain of substances so as to destroy the dependence of the accidents. If to say that something is white is to say that this whiteness as an individual abstract is in another concrete individual, namely, a substance, we must dissociate the instance of whiteness from the instance of substantial predication (a man, a flower, etc.) in which it is. Consequently, the predicate 'white', as any prima facie one-argument accidental predicate, will in reality be a three-argument accidental predicate, 'white (y, t, x)', where the variables y, t, x, must respectively be filled by a term referring to an instance of whiteness, a determination of time and a term for the substance in which the instance of whiteness is at time t. The former paraphrases will then read respectively:

'$(\exists x)$ $(\exists t_1)$ $(\exists t_2)$ $[L(|t_2 - t_1|).$ (t) $(t_1 \leq t \leq t_2 \supset$ is-a-man-at $t,\ x)]$'
(unchanged),

'$(\exists x)$ $(\exists t_1)$ $(\exists t_2)$ $[L(|t_2 - t_1|).$ (t) $\{t_1 \leq t \leq t_2 \supset$ (is-a-man-at $t, x.$ $(\exists y)$ y is-an-instance-of-whiteness-at $t,$ in $x)\}]$, and

'$(\exists x)$ $(\exists t_1)$ $(\exists t_2)$ $[L(|t_2 - t_1|).$ (t) $(t_1 \leq t \leq t_2 \supset$ is-a-man-at $t, x).$ $(\exists y)$ $(\exists t)$ $(t_1 \leq t \leq t_2.$ y is-an-instance-of-running-at $t,$ of $x)]$.'

Simpler paraphrases, which will be useful for circumstantial predication, would be obtained by introducing a new two-place predicate: 'x is-at t'. The advantage gained would consist in leaving the substantival predicate as a one-place predicate and in reducing the paraphrase of previous three-place predicates to two-place predicates. There would be, however, a price to be paid and a risk of category-mistake when using the newly introduced two-place predicate, where the variable x should at one time be replaced by a proper name referring to a substance and at another be bound by quantifying over an accident (the state of a substance). If we sacrificed clarity to simplicity and ran the risk, we should then obtain the simpler expressions:

'$(\exists x)$ [is-a-man $x.$ $(\exists t_1)$ $(\exists t_2)L(|t_2 - t_1|).$ $(t)(t_1 \leq t \leq t_2 \supset$ is-at $x, t)]$',

'$(\exists x)$ {is-a-man $x.$ $(\exists t_1)$ $(\exists t_2)[L(|t_2 - t_1|).$ $(t)(t_1 \leq t \leq t_2 \supset$ is-at $x, t).$ $(\exists y)$ (y is-an-instance-of-whiteness-in $x.$ is-at $y, t)]\}$',

'$(\exists x)$ {is-a-man $x.$ $(\exists t_1)$ $(\exists t_2)[L(|t_2 - t_1|).$ $(t)(t_1 \leq t \leq t_2 \supset$ is-at $x, t).$ $(\exists y)$ (y is-an-instance-of-running-of $x.$ $(\exists t)$ $(t_1 \leq t \leq t_2.$ is-at $y, t)]\}$.'

But it is not certain that these quantificational paraphrases have eliminated the modalities. A time-indexed predicate may be interpreted by a rather transparent relation of contiguity or togetherness between the predicate deprived of indexation and a time. But when we say that whiteness is *in* a substance or that running is *of* a substance, we exclude such simple relations. We mean that whiteness and running cannot be or be thought of without their corresponding substances while substance can, in a sense, be thought and spoken of without its accidents. It is highly doubtful that this distinction between the abstract and the concrete can be expressed without giving verbal modalities their full use.[35]

(3) The substantial prism may be construed in two different ways: either it is continued *in infinitum* in both past and future, or it has a beginning and an end.

When a substance has a beginning and an end, it is corruptible and therefore composite as is its corresponding substantial predication. The correlate of such a substantial composite predication is a simple accidental predication, the accident being interior to the substance itself because of its being composite. The scheme of accidental predication reduces, then, to one prism.

Sempiternal substances, on the contrary, being never internally associated or dissociated, afford a strong presumption of simplicity, and their substantial predication will also be said to be simple. Its correlate is given by a composite accidental predication. An element – be it a star or an atom – remaining indefinitely what it is, only an aggregation or a relation between such elements is subject to corruption. The scheme of composite accidental predication requires, therefore, the intersection of several substantial prisms. Such an intersection would figure the duration of the composite accidents, be they atomic *concilia* or planetary conjunctions, oppositions or quadratures or, by analogy, heaps of sand and fighting regiments.

Simple accidentality and substantial composition have always been considered the traits of contingent beings, while substantial simplicity and composite accidentality characterize necessary beings. These obscure and important thoughts will have need of religions and philosophies to develop them into views which might at best be self-consistent though surely mutually incompatible. But it is by no mere chance that proper names and substantial and accidental predications are so thoroughly committed to modalities. Substance and accident on the one hand and extensionality on the other are like fire and water. Extensionality admits of any identification bound to a transitory and isolated state of affairs. Speakers using substance and accident join virtual reidentifications to actual identifications. They survey continuous temporal developments, finite and indefinite, and every local reference is always made by thinking of the references which it makes possible or presupposes. The identification at stake would be missed were the speakers to forget, for mere extensions, the ways and intensions by which their words determined the classification.

Accidental predication and substantial predication are respectively suited to expressing the two kinds of perceptual representation.

The predicate of substantial predication stands for the species or the genus, and its singular term names this or that instance of this potential universal. Substantial predication therefore directly and exactly pictures the second level of representation.

The situation is not so simple with accidental predication, since the predicate stands for the properties of the perceived substance while the singular term names this substance. In perception it was the properties which represented the substance. In the accidental sentence it is the individual subsumed under the universal which represents the property.

Natural language then realizes a spontaneous regimentation. Pure predication imposes its pattern upon substantial predication and it is at the level of substantial predication that language gives its most faithful picture of perception. The same predicative pattern is then forced upon accidental predication, even if the linguistic signs cannot express the respective roles of the perceptual signals without exchanging them.

Circumstantial predication

If the material chain of the sentence must determine the singular term, it can do so only by its physical properties, the offices of the signs as such being elsewhere invested. Therefore the problem is that of borrowing the function of unique designation characteristic of the singular term from the salient perceptive feature of a given chain of sounds. Now, what is perceived is a message as an event and an event produced by a speaker at a determinate place and moment. The noise of the utterance then automatically shows an absolute space–time origin for localizing the universals. Thus language reuses its own waste. If speaking were replaced by writing, it would then be the place where the inscription has been engraved and its time computed according to the wear of the stone that would be taken into consideration.

All the verbal determinations permitted by substantial and accidental predications entrust the referential identification to the substance itself as a frame of coordinates for its own change. In order that the remaining objective verbal determinations may be exploited in an essential way, a new elementary sentence form is needed, namely, *circumstantial predication*. One innovation settles everything. The speaker actively converses with others and dialogue takes the place of narration. This innovation, it will be shown, is connected with the use of egocentric particulars. Every natural language recognizes a formal class of such signs. It is by their use that sentences such as 'It is raining' are expressed.

An objection, however, is raised by philosophers. Egocentric particulars, they say, may always be eliminated as such, certain general terms taking over the function of the previously admitted egocentric particulars, so that the explanatory power of the language containing egocentric particulars does not exceed the explanatory power of the regimented language in which the elimination paraphrase is made. Such is the case when I replace the sentence 'It is raining' said in Paris on 1 January 1981 by the sentence 'It is raining in Paris on 1 January 1981', a sentence whose truth-value never changes.

Imagine a man some centuries hence deciphering this eternal sentence printed in a book. (The occasion of the interpretation of an eternal sentence does not matter.) He will use two methods for reaching an understanding of the sentence.

According to the first, he will try to reconstitute the frame of reference used in the book, namely, the Christian chronology, just as we do for older Egyptian or Chinese chronology. The proper name 'Paris' will evoke for him some archaeological site or perhaps the intersection of a meridian with a parallel. Through the aid of such chronological and geographical systems of coordinates he will understand the sentence. If it is supposed that there is no concealed use of egocentric particulars in his understanding of both frames of reference, he will then objectively assign the described event by merely putting its time and place within a certain undetermined distance from his own time and place.[36] Such undetermined assignments occur every time archaeologists succeed in establishing only relative chronologies: when they know how to organize a story without knowing when and where the story took place with respect to them.

According to the second method, the reader of future centuries is supposed to have reached an exact agreement between our Christian chronology and his own and to have visited the Parisian field of excavation. He then gets another understanding of the sentence and he is able to translate the printed eternal sentence into the following statement: '2,521 years ago, in that city whose ruins I have visited, it rained'. The possibility of the translation shows the reference to be now determined. But the determination has merely resulted from reusing egocentric particulars.

What would make the elimination of proper names critical is the difficulty raised by putting the extended linguistic code on the same level with the proper code when universals such as 'Socratizes' had to be admitted along with universals such as 'is raining'.[37] This is another difficulty incurred by the elimination of egocentric particulars. Now, there is a sense in which we are indeed never sure that the information we convey is determinate. We are indeed never sure that people will be able to connect their own frames of reference with ours. When we used proper names, our message may well have been confined within descriptions, since proper names, by themselves, do not convey features of acquaintance. Were we deprived of egocentric particulars, we should be unable to use our acquaintance in order to give our message its full determination.

Such an answer to the objection may be rebutted. Firstly, that a future reader will know or not know how to connect our frame of reference to his own is imputable not to an objective state of affairs but to the subjective state of his knowledge. Secondly and more importantly, his own use of egocentric particulars may be eliminated by choosing, once for all, an objectively determinate event – the big bang or our geological periods – as a time origin and by indexing the successive 'now' as values of a time variable. Egocentric particulars are a pragmatic convenience, not a theoretical requirement of communication.

Such a rebuttal, however, valuable as it is for science, has no value with respect to the deduction of linguistic categories. Messages which make sense because they inform us of an immediate and intuitive way towards identification lose their sense when they are transformed into messages having the same truth-value but where the way towards identification would depend on a hypothetical conceptual apparatus and, therefore, would always risk missing its point. We cannot without absurdity expect the categories of spoken language to reduce to those of written language, a language amputated from dialogue.

Dialogues occur when the common origin of the coordinate system is fixed for the speakers by the utterance of the sentence. Everything the message is about will be organized about the utterance. The tenses of the verb are related with the specious time of the utterance; the distinction of time's parts depends on it and flows with it. The proper egocentric particulars – 'now', 'a while', 'long ago', 'here', 'there', and the cohort of the adjectival and pronominal formations that they bring about in language – bear witness to a pervasive presence of the speaker-centred coordinate system. The very determination of person depends on it.[38]

Egocentric particulars *qua* arguments manifest their strongest use, in the circumstantial form, when the argument-sign does not refer to a substance but to a time and place. The question is how such an argument can identify a reference uniquely. An egocentric particular refers only for the duration of the message, even if the reference is one to a substance as happens when the egocentric particular is appended to a universal concept ('this man'). The truth-values of the sentences change, therefore, with the occasion. *A fortiori*, when the egocentric particular functions as an adverb, it can only determine its reference, without claiming to survive the utterance, exactly as a gesture of showing does by exhausting its own referring-force at the very moment of its occurrence. As a counterpart of its brevity, which will result in transitory sentence truth-values, the egocentric adverb enjoys the privilege of directly and uniquely determining the reference of any verbal predicate, however short-lived and seemingly unrelated the reference may be. Since this referring apparatus is now built into the very matter of the message, the adverb can bear the burden of the determination of reference by itself. No additional conceptual device is needed: a time and, possibly, a place are explicitly and intuitively fixed in relation to an utterance's time and place.

Loosely structured arguments fit well with verbal commitments. A fully developed verbal predicate apparently does not need the same regimentation which governed accidental – and, *a fortiori*, substantial predication. When instances were substances, sentences had to enter into a pre-existing structure; and predicates at work have been rightly compared to atoms being given a fixed valency.[39] But with predicates whose reference depends on a framework fixed by the utterance, where universals are exactly but insubstantially instantiated, a more flexible policy is better adapted to describing the circumstances of what takes place in the play (the number of which is, *a priori*, unlimited) in contrast to giving a determinate list of the actors. It would suffice neither to express this variability at the level of molecular sentences nor to understand the adverbs as conceptual restrictions placed on predicates, by which one would determine sub-properties of the property which is instantiated. Precisely because places and times are not instances of universals, which they merely *locate*, several instances of different such universals may simultaneously coexist at the same place. (This of course cannot be the case for substantial instances.) Moreover, they necessarily fall under a complex spatio-temporal organization, whose structure, be it conceived as conceptual or intuitive, has nothing to do with the classification characteristic of either substantial or accidental predication. The instance of the predicative universal that is located by a circumstantial predication becomes *ipso facto* part of this organization. Consider the sentence 'Just after the second thunder-clap it began to pour with rain without stopping until now.' Rain is instantiated relatively to now. Although, if need be, the predicates 'pour' and 'thunder' might be regarded respectively as ordinary conceptual restrictions on the predicates 'rain' and 'clap', the other determinations of the instance of raining are clearly added in as the space–time inspection proceeds from the second thunder-clap towards the utter-ance's time. Now, our sentence-building would be at a loss were we not sure that all those determinations were contingent upon one and the same instance, however short, of the universal, located as it is by egocentric particulars. Moreover, nothing is said about the instance beyond its duration or place relatively to the utterance. It is said to be *at* this place and *at* this time. The egocentric particular then allows us to point it out and to make it singular. But as an instance of its universal, it is left determined without yet being singular. It therefore requires the introduction of a bound variable and an existential quantification. This instance of rain is simply the binding of the propositional function 'raining at a given place and time'.

In the case of accidental predication, when a verb's action was referred to a substance, for instance, that action could give way to adverbial constructions. This was seen to be the case when the verbal universal which was previously considered as a one-place predicate came to be interpreted as a two-place relation, or even as a three-place relation where the substantival predicate was itself transformed into a propositional function of time. One place had to be filled by a substance term, the other by a term standing for what would be an instance of the universal in so far as this abstract instance 'is-in' the substance, the third place being potentially reserved for the time assignment. Choosing a two-term interpretation resulted in introducing a new and systematically ambiguous two-term predicate 'is-at (x, t)' where x takes its values in two different categorical domains, the domain of substances and the domain of accidents, whether they are permanent, as a man's whiteness, or transitory, as a man's action. The three-term interpretation entailed more cumbersome predicates, but the ambiguous time localization disappeared. Nothing in the three complex predicates 'is-a-man-at (x, t)' 'is-an-instance-of-whiteness at, in (y, t, x)' and 'is-an-instance-of-running-at, of (y, t, x)' implies that a man has the same kind of time localization that either an instance of his whiteness or an instance of his running has. Moreover, the strong and closed structure of substantial and accidental predications urged the latter interpretation.

On the contrary, because it is free and not correlated with substantial predication or, more accurately, subordinated to it, circumstantial predication calls for the other interpretation. Formally, we may translate 'It is raining', if 'A' designates the enunciation of this sentence either by the form:

'$(\exists x)\,(\exists t)$ [is-an-instance-of-raining x, x is-at-time t. A is-at-time t]',

or by the form

'$(\exists x)\,(\exists t)$ [is-an-instance-of-raining-at x, t. A is-at-time t].'

What recommends the first version here is that the predicate 'is-at-time t' is a predicate naturally defined for events, and that the loose structure of circumstantial predication leads us to expect the instance of raining to be further determined by an arbitrarily long sequence of qualifications – this instance being at such-and-such a place and having such-and-such properties.

The two competing interpretations result from the categorical meanings of the predications at stake. Events are fully individuated by a simple localization. Actions and *a fortiori* permanent accidental properties require a much stronger condition. They have indeed to be *of* or *in* substances, and it is only in the relation of *inesse* that their time determination may be systematically reached. The occurrence of an instance of raining is connected with time by a simple relation of togetherness. There is much more in *inesse*.

The doubling of the variable for the running-instance proceeds from this instance's being thought of as inherent in its substance. The difference is glaring between a pseudo-relation such as 'is-an-instance-of-running-of x, y' and a genuine relation such as 'is-older-than x, y'. There is therefore also a difference between localizing an event and localizing an accident, even if the accident has the transitory feature of the event. It is precisely this difference that is exactly adapted to expressing the opposition which perception draws between images and representations.[40]

Let us start from a universal which is closed with respect to negation. And suppose that for this universe of discourse neither the proper linguistic code nor its extension by convention furnishes singular terms. We must therefore give up the search for genuine instances that could exemplify the universal in the way humility or Socrates respectively exemplified virtue, humanity or running. All that we can do is to use the noise produced by our utterance of the sentence. The wave propagation starts from the speaker's mouth which may thus fix the point of origin of a spatio-temporal coordinate system.

Let us then introduce into our language some words building a system, i.e., interrelated by paradigmatic connections of mutual oppositions, and grading the different possible spatial and temporal distances from a still undetermined origin. These words are called indexes. When they are associated in the right way with an ordinary predicate, they give its relative localization with respect to a frame of reference whose origin is still not fixed and cannot be fixed in so far as we resort to ordinary paradigmatic universals.

What does A do, then, when he says: 'It rained near here yesterday'? He draws the circle corresponding to the universal 'is raining' in the universe of discourse. He uses two redundant monemes (the imperfect and the word 'yesterday') to index the predicate 'is-raining' with respect to time and other monemes (the words 'near here') with respect to space. The assertable syntagm, thus obtained, says that an instance of raining has occurred one day before a given event and at the same place where this same event occurred. The truth-value of all these universals is still not assigned. What assigns it is the enunciation of the sentence which fixes the origin of the localizations. The event of the speaker's utterance determines from where and from when the event of raining must be indexed in space and time. Universal predicates and indexes as well as their respective adjustment belong to semantics. Pragmatics is necessary for identification, and pragmatics resorts to using these words which fix the scheme. (See figure 4.)

The hearer B understands the ordinary linguistic code as well as the code of the indexes which are integrated in semantics. But he can determine and

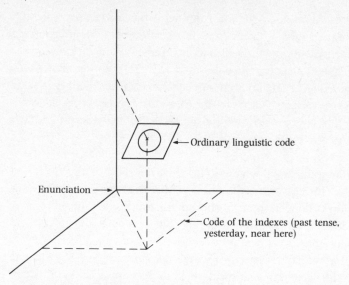

Figure 4 Scheme of circumstantial predication

make the relative localization absolute only if he knows where and when to put the origin of the frame of reference. This occurs only if *B* hears *A*'s sentence and if therefore *B* is a partner in a dialogue with *A*.

Nominal, substantial and accidental predications did not put any particular limitation on the access *B* had to the truth conditions (with the exception of his participation in the group's conventions when proper names were used). The reason is that space–time determinations were either absent or occurred relatively to the sentence's 'subject', namely, the substance. Now that localization is pragmatically fixed, all persons who are not present at the enunciation are excluded. It is then understandable, in linguistics, that the 'persons' are produced by dialogue, and that, because the correlation of dialogue is promoted by circumstantial predication, the only recognized persons are I (and we) as well as you (singular and plural), the person or the persons who utter and those who hear the sentence. The same reason explains why, while the truth-values of the sentences are fixed in narrations and, *a fortiori*, in speeches and treatises, they are always changing in dialogue. Nevertheless, though by determining persons and by changing truth-values the egocentric particulars almost irresistibly tempt the linguist to count their organization as belonging to the 'correlation of subjectivity',[41] this is a misleading qualification, since the identification of the speaker and therefore of his utterance and of the localization of the universal has by itself nothing subjective about it.

Circumstantial predication is a localization rather than a genuine predication, and that is why it accords so well with the communication of perceptual images.

But not all images throw in their lot with one another in this respect. Firstly, there are the geometrical images grounded on compensation. The equivalence classes thus determined are expressed by ordinary universals which then occur either in pure predication when they give rise to singular terms, or in accidental predication when they are employed only as predicates. Secondly, there are the absolute places and moments as related to the perceiving Ego. These are unmistakably the proper objects aimed at by circumstantial predication whose procedure confirms and marks out the ways in which imagination sets the course.

Several derivative singular sentences result from mixing circumstantial predication with accidental predication and even substantial predication. Three cases are especially important.

(1) Very often proper names are replaced by the combination of a moneme expressing a universal and an adjectival egocentric particular ('This man runs'). We then start from the intersection of two universals, but instead of identifying by quantification, we use the utterance of the sentence as an origin to identify the man of whom we speak, namely, the man who is here.

(2) The same procedure is used when we say: 'You run.' The whole prism of a simple accidental predication is related to the enunciation and the identification takes place by this means.

(3) When we say 'this is a man', we still reduce the construction, 'this' designating the instance – whatever it may be – of any undetermined universal localized near the enunciation.

Despite their practical importance, these sentences do not count as elementary, because they have a mixed origin and do not exploit all the peculiarities of circumstantial predication, which they use for other aims. By the way, it happens that our elementary sentences may be formally analysed in terms of quantification, a reason for which the formal condition of atomicity has to be relaxed. But the paraphrases in terms of quantification, useful as they are in characterizing the category we deal with (substances, accidents, events), are not to be taken too seriously within natural language. The person who hears the sentence 'It is raining' does not, in order to get its identification, have to quantify over an instance of raining and to locate this instance in a place and at a time that are identical with the place and the time where the occurrence of the enunciation is itself localized. He and the speaker use egocentric particulars precisely because intuition is, even within language, the shortest way to identification.

To sum up, circumstantial predication ends the first or dogmatic series, where any involvement of the subject in the assertion is neutralized. Since nominal sentences neutralize all verbal determinations as well, they eternally instantiate universals by ideas. With participation sentences we leave eternity for space and time. Substantial predication imitates nominal predication, but substances take the place of ideas, and proper names are required for some of them. With accidental predication another part of the verbal determinations emerges; universals are instantiated by adhering to substances previously given. Finally, circumstantial predication locates universals with respect to the egocentric framework around the material occurrence of the sentence.

The deduction of the dogmatic series of categories is thus completed. This series indeed supposes that the sentence gives a 'living picture' of the state of affairs. Once the universe of discourse is determined – which requires, in the case of accidental predication, a subordination of universals – the singular term comes, so to speak, by itself to put itself inside the circle which stands for the universal. In so far as the individual spontaneously places itself under the universal without allowing interference from the speaker's subjectivity, there are as many categories as there are kinds of objective individuation. There are in fact three such kinds. Individuation by the code proper requires a unique universe of discourse. Substantial and accidental individuation require a solid prism of universes of discourse united by proper names. Circumstantial individuation depends on enunciation. There remains no further element or presupposition of language which can be exploited for dogmatic identification. Since the persons of the speaker and of his audience have been used until now through their objective determinations – which was the case with circumstantial predication in dialogue – it remains for them to occur through their subjective determinations, an occurrence which opens a second or subjective series within the deduction.

The judgment of method

Language has to settle a final question if it is to express subjectivity as well as objectivity.

The dogmatic series does not ignore the assertive role of predication, without which there would be no complete declarative message. Rather, it presupposes that for a sentence to be true the subsumption of the reference under the universal is predetermined in the things themselves, and it automatically entails the correspondence of the described state of affairs with reality. Our thought, as expressed by means of linguistic signs, is considered to be a picture in the strictest sense. A sentence shows what is the case; and the unifying and ontic force that the predicate expresses merely mirrors, independently of our thinking, the self-construction of reality. In the same way, Spinoza – over and against Descartes's distinction between the understanding and the will – maintained the self-asserting power of ideas, so that, since the idea of the idea is completely determined by the idea itself, no freedom of reflection and no methodological primacy of the *cogito* have to be acknowledged.

The dogmatic prejudice which reduces elementary singular predication to elementary singular objective predication has a certain foundation in natural language. The two permanent functions of the verb by which assertable syntagms are unified and are asserted remain implicit in the present state of Indo-European languages. Only the variable functions are positively expressed, and all of them are objective. In order that predication and subjectivity may be related, the examination must therefore bear on the two permanent functions of the present-day Indo-European verb.

The correlation of subjectivity may indeed affect predication by two different means.[42] Firstly, the semantic function of assertion may be held invariant while the syntactical unity of the universal and the individual is referred to some subjective performance by the speaker. Secondly, this syntactical function – whether it is conceived of as dogmatic or as supported by a subjective performance – is maintained invariant, and it is now the semantic function which is referred to subjectivity. This reference is to occur, however, under the condition that the elementary sentence, thus obtained, still has a truth-value, since, owing to a violation of this condition, the genuine assertion would be destroyed and predication itself, as making knowledge possible, would disappear.

Both procedures correspond to what classical philosophy called *judgments* as opposed to propositions. The first will be called instructions or judgments of method, the second, judgments of appearance. The examination of the judgment of appearance will show why a third case is not possible, and the complete deduction of linguistic categories will be achieved.

How can the syntagmatic unity of the sentence determine the singular term? This unity has as its function to show how the several monemes expressing universals hang together to produce an assertable syntagm, that is, picture a certain state of affairs.

When language uses devices such as proper names or egocentric particulars, it is immediately clear how the predication works, since the conventions of the group in the one case and the situation of the speaker in the dialogue in the other completely solve the question. Consequently, if the determination of the singular term by the syntagmatic unit of the sentence really gives rise to a new category of identification, it is not by opposition to substantial, accidental or circumstantial predication that it must be conceived.

Let us then look on the side of pure predication. Here a transformation of a universal into a singular term occurs, which supposes a lawlike partition according to which the universal, so to speak, produces its different instances and in a way completely foreign to individuation by realization. Thus there are just the five regular polyhedra. Nevertheless, that the instances subsumed under the universal obey a law does not mean that we know how to apply it. Between universals and particulars born of universals, pure predication is thus seen to allow of and even harbour an obscure no man's land.

Under these conditions, a recommendation to determine the singular term by the syntagmatic unit of the sentence amounts to entering into the actual working of predication. A singular term thus determined is called a *construction* and the corresponding predication, in contradistinction to pure predication, which is committed to pure existential reference, has to construct its reference and is called a *judgment of method*.

In what terms would the question of judgments of method have to be put, supposing they had to do with a formal linguistic class?

The requirement of a subjective performance for unifying the predicate and the singular term into an assertable syntagm has a distant counterpart within the dogmatic series in the opposition between egocentric particulars and proper names. Whereas substantial and accidental predications depicted a state of affairs by themselves without assuring the speakers of an ego-referred way for their identification, circumstantial predication did afford them such assurance. Let us now reconsider nominal predication. Nominal sentences such as 'Eight is an even number' or 'Humility is a virtue' speak the truth without giving us a way of establishing their truth. We are not shown how the subsumption they assert may be realized, or even whether it is possible.

In order for the elementary sentence in question to have a relation to the nominal sentence similar to that which circumstantial predication bears to substantial and accidental predication, the singular term must inform the speakers about its own subsumption under the universal. The predicate 'is even' means 'is a multiple of two' and, therefore, may be put in the form: 'belongs to the class of all ys such that $(\exists x)\, 2\, x = y$'. Suppose, now, that instead of saying that eight belongs to this class, a sentence which by itself does not show why it is true, we replace 'eight' by the singular term 2^3 (or 2.2.2). Then we 'see' that the singular term exemplifies the law expressed by the universal.

The question of whether there are formal criteria that distinguish a judgment of method would thus reduce to the question of whether there are universals, turned into singular terms by the general device of nominal sentences but such that the method of their construction belongs to their very meaning. 'Regular' number names such as 'eighty' (8×10) would afford good examples of this, in contradistinction to the proper names of the ciphers, such as 'eight'. Similar remarks would apply to geometry and to other domains: there are words such as 'triangle' or 'pentagon' which tell us how their referent is constructed, and other words such as 'circle' or 'sphere' which do not.

The validity of such formal characterization would be illusory. First of all, it would amount simply to an objective and *ad hoc* procedure for reducing a nominal sentence to an analytic truth. We should thus determine only a proper part of the class of nominal sentences and we should remain within the dogmatic series. Secondly, if our nominal sentences are comparable to cheques, what we require from judgments of method is not that these cheques should be authenticated – that they have the right signature – but that they should be cashed. But the possibility of exchanging words for things can never be borrowed from the words themselves or be printed on paper. It requires a subjective commitment going beyond morphological criteria.

Since judgments of method must show intuitive ways of accessibility to the truth conditions of nominal sentences, we may expect to find examples of them in demonstrative sentences, and especially in geometry and arithmetic.

Theorems of geometry, as universal categorical sentences, are comparable to banknotes. If there is a provision to know them, it is to be established by the demonstration. Now, geometrical demonstration, according to Aristotle, Locke, and Kant, possesses a specific and astonishing feature: it is made up of singular sentences. The geometer uses the *dictum de omni*, according to which what is demonstrated for whatever individual is demonstrated for all individuals. The 'whatever individual' corresponding to the geometrical theorem is the figure. According to the *dictum*, we shall be permitted to substitute for the universals occurring in the categorical sentence any individual whatsoever, that is, a figure which retains only universal features entering into the definition of the individual. 'Any figure whatsoever' is thus a rule of construction, giving instructions to produce an individual conforming to the universal.

Let there be, says the geometer, a triangle *ABC*. 'Any triangle whatsoever' excludes all roles for particular determinations: an isosceles triangle would not do. The drawing of *ABC* retains only the proper elements (*per se*) constitutive of the triangle in so far as they are explicitly given in it itself (*in ipso*). These are, namely, the three straight lines *AB*, *BC* and *AC* which are

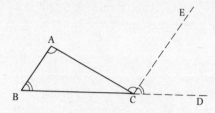

neither parallel nor intersect in a single point. Extend *BC* in the direction of *D*. Through *C* draw the parallel *CE* to *BA*. Once the construction is drawn or imagined, it is immediately seen, owing to the equalities of required angles, that the sum of the angles of the individual but any triangle *ABC* is equal to two right angles. The geometer uses imperatives. His requirements of construction are those actions which allow him to honour this banknote that we call a theorem. Such imperatives differ from genuine performatives, inasmuch as they do not, properly speaking, do things with words. But they differ also from ordinary imperatives which are efficient or not, but have nothing to do with truth conditions. A construction imperative – the instructions – makes the theorem true because it makes a universal (the predicate: 'has the sum of its angles equal to two right angles') possible.[43]

Though it is borrowed from an already developed arithmetic, the following example deserves attention because it gives a good illustration of what a subjective universe of discourse may be. The sentence 'The number $\sqrt{2}$ is an irrational' is a nominal sentence. When, instead of this singular term, we express its development by an infinite continuous fraction, *viz.*:

$$\sqrt{2} = \cfrac{1}{2 + \cfrac{1}{2 + \cfrac{1}{2 + 1}}}$$

the nominal sentence is transformed into a judgment of method. Whatever may be the rank *n* of the reduced r_n which approaches the irrational number by excess and by defect:

$$r_1 = 1, \ r_2 = \tfrac{3}{2}, \ r_3 = \tfrac{7}{5}, \ r_4 = \tfrac{17}{12}, \ \ldots$$

the rational number, thus obtained, leaves a remainder. The numbers of the sequence are approximations converging towards the number $\sqrt{2}$, which is irrational. This procedure of construction, known to Theodorus and to Plato, contrasts with the *reductio ad absurdum* used by Pythagoras for demonstrating that there is no ratio between the side of the square and its diagonal. A *reductio* is dogmatic, because, from the fact that an individual is not subsumed under a universal, we infer that its representative point falls outside the circle representative of the universal.[44] On the contrary, with judgments of method, we abandon this right of closing the universe of discourse as long as we have no procedure of construction. The closed universe is replaced by a universe open and only determined by the subjective rule of construction of the individual, the most interesting cases being those where the intuitive infinity of the procedure shows that and how the individual is subsumed under the universal.

Reduced to a scheme of nominal sentences, the categorical geometrical sentence is a complex one saying that there are no triangles which have not

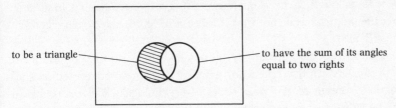

the sum of their angles equal to two right angles. For this scheme is substituted another, apparently similar to the scheme of circumstantial predication, since the categorical sentence must be replaced by a singular sentence and the universal 'is a triangle' is to be replaced by any singular triangle. But individuation is no longer produced by deictic localization. The predicate, left to itself, is denied any power of attracting into its scope the arguments that it will subsume. An act of subjective synthesis is required for this subsumption. Only – note such an act is able to produce a particular triangle *ABC* of any type whatsoever. Therefore the subsumption of the individual under the universal 'closes' such a universe only because it results from our constructing or being able to construct the required figure. In the case of the arithmetical example, we no longer start from a complex nominal sentence. But the judgment of method is still obtained from our capacity to construct the individual according to the general instructions: continue indefinitely to reckon the fraction. Whether it is any representative whatever of a universal as in the first case or a determinate product of a rule as in the second, the individual is always assigned by a constructive performance of subjectivity; and it is only this performance which is able to close the universe of discourse.

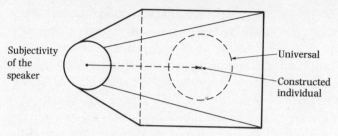

Figure 5 Scheme of the judgment of method

Every time the speaker *A* identifies an individual under a universal in the sense of the judgments of method, he asks *B* to construct the same subsumption, without which he would not get the kind of access to the truth conditions which is promised by such judgments. *B* can understand *A's* instructions only if he is able to make the same constructions. The agreement between them has, then, necessarily something subjective about it, in so far as neither the linguistic code nor the procedures of verbal objective predication can justify it.

For such a subjective agreement to be possible, the subjective performances that are considered must claim a universal validity and count as methodological actions foreign to the vicissitudes of psychological life. Let us call a 'cognitive subject' such a subject which has been deprived by abstraction of all these vicissitudes and whose only role is to support the acts of synthesis. In order to get a more determinate notion of what it is or rather what it does, it may be helpful to construct from some elementary judgment of method its corresponding particularization. What must we admit for x, for instance, when we start from the judgment '$\sqrt{2}$ is an irrational number'? Such an x must be constructed by a progressive action, which is nothing other than my own act in so far as I think, on the condition that such an act of the *cogito* can claim universal validity, i.e., contains in itself the principle of its indefinite repeatability by any other possible subject. If '*F*' designates the universal (here: 'is an irrational number'), we may then paraphrase the required existential judgment of method by the following statement:

'$(\exists x)$ x is constructible as an instance of F by an act of the *cogito*.'

The *cogito* itself cannot be regarded as a singular value of a variable, and an act of synthesis cannot, in this respect, be compared with an ordinary action. The instances of running are of substances that may be identified as such independently of these particular instances, as being, for example, of such-and-such a speaker participating in the dialogue and thus objectively given. The *ego cogito* is not identifiable by itself and has no substantial existence beyond its acts of knowledge. When I perform such an act, I never capture what I do by saying that I did it. In order for anyone else to understand what I say he must himself perform the act which was hinted at by what I said. Imagine, indeed, what would happen if the *ego cogito* were to be taken as a value of a variable in the following expression:

'$(\exists x)\ (\exists y)\ x$ is constructible as an instance of F by an act of y'

where y designates a thinking speaker. Such an expression would paraphrase a sentence belonging to the dogmatic series and resort to accidental predication. It would *describe* the performance of an intellectual construction as attributed to a substance; but the state of affairs thus described would no longer depend on the speaker's construction. Judgments of method do not describe constructions. They *perform* them. And it is because they perform them that they are expressed in the first person of the present tense. If we may speak of the language games in which judgments of method occur, it is only *cum grano salis*, and these games are called reflections, meditations and soliloquies. Those are the places where knowledge is turned into action and where the new category of mental construction flourishes.

Such construction is specifically linguistic. Certainly the percipient knows how to distinguish between events or objects on the one hand and the ways he perceives them on the other. But the unseparated universals in images and representations are always given and we cannot be acquainted with perceived events or objects without being acquainted with the ways of perceiving them. The separated linguistic universals split acquaintance from description. Since, however, the individuals designated in all the kinds of predication which have been enumerated, excepting pure predication, are or may be completely and constructively determined in space and time as events or things, as soon as the singular terms which designate them close the assertable syntagm, the only singular terms which may be involved in the constructive identification of judgments are these very singular terms that belong to the proper linguistic code and have been introduced by pure predication. In so far as pure predication and judgments of method have no perceptual counterpart, they express that objective and subjective part of cognitive communication which transcends perception.

An objection might come from physicists who adopt an operationalist methodology. Do they not indeed require judgments of method with respect to substances, accidents and events? The objection is not without foundation. It has already arisen, at the level of proper names, with the pseudo-proper names, and, in its turn, simultaneity at a distance is as mythical as Zeus. Every time descriptions go beyond appearances either within pure predication or when we merely communicate perception, the judgments of method seem to be near at hand. There is, however, a difference. When I report my own experience, I can use ordinary constructions of language – adjectives, adverbs, relative sentences and so on – to describe what I was acquainted with. My hearers will rely on analogy to interpret my speech. On the contrary, pure predication speaks of what bypasses experience and may not be seen, but only known. Within knowledge, however, a kind of acquaintance is still opposed to description. Here the judgments of method are useful, and only here are they technically irreplaceable. My hearer immediately knows how to handle the gardener's ellipses, whereas long explanations will probably be needed for him to understand a description in terms of a locus of points obeying an analytical equation. In the same way, once he has released our collective emotions by uttering the word 'justice', the political leader begins to control and to lead our collective actions by entering into judgments of method and specifying whether justice means isonomy or equalitarianism.

Judgments of appearance

The semantic unit is the final element of the sentence which may determine the singular term. Now, this unit has as its function the transformation of a complete assertable syntagmatic unit into an asserted sentence by attributing a truth-value to it, for instance transforming the syntagm: 'that here is a man' into the sentence: 'That here is man, is true.' How can the attribution of a truth-value, the being true of 'that here is a man', determine a singular term? Neither the syntagm itself, considered as complete, nor the semantic assertion contains such a term. The only individual which interferes during the attribution is the speaker when he changes from the *Annahme* to the assertion and gives a thought its value, or, more accurately, the subjective estimation of the value which he is ready to attribute to his thought. Now, pondering the truth-value of a syntagm is nothing for the subject but introducing into this closed syntagm a term expressing how the state of affairs looks to him. The resulting sentence will have the form of a judgment of appearance and the sentence: 'There seems to be a man here' will fill the place of the dogmatic sentence 'Here is a man.'

If human language is distinguished from all animal systems of communication by its capacity to transmit the message of an absent speaker and to provide an indefinite number of new interpretations for it,[45] one must not be surprised to find in discourse so many occurrences of what Russell called 'propositional attitudes'.[46] These attitudes go from the simple report and the literal quotation of a given message to the reconstruction of what might have been a message, had it been uttered. A confusion easily arises here – comparable to that which occurred when the *cogito* was interpreted as the value of a variable in judgments of method – if no distinction is drawn between referring to subjectivity and expressing the speaker's subjectivity. The former kind of reference lies within the province of the complex sentences of the dogmatic series, whereas the latter type of expression excludes, by definition, its being realized by anyone other than the speaker.[47]

Consider propositional attitudes expressed in the first person and the present tense and compare the two sentences 'I have the feeling that the weather will change' and 'I believe that the weather will change.' Despite a complete formal symmetry, 'I have the feeling' describes myself as feeling, whereas 'I believe' does not describe myself as believing, but merely weakens my assertion and transforms 'into a subjective stating the fact impersonally asserted, namely the *weather will change*, which is the genuine proposition'.[48] The role of expressions such as 'I suppose', 'I presume' , 'I conclude', in their standard occurrences, is analogous to the role of 'I believe': they *change* the assertion, whereas the forms 'You suppose', 'You presume', 'You conclude', as well as 'You believe' or 'I believed' *describe* subjective states in the same way as does 'I have the feeling.'

When expressed in the present tense and in the first person, propositional attitudes are distinguished by two characteristics from the describing propositional attitudes. Firstly, when I assert 'I believe that *p*', I commit myself to asserting *p*. Secondly, while a describing propositional attitude appears to express a function of its object, the reflexive form 'I suppose that you are Mr X' may be translated into 'You are, I suppose, Mr X', where 'You are Mr X' occurs as a genuine sentence rather than as a function of 'I suppose.' This paraphrase, which is impossible in other tenses and persons, is all the more paradoxical since there seems to be no middle ground between asserting a sentence and translating it into a name – a that-clause – which then occurs as an argument in another sentence. Cassirer noticed the same difficulty about the pronominal designation of 'I' with respect to the opposition between the verb and the noun: we may give his remark a general application. An exact designation of the subjectivity at work in a sentence's relation to reality 'can only be found if it opposes itself to the designation of its objectification on the one hand, but on the other hand goes through this objectification'.[49] Now, for subjectivity to be expressed through the that-clause, the predicate occurring in this clause – a predicate which ordinarily would assert the objective property of being Mr X – is made incomplete with respect to its assertive power as long as the speaker's attitude is not considered. What goes through the that-clause is the attitude of the person for whom the state of affairs is asserted, believed, maintained, supposed, surmised, doubted and so on. Although the objective part of such a sentence expressed in the that-clause, and its subjective part expressed by the speaker's attitude, are formally split up in our languages, they are not really independent and must rather be considered as forming one predicate. We cannot sever the seeing of a red patch from the appearance of a red patch; nor can we separate the expression of our belief from what we believe. Utterances of the form 'I swear', 'I promise', 'I witness' are performances, which bind the ego in such a way that the social and juridical consequences of my swearing, my promising or my witnessing begin with and result from my very utterance of those sentences.[50] In the literal sense required by human institutions, we 'do things with words'.[51] The things thus created by – or rather through – formulas are characteristic of situations which depend on social contracts, conventions and rules. A sentence which expresses a positive correlation of subjectivity does not create such an objective institution, but it uses in a comparable way *a dictum* or a that-clause in order to make known my adopting of the attitude, which is merely described by propositional attitudes in the third person or in a past tense.

Doubts, however, arise as to whether the formal class of sentences which has been delimited captures the whole spectrum of the judgments of appearance. Verbs such as 'appears' or 'seems' play a similar role of modifying the assertion and expressing propositional attitudes in sentences such as 'The weather seems to change.' Adverbs, too, may produce the same result.

Whatever the formal expression of a judgment of appearance, it may be further characterized by opposing it to circumstantial as well as to accidental predication.

In circumstantial predication, the predicate receives its verbal determinations from the relation that the egocentric particulars establish between the course of things as described by the sentence and the sentence's utterance. What comes into play with predication of appearance is no longer the assignation of the objective indication that the predicate lays on a given course of things. We are now concerned with the relation between the course of things just described and reality. The objective egocentric particulars that are centred around a sentence's utterance are by themselves unable to fix and to qualify the new relation, which we hold responsible for establishing the assertion. The new positive correlation of subjectivity goes through the sentence for the purpose of relating it to the action of the subject of the utterance, as the correlation of speakership went through the predicate for the purpose of relating it to the utterance itself. The first correlation therefore proceeds further than the second and severely restricts the egocentric system of tenses and persons. To adopt Wittgenstein's terminology, a dogmatic sentence shows, but never expresses, the sign of assertion. Predicate and arguments are enough to produce both the unity of the sentence and its truth-value. But as soon as the truth-value is detached from the predicate in order to be ascribed to the action of the subject, this subject becomes as undeclinable in its assertive function as it proved to be, in judgments of method, with respect to its syntactical function.

Accidental predication obeyed a double principle of classification: strict predication or subsumption under a verbal universal and inherence in a substance given by a foreign classification. In a similar way, in reflexive predication, the predicate contained in the that-clause expresses the sub-sumption under the universal, while the propositional attitude conveys the inherence of the whole clause in the subject's activity. Comparison, however, is no reason.

Firstly, the predicate at stake must be made from a that-clause, i.e., from a consideration, an *Annahme* that is a complete assertable syntagm. In order to get a universal able to play the role of a predicate, the that-clause has itself to be regarded as a kind of singular term which is transformed into a predicate when it is appended to classifying words such as: 'It is my belief', 'It is my doubt', and so on. From the sentence 'It will rain', we form the that-clause 'that it will rain', and from the that-clause we form the predicate 'is my belief that it will rain', the final singular sentence being obtained when the pronoun 'it' is prefixed to the predicate. The second peculiarity of judgments of appearance is then evidenced from the existential generalization which such a singular sentence authorizes. Suppose, indeed, that we should paraphrase the literal generalization 'There is an instance of my belief that it will rain' by localizing this instance in a substance. Such a paraphrase would read: 'There are an x and a y such that x is an instance of belief of y that it will rain', where y would refer to a substance. This last paraphrase, however, would lead us back once more to the dogmatic series. We would be describing, not expressing, a propositional attitude. The only admissible paraphrase is therefore compar-able to that allowed for judgments of methods:

'$(\exists x)$ x is an instance of belief entertained by the *cogito* that it will rain'

or, more generally:

'$(\exists x)$ x is an instance of propositional attitude entertained by the *cogito* that it will rain',

where the *cogito* is not a possible value of a variable.

In judgments of appearance, the assertion no longer arises from the subsumption of the individual under the universal, whether this subsumption is dogmatic or results from a subjective performance. It becomes a subjective attitude posited by reflection. What is now asserted is no longer a state of affairs, be it devoid of subjectivity or a construction, but some modification of what would have been the primitive assertion. Such a predication is called a *predication of appearance*, not because we would affirm that the described state of affairs is an appearance, which is a particular case, but because the state of affairs is asserted inasmuch as it appears to me and such as it does appear to me: that is, as certain, likely, probable, doubtful, apparent, and so forth. That is why such propositional attitudes are expressed in the first person of the present tense. That is why, though such a predication belongs to a second linguistic level (an assertion about an assertion), it is genuinely elementary. We do not describe our attitude in the face of a previously given state of affairs. We constitute the state of affairs by our reflection. To objectify reflection – as is done by all other uses of propositional attitudes – is one thing, to produce it *in statu nascendi* and to actualize it by positing the state of affairs itself is another.

Figure 6 depicts judgments of appearance. It shows how the subjective attitude builds the predicate of such judgments and how its instantiation is referred to subjectivity.

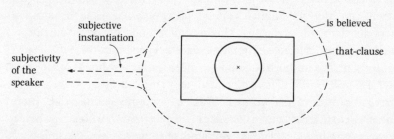

Figure 6 Scheme of judgments of appearance

When the speaker *A* utters such a judgment, he therefore makes explicit the way some propositional content appears to him and asserts this way of appearing. He cannot then not commit himself to the appearance which happens to be given to him. This self-pledging of *A* is the reason why reflection still remains an assertion.[52] As for *B*, he may perfectly well understand what *A* says without participating in *A*'s commitment. He may, in particular, not be ready to say 'I believe that *-p*' and nevertheless have access to the truth conditions of the sentence as asserted by *A*. This last sentence is true for *B* if and only if *B* is assured that *A* believes that *-p*, without his having to share the belief. When uttering a judgment of method, *A* instructed *B* to perform the same subjective operations that he performed himself. A judgment of appearance expresses *A*'s belief and, therefore, the way he commits himself with respect to being. It does not require of *B* the same self-pledging, and it suffices that *B* accepts *A*'s self-pledging as a fact. Now, when *B* takes as true *A*'s belief that it will rain, he analyses it and distinguishes in it a described propositional attitude whose instance is of the subject *A*. Such a subsumption is in the second (or the 'third' person) and possibly in the past. It differs completely from *A*'s judgment of appearance and belongs to the dogmatic series. There is no need to add that the logical consequences of such a statement are completely different from the consequences of the original judgment of appearance itself. The proclamations of faith, which need not always be solemn, illustrate the case. Again, just as in judgments of method, the speaker's ego is beyond the opposition and the relativization of the persons taking part in the dialogue. But furthermore, here, in contradistinction to the individuation of a construction, the individuation of a propositional attitude is understandable without participation and finds its cognitive counterpart in a simple sentence of the dogmatic series.

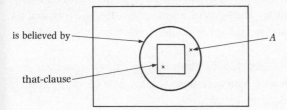

Figure 7 How *A*'s judgment of appearance is received by *B*

Among the different kinds of perceptual presentations that have been distinguished, the most simple, the impressions organized into signals of position and qualities of state merely given as such, has still not found its counterpart in linguistic communication. It may indeed be doubted whether percipients should have any interest in communicating mere appearances. But it has already been remarked that in situations of uncertainty, when we wonder about localizations of images and references of representations, we tend to reanalyse perception into the constituents of its first-level organization, so that our subjective perceptual settings are spontaneously interpreted through those appearances. In any case, this form which I see in fog now as a man and now as a bush is for the time being seen as a medium-sized shadow. It is understandable that, in similar circumstances, persons hesitating to pronounce about what they are perceiving may none the less want to communicate the appearances to which their doubts have reduced their perceptual organization. This is the part of perception that judgments of appearance intend to express.

The deduction can go no further for, if it did, it would overstep all access to the truth conditions to which it has been bound. Suppose, indeed, that a remaining subjective engagement were possible. It could only consist in suspending itself, since otherwise we would either have to assert simply the state of affairs (dogmatic case and judgments of method) or have to assert the propositional attitude itself (last case examined). As we have seen, the predication of appearance projects the speaker's activity into and through a state of affairs, so that the objective claim of this state to show reality could not be separated from the subjective attitude itself. Nevertheless, it remained true that reflection intended to tell something directly about reality, even in spite of mitigating or doubting the assertion. Dogmatism, not *doxa*, was renounced. Thus the predicate of the judgment of appearance has in common with the predicate in the whole preceding series a general world-thesis, according to which a sentence may or may not depict a state of affairs as it is but must none the less tell us something about it. Sentences, including sentences modified by reflection, do not count among the signs of language, for they directly tell us by means of signs that stand for things how the world is or how, at least, it appears to be.

Suppose there remains a last step: to neutralize any doxic commitment. This neutralization entails two consequences: predications become fictions, and fictional sentences become virtual signs.

Although fiction generally takes the form of dogmatic predication, it is easy to establish the tacit conventions that condition make-believe. The teller's subjectivity appeals to that of the listener in order to give the story its proper determination of unreality. Special conventions may designate the framework which delimits the pseudo-space and time of fiction as opposed to the real world. Every sentence is then interpreted as deprived of its doxic import. If the teller says of one of his characters 'I believe he is angry', everybody knows that he does not actually believe it. If he says 'there was singing and dancing', it is understood that this happened nowhere. Does he use proper names or descriptions? It is a part of language learning to have lost any doubt as to where and when Tom Thumb was left alone and hungry. Substantial and nominal predications themselves lose their sense and no longer confine beings within their defining boundaries. Oaks speak to reeds, and – why not? – men marry otters and fish.

It has been questioned whether fiction really does neutralize reality. Images which result from a memory's being neutralized, it has been said, merely modify the presentation of a previous positive attitude so that this act of neutralization itself still expresses a reflexive predication and takes place, as suppositions or considerations (*Annahmen*) do, if not within the dogmatic, at least within the doxic, series.[53] A true neutralization, the argument goes on, is not comparable to a particular portrait that would present us with quasi-, but still objective being, as do Dürer's engravings, with their imaginary characters.[54] Neutralization requires something more, namely, the working of a general disposition specific to human consciousness, which consists in its absolute freedom to adopt or to abandon the doxic attitude.[55] While we are supposed to know how to reiterate an image (a novel within a novel, a play within a play), true neutralization is beyond reiteration; it obeys the law of all or nothing.[56]

Two remarks will suffice to challenge this specious argument.

Firstly, if the objects of fiction may in particular cases be reiterated, this does not concern fiction itself. When Hamlet asks his mother 'Madam, how like you the play?', we are presented with Hamlet, the King, the Queen, a King-actor and a Queen-actress, all five players, without our having to repeat the general neutralization which is already supposed to work when we look at Bernardo meeting Francisco on Elsinore's platform. It is therefore not without reason that the absolute power of neutralization, thus recognized as the privilege of consciousness, was later identified with imagination, understood as the 'nihilation' of being.[57] The so-called true neutralization, then, can no longer claim the privilege of a predicative neutrality which would warrant a possible philosophical objectivity. Among the other predications, fiction is, by definition, certainly not committed to the *doxa*, as the others are. It is nevertheless committed to images and to the presence of absence which images introduce into the world of things. Accordingly, some philosophers have identified imagination with the proper commitment of human existence, an acceptable representative of neutralization but an unexpected candidate for neutrality.

Secondly, this specious argument aims at giving an alleged new interpretation of the suspension of judgment practised by the sceptics. Thus a distinction between two kinds of doubt will here be germane. One kind of doubt, as propositional attitude in the first person and in the present tense, was enlisted in judgments of appearance. This is Descartes's doubt, or an incentive to it. Another kind of doubt, or rather another type of behaviour included in the term 'doubt', is the indifference towards a world of which the reality is systematically held suspended. Listen now to Montaigne describing the difficulties we get into when we try to speak about indifference:

'I see the Pyrrhonian philosophers', he says, 'who cannot express their general conception in any way of speaking. For they would need another language. Ours is all formed of affirmative sentences, which are entirely enemies to them, so that when they say "I doubt" they are forthwith pinned by the throat and forced to avow that at least they assure and know that "they doubt". They have thus been obliged to take refuge in the following medical comparison, without which their humour would be inexplicable. When they utter "I don't know" or "I doubt", they say that this sentence allows itself to be carried away at the same time as the rest, neither more nor less than rhubarb that pushes the bad humours out and allows itself to be carried away at the same time.'[58]

There is indeed no better comparison to show how sceptical doubt results in seeing the whole world as a fiction, where doubt's activity itself happens to be carried away by the universal neutralization of reality.

We constructed the entire doxic series by progressively adding more and more verbal determinations to the sentence's predicate: pure tacit copula, spatio-temporal existence of the subject, spatio-temporal affection of the verb, egocentric reference of the verb, reflexive constitution of this reference and of our belief. Fiction transforms the whole of this construction into a simulation.

Because doxic or belief sentences are pictures of reality, they cannot count as signs among their proper signs, that is, among their constituents. But suppose this claim to *doxa* is renounced. Predicates still maintain a sentence's unity and retain their function of sealing a complete message. They cannot therefore pass for proper and actual signs. Their lost dimension, however, frees from the ordinary doxic burden. Since their explicit as-if picture does not refer to a reality, it may direct us to another reference not actually given and perhaps never accessible or completely assignable. Every fiction is therefore a virtual sign and speaks to us by allegory in the strict sense of the word. The impossible dialogue between the oak and the reed, as well as the impossible marriage of men with frogs, still has reference to reality and demands a hidden interpretation. Art and myth are thus condemned by neutralization to a double-talk which is responsible for the peculiar feeling of depth that art and mythology may arouse and that is lacking in plain doxic or belief sentences. Naturally the opposition between *doxa* and fiction does not solve, but merely poses, the difficult question of what the real reference is that is both hidden and symbolized by fiction's imaginary reference.[59]

All verbal determinations have been displayed, including their general neutralization. The deduction is now complete and has even overreached itself. We cannot, indeed, count fictions among our elementary singular sentences without destroying the very defining character of statements, namely, that they have truth-values. Fictions violate categories and an access to truth conditions – which was the leading thread of the deduction – can be defined for sentences having truth-values, not for pseudo-sentences that are treated as signs and thus are beyond the field of knowledge.

The following scheme summarizes, better than further discourse would, how language constructs our sensible world.

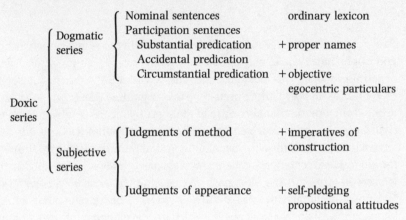

Doxic series

Dogmatic series

Nominal sentences — ordinary lexicon
Participation sentences
 Substantial predication — + proper names
 Accidental predication
 Circumstantial predication — + objective egocentric particulars

Subjective series

Judgments of method — + imperatives of construction

Judgments of appearance — + self-pledging propositional attitudes

3 | AXIOMATICS, ONTOLOGIES, PHILOSOPHIES

There are civilizations without philosophy, and there are civilizations where philosophy never could, and those where it never can, disentangle itself from a certain bondage to custom, law and social utility. Free philosophy, therefore, as opposed to Church- or state-organized ideology, must have arisen from a revolution in the use of the signs by means of which, for every civilization, language represents the sensible world. What was and still is the force which protects the old order of signs? What is the weak point in the net of the elementary sentences? Where can we expect innovations to subdue this conservative force? The first part of this chapter seeks to answer these questions by analysing the nature of myth: the development of free philosophy will appear as correlated with the development of the axiomatic method. The two go paired together like the Dioscuri. The second part of the chapter will examine the manner in which philosophy and axiomatics give signs a new interpretation.

I FROM MYTH TO PHILOSOPHY; THE ROLE OF THE AXIOMATIC METHOD

According to Helmholtz's principle, the signals which constitute perceptual organization are spontaneously interpreted as objective things. An analogous principle is valid for language and the sensible world. The elementary sentences certainly admit of local distinctions between appearance and reality. But appearances are spread out as so many puddles which never conjoin into one and the same river. Judgments of method sometimes hint at their dogmatic counterparts as empty sentences that need subjective animations. Or the performative energy which propositional attitudes in the first person of the present tense use contrasts with the dead belief expressed by the corresponding descriptive dogmatic sentence. But the judgments of the subjective series are opposed to the propositions of the dogmatic series neither as appearance to reality nor as reality to appearance. As to genuine fictions, they are not presented as appearances which would deceive us. For a systematic opposition between appearance and reality to develop, men as a group have to come to believe in some order hidden from their perception and taken as supporting permanent features of reality that they would otherwise

96

lose sight of. How could hungry tribes accept the hard discipline of scarcity during long winters if, behind the apparent death of Nature, they did not imagine some adventure, some descent into Hades and some exile there promising – possibly on the condition of some performed rites – the return to life? Now, for fictions to raise in our minds the general question of appearances, two conditions are required. Firstly, fictions have to be taken seriously: beyond their explicit, imaginary reference, we have to recognize a second, real and concealed reference. Secondly, they have to be collected into a complete and closed story, where the whole imaginary reference stands for the whole of reality. Both of these conditions are met by myth. But myth, as will be seen, obeys the generalized Helmholtz principle. It is not experienced as appearance which would contrast with reality. It still pretends to be a picture of reality – a picture rivalling the picture based on perception, or rather supplanting it by interpreting it and assigning it its place in completely new surroundings.

Contemporary studies in mythology have profoundly changed our notion of myth. Primitive societies have become better known, and ethnographical methods have been applied to our own societies. Moreover, the concept of irrational behaviour has raised doubts among scientists who are prone to profess the principle of charity. But above all, a widespread feeling of resentment against their own traditional values has come to characterize Westerners.

The exaltation of mythical thought progressed by stages. First the idea of a 'primitive' and 'prelogical' mentality was abandoned by its author.[1] Then the fundamental concept of theory was extended to the world image expressed by myths[2] considered as a form of rationality paving the way for science.[3] If myth and science were kept distinct among symbolic forms, it was because they were thought to use two different kinds of signs: signs of things and signs of order.[4] Myth has its signs rooted in things, it was claimed, since ritual actions take precedence over mythical representations.[5] But even this alleged precedence may be questioned, as can its consequence. The systematic knowledge presupposed by the Neolithic revolution when man mastered the great arts of civilization (pottery, weaving, agriculture, animal domestication) is hardly compatible with the hypothesis of a thought subjugated by concrete rites and things.[6] On the other hand, the exuberant exercises of natural classification which are common to each savage society cannot uniquely or even principally aim at practical utility.[7] Even totemism, where signs of things seem to overwhelm rationality, shows that mythical concepts resist any reduction to substance-concepts (as opposed to functional concepts, which would be the prerogative of science). Though once it was thought that persons or groups themselves were identified with vegetables and animals, a more accurate analysis reveals that there are rather differences or oppositions between persons or groups which are correlated with representative differences or oppositions between vegetables or animals. More generally, a given myth, construed as a relation between determinate things, may through a system of transformations (almost in the sense in which geometers speak of groups of transformations) be mapped on to another myth, in which all things and their properties may have been changed, while the structural code (which is nothing but the meaning of these myths) has been preserved.[8]

Once myths have been incorporated into the field of rationality (conceived as the power of signs), according to Hegel's programme of identification between rationality and reality, the problem arises as to how to distinguish myth, which is now assimilated to the science of the concrete, from modern science. It may indeed be provisionally rational to believe that a tooth-shaped seed protects from snake bites,[9] but this is precisely the kind of sense-given relation which is rejected by science. Let us, therefore, with the aim of simplifying the discussion and of fastening on the essentials, subordinate cult to myth and idealize myth into an image of natural classification. Then the divisions of the group which cults bring directly into play only mirror the abstract system of divisions which mythical reason puts into reality. In consequence of this interpretation, the actual imaginary content of the myth refers to the code according to which our minds get a first classificatory mastery over the world. Thus myth, considered in its real referential dimension, aims at reinforcing reason's code, rather than at holding man's grip on reality.[10] Now these reinforcements immediatley contrast with what we today call a science. Mythopoiesis has therefore been compared with tinkering.[11] Just as any bit of material is used and reused to mimic the proper piece of a working whole, so there are signs which are used and reused to mimic the pieces of a coding system of classification. But this utilization has three consequences for mythical signs.

First of all, the transformations which map two myths (considered as equivalent coding messages) on to one another do not belong to an *a priori* well-defined class, as do geometrical transformations; moreover, they may be borrowed from the most heterogeneous domains.[12] In the same way, the class of substitutions is no more well defined for correlated signs than, in tinkering, it is for corresponding things. Since contents are disregarded in favour of differences or oppositions, and since differences and oppositions generally give way to equivocal comparisons, there is no biunivocal relation between signs and differences, or oppositions, of things – and, *a fortiori*, no biunivocal relation between signs and contents. On the contrary, the 'well-made language' of science will require a well-defined identity for its signs and there will be no science without foundational instructions concerning at least the requirement of linguistic univocity.

Secondly, myth and science are brought closer together, because the meaning conveyed by myth is felt to be more abstract and systematic than the appearances suggested. Nevertheless, abstract systems fundamentally opposed to science may easily be found, as is evidenced by late developments in Greek philosophy and various constructs of German absolute idealism. As for the mythical systems, their comparison with tinkering shows them to be repetitive[13] and simply aggregative. New concepts can be used only to reinforce old oppositions so that the system runs no risk of revision or extension. Although the system admits of content enrichment, it is kept formally closed and fixed. Or rather it is impossible to speak, except by analogy, of theoretical determination for such systems.

Thirdly, for myths to be genuinely amenable to rationality, rationality cannot be added to them from outside, as happens with allegorical interpretations, according to which a sensible sign carries an ideal message subject to a subsequent intellectual deciphering. Only the story told is explicitly given. The coding message, however, while aimed at as a latent interpretation, must be actually even if obscurely grasped in the living experience characteristic of mythical consciousness. Through its surface meaning a sign of myth – whether it is considered as a thing-sign or as a code's reinforcement – must therefore hint at the real reference. But it could not make its way to the inner meaning and the deep reference without referring to the closed totality.[14] Every sign therefore supports every other sign. This mutually constant and circular support of its signs makes a myth meaningful, and meaningfulness is its unique law. To understand a myth, we need not know in what circumstances the story would be true. We need only surmise the code at which this story hints. As shown by modern myths, alien as they are to any form of disconfirmation, meaning here leaves no place for truth. This contrasts with science, where, when new concepts are introduced, a rule must be respected according to which the old concepts that are thus replaced may still be regarded as approximations valid on a coarser scale; in this way the truth-values of sentences are conserved even if they are relativized to a given stage of measurement. It is this fundamental rule which is overlooked by those who, on holistic pretexts, unduly bring together scientific structures and mythical systems.

Therefore, even if myths are exalted as a 'savage' science, the reason which produces them has to the reason at work in science the same relation that a lifeless imitation of life has to life itself. The substance of the pattern is lacking. In order to be possible, science required a complete revolution in the use of linguistic signs – something which amounts to creating a new language with respect to sign identity,[15] theoretical determination[16] and truth. Axiomatic method and philosophy gave this revolution its expression in both the domain of the particular sciences and the domain of rationality in general. The revolution resulted in man's struggle to disentangle reality from appearances.

Free philosophy and axiomatic method arose simultaneously in Greece.

There have been other countries where particular sciences – grammar, logic, arithmetic, algebra, geometry, astronomy – developed and even flourished, where social conflicts raised a systematic discussion of the principles governing the organization of the city and where the 'sacerdotal class' – to come back to Benjamin Constant – did not impose its severe control on people's opinion. It was in Greece alone that sciences were taught and practised as parts of liberal education. Only the Greeks conceived of a rational way of dealing not only with scientific but also with religious, political, ethical and artistic subjects.

Greek science was a unique event in the history of mankind because of the axiomatic method it applied in arithmetic, geometry, logic, astronomy, harmonics and statics. It was an immediate cure for the three defects of mythical signs regarding foundations, procedures of extension and truth, even at the risk of appearing indifferent to experience and the sensible world. Firstly, it strictly delimited and identified the domain of elements, which myth left open. Each science was to determine its irreducible and fundamental concepts ($\sigma\tauοιχεῖα$) and principles ($\dot{α}ρχαί$). Secondly, rules of construction and definition were introduced, according to which new concepts were produced from the primitive concepts and were eliminable in terms of them. In the same way, a list of deductive rules was given, a list which allows us from the given set of primitive principles to draw the set of its logical consequences. Thirdly, just as the set of these principles was recognized by the Greeks as true, and just as the rules of deduction were seen to preserve truth-values, so the logical consequences of the principles were themselves recognized as true. They were taken as constituting the theorems of Greek science.

There is no awaking to life and leaving the cave's darkness for the sun's light without waver and dazzle. Who, if anyone, was the first man to take the decisive step? According to Proclus, it was Pythagoras, who 'transformed the science of geometry[17] into the form of a liberal education, examining its principles from the beginning[18] and tracking down the theorems immaterially and intellectually',[19] in opposition to Thales, whose method was 'in some cases more general, in others more empirical'.[20] Whatever answer was to be given to the anecdotal questions of priority, a host of intellectual difficulties had to be met by a man tracking down the theorems in a completely demonstrative way, without borrowing from experience.

Firstly, there is the impossibility of regressing to elements without encountering principles which cannot themselves be demonstrated and concepts which cannot themselves be defined. Now, this impossibility is difficult to accept for a mind just freed from the circularities of myth. The seventh and the third books of Euclid's *Elements* – books on Pythagorean arithmetic and geometry – contain pseudo-definitions of such indefinables as *unit*,[21] *point*[22] and *line*.[23] These pseudo-definitions contrast with genuine definitions of derived concepts such as *even number*[24] or *rectilinear figure*.[25] As for the truth of first principles, the Greeks soon came to distinguish between postulates and common notions[26] without coming to agree on the exact meaning they gave to the distinction. While they do not seem to have doubted the truth of the fifth postulate, they certainly wondered whether the truths pertaining to the formal properties of equality had the same origin, bearing and foundation as the truths pertaining to the existence or the uniqueness of a particular geometrical construction. Furthermore, the discovery of irrationals made the Greeks ask how to reconcile Thales' theory of geometrical proportions with the existence of geometrical lengths that had no proportions or *logoi*. Eudoxus' celebrated definition[27] in Euclid (v 5) stipulated the conditions which any analogy must obey, that is, it defined equality of proportions without referring in the *definiens* to a previously defined concept of proportion – just as in modern set theory we are told what we can do with sets without being told what sets are. Proportions and sets only admit of contextual definitions, so that material axiomatics, which presents or constructs each of its objects, gives way to formal axiomatics, where, to put an end to a mathematical crisis, we decide to ignore what we speak about and to renounce any material determination of objects that would go beyond the formal operations allowed by the axioms.[28]

In the second place, the rules which may be used to construct and to demonstrate afford material for discussion, as is shown by the different interpretations of geometrical constructions as well as by the recourse to a deviant logic. For Speusippus and the Academy the existence of the objects of science does not depend on the particular ways in which our knowledge approaches them. So ruler and compass are useful only because they imitate Ideas, which alone exist by themselves. By contrast, the geometers of the school of Cyzicus, like Menechmus, require before admitting an object as existent an effective construction, understood as a controlled progression of knowledge. When Menechmus met problems beyond the reach of ruler and compass, for instance, the duplication of the cube, the trisection of the angle, and the construction of the regular heptagon, he reduced them to the problem of simultaneously solving two equations of the second degree by constructing the intersection either of a parabola with a hyperbola or of two parabolas. His method pushed construction by ruler and compass as far as possible by extending it from the plane to space. The mechanical constructions of Eudoxus and Archytas were still further removed from ruler and compass.[29] We do not know how the Greek geometers, when venturing beyond the domain of algebraic expressions containing only square roots, legitimated these extensions. Yet the care with which Menechmus managed to remain as faithful as possible to the constructions licensed by the theory of Ideas discloses doubts to which only Descartes's *Geometry* was to put an end. On the other hand. Anaxagoras is known to have denied, in consequence of his physical doctrine of homoeomeries, the validity of the principle of the excluded middle.[30] Since there is some evidence of his having conceived the physical continuum and the mathematical continuum in the same way, we are authorized to trace modern intuitionism back to Greek mathematics.[31]

A further price must be paid when the axiomatic method is used. Each myth, while expressing an immutable code, grows by aggregation without fixed limits. In the same way, different myths enter, without conflict, into a process of juxtaposition that results in a mythical system, a 'science of the concrete' which Bergson labelled 'the proliferation of the absurd'.[32] For overlapping classifications lead to conceptual crisscrossings; they cannot produce contradictions. As for axioms, they enclose a subject-matter in a predetermined closed space. But the relations between different axiomatic domains very often contain surprises and clashes which engender the most important forms of scientific progress. The same Pythagorean theorem which demonstrated that the lengths of the sides of a right triangle are related through their squares introduced the irrationals and obliged mathematicians to renounce the previous Pythagorean identification of geometry with the arithmetic of the rational numbers. This demonstration of impossibility characteristically opened on two ways out. Theodorus and Theaetetus introduced the irrationals by means of infinite definitions grounded on the approximation by continued fractions. Eudoxus established his new method of formal axiomatics.[33] There is an analogy when the axiomatic method is applied to the observational sciences. Eudoxus[34] recognized that planetary motions imitated a certain curve which he called 'hippopedes' (a spherical lemniscate, a kind of figure of 8), of which one loop is withdrawn to infinity. This suffices to describe the phenomenon of the planetary retrogradations. Now axiomatics comes into play to integrate the phenomenon into a deductive system. Classification is thus transformed into explanation. Plato had fixed the terms of axiomatic astronomy by requiring that every celestial body should be moved with circular, uniform and unidirectional motions. The mathematicians had therefore to solve the following problem: 'What are the uniform and perfectly regular motions which it is fitting to take as hypotheses, in order that the phenomena offered by the wandering stars be saved?'[35] Eudoxus himself and his followers built and refined a model of homocentric spheres centred around the Earth. The axiomatic method shows its revolutionary force if we consider how, when and in what order new astronomical systems appeared to explain the phenomena more simply, or to approximate them more accurately. Firstly Heraclides, by putting the Sun at the centre of the motions of Mercury and Venus, anticipated Tycho's hypothesis, at least for the inferior planets. Then Aristarchus articulated a Copernican-like heliocentric system. When, finally, Ptolemy made use of the quantitative data of the Babylonians, he subjected them to a model obeying the same axiomatic method typical of Greek science. Using eccentrics revolving around the Earth, he refers back to Apollonius' theorem,[36] according to which there is kinematical equivalence with the semi-heliocentric device of the epicycles, an equivalence that is easily extended to the proper heliocentric hypothesis but which excludes the geocentrical systems of homocentric spheres. Thus, whereas myths are protected beforehand against revision and insulated from experience, axiomatic systems in pure and applied mathematics proved to be rooted in a perfectible and self-correcting reason. These systems form an open sequence in which each of them contains its predecessor and gives a better approximation of reality.

2 AXIOMATICS AND PHILOSOPHICAL ONTOLOGIES: THE ANALYSIS OF THE MOTION AND THE ANALYSIS OF FREEDOM

The axiomatic method awakened the restless mind from its mythical slumber. It is no wonder that such an awakening was correlated with a complete reorganization of reason as the power of signs.[37] Myths had to yield to philosophies.

At the same time that science was born, Greek myths underwent a profound change. The Milesian naturalists introduced the quest for true principles[38] into myths and thus constituted what has been rightly called a theology. Having characterized the Divine as omnipotent, eternal, just and so on, they and their successors in Greater Greece or in Athens drew definite conclusions which questioned the validity of the old myths. While the word *muthos* 'had originally been a harmless designation for any speech or narration', it started then 'to take on that negative sense which was to become almost universal by the time of Thucydides . . ., the sense of the fabulous and unauthenticated, as contrasted with any verifiable truth or reality'.[39] Even those who tended to restore the traditional faith did it from positivist arguments and according to demonstrative schemes in agreement with the new scientific method.

But between axiomatics and philosophy there are deeper relations than this penetration of myth by reason, a penetration characteristic of Greek religion since the time of the early Greek philosophers. These relations will appear if we recall the three advantages and drawbacks of the axiomatic method concerning foundations, demonstration and truth.

Firstly, the axiomatic method precisely determines a field by listing a set of premises from which theorems follow with certainty. But it ignores the nature of its undefinable concepts and the justification of its indemonstrable principles. For concepts, formal axiomatics goes so far as to make a virtue of necessity. The Socratic question is thus unavoidable: how do irrational and uncognizable elements combine into reason and knowledge?[40] As a hypothetico-deductive system, axiomatics is thus completely foreign to ontology. Many working mathematicians admit – as did even the ancients – the reality of the objects about which they speak, be they polygons and polyhedrons, or circles and spheres or more abstract structures such as Eudoxus' system of magnitudes.[41] But such an interpretation is never forced upon us by the axioms themselves, which do not tell us what the elements are. It was left to Greek philosophy to inquire into the nature of the things presupposed by axiomatic systems but not included within them. What are numbers, points and lines? What kind of existence may be claimed for them? These are philosophical questions. But the ontological inquiry could not be confined to the objects of proper axiomatized systems. The world of myth had crumbled: its materials had to be reorganized. Explanatory concepts and principles – material, causal, formal, final causes – were sought for, whose consequences could fit the phenomena. The four elements, their four constituent sensible qualities and long lists of paired abstract entities (atoms and homoeomeries, becoming and being, motion and rest, multiplicity and unity, *mixis* and separation, continuity and discontinuity, illimitedness and limitedness, love and strife) cooperate or compete in order to explain the constitution of things.

Myths had two referential dimensions. Their explicit signs designated fabulous entities, while their implicit interpretation in terms of reality was left undetermined and equivocal. Axiomatics, so to speak, overturns this setting. The ontological interpretation is left out. As for the mythical story, it has its counterpart in the process of deduction. The possibility of a third figure is contained in these data, if an ontological posit borrowed from myth, but now made clear and distinct, may be put to the test by uncoiling its consequences in a deductive chain. For this combination to be possible, it is necessary that reality should be analysed into a few concepts and principles which will be taken as premises, and it is sufficient that from these premises one can draw results which, when compared with how reality looks, either are not distorted or obey a received rule of distortion. As every axiomatic system has in common the deductive apparatus which is called formal logic, we may define the system of signs which is peculiar to philosophy as an ontology subjected to logic. It is then no wonder that the first parts of logic – syllogistic and sentential logic – found their scientific expression within Greek philosophies. Moreover, the two dimensions which are attributed to philosophy as a presumptively coherent combination of ontologically interpreted signs explain why each free philosophy has the form of a rational system. Since logic applies to ontology, philosophy is systematic in the same way that material axiomatic systems are. Besides, any set of premises which contains an ontology continues to embrace the whole of reality, and philosophy may be said to be systematic in a second sense, which recalls and metamorphosizes the universality of myth.

Objections to the systematic character of philosophy will be raised from different sides and must be answered before going further.

Some objectors will even deny that philosophers ought to struggle for consistency. Aristotle, they say, defends the validity of the principle of non-contradiction. But is it not the case that what was defended had been and may be attacked? Now, according to the letter of Aristotle,[42] it is impossible to conceive that the same thing is and is not, as some people believe Heraclitus to hold. This reference is interesting, because, if we forget about the sophists, who do not find themselves committed to thinking what they assert, the unique ground for all serious objections to the principle of non-contradiction arises from one and the same Heraclitean theme, repeated *ad nauseam* by Hegelians and Marxists. Reality and motion, it is affirmed, result from the unity of opposites. As for Heraclitus, it would be surprising if the principle of logic without which any conclusion might be drawn from any set of premises had been questioned by the philosopher who wrote: 'The sun will not overstep his measures; for otherwise the Erinyes, Dikē's deputies, will find him out.'[43] As for the objection itself, it deserves no further examination and simply results from a confusion between logical contradiction and factual opposition or conflict – a confusion sometimes supported by other confusions suggested when using infinitesimals for explaining motion or continuity.

Three main objections concern the second sense of philosophical systematization.

The first objection comes from those who oppose monism and who confound system and monism. Now, when from the existence of material substances which sometimes move and sometimes do not Aristotle concludes that there are also sensible but ever-moving substances as well as an immobile and immaterial one, his demonstration amounts to refuting monism; but nevertheless, it covers the whole range of possibilities and proceeds systematically.

A second mistake arises from confounding system and dogmatism. A universal ontology, it will be said, bypasses the possibility of experience and leads to antinomies. These antinomies express themselves in the opposite concepts which often appear paired by the early Greek philosophers: finite–infinite, indivisible–divisible, freedom–determinism, contingency–necessity. But even if the concepts of the pure understanding lose all ontological reference when used beyond the limits of possible experience, and even if therefore universals have nothing to do with the universe in itself, restricted as they are with respect to their objective value to the possibility of experience, universals none the less retain their architectonic role since they build a complete system of phenomena.

Finally, there are philosophers who reject any form of system. Apart from stylistic preferences for aphorisms, they criticize systems for their predetermined character of conceptual and lawlike divisions, which, on their view, are unable to account for life's looser situations, better described by family resemblance concepts or by language-games. Systems of concepts and laws, they say, are idealizations that philosophical analysis must break in order to discover how they twist the data as given in our immediate presystematic experience. However, once phenomenological consciousness, life, existence and language-games have entered into philosophy as its true principles, they necessarily comply with the ordinary systematic duties, since they must be shown to suffice for producing what, in the world, is recognized as authentic reality and for explaining away the intellectual constructions that have traditionally been mistaken for philosophy. Open, piecemeal, rough philosophical systems are still systems in both of the senses we gave to the word.

The second benefit stemming from axiomatics concerns demonstration. Technical disputes about methods of construction and local reservations about the principle of the excluded middle did not hinder Greek science from reaching universal agreement on what a scientific theorem is. Queries and discussions could always be put to an end, at least within the hypothetico-deductive method, by locating the debatable point in the chain of deduction. But ontological concepts seriously call into question the validity of the excluded middle, because they may apply to infinities, which are not apprehended as given totalities. Moreover, in consequence of their inexactness and above all of their unsuitability for entering into specific processes of construction, they restrict the use of the axiomatic method to some patterns of refutation such as the infinite regress and the *reductio ad absurdum*. In the regress elements can never be reached, while in the *reductio* the principle of non-contradiction is broken, contrary to the very requirements of the method.

Since philological evidence is too scanty to support simple and definite conclusions concerning the negation of the principle of the excluded middle, it will be safer to concentrate on two famous cases in which the *reductio ad absurdum* was used in connection with the main concepts of physics and ethics: motion and freedom. Let us examine how Greek philosophers used deduction in the case of the celebrated example of Zeno's principal[44] and simplest argument: the arrow. When extraneous comments are removed, it reads: 'The moved is moving neither in the space where it is nor in the space where it is not',[45] a sentence in which the continuous present has an essential occurrence. Aristotle's version says: 'If everything is always resting or moving and if it is resting every time it is in a space equal to itself, then since what is carried is always in the now, the arrow in the process of being carried is unmoved.'[46]

Zeno's own argument has the following form:

(1) For an accomplished motion to be possible, it is necessary and sufficient that the arrow whose head was assumed to coincide at time t with the point x

should have at the time $t + \triangle t$ its head coinciding with the point $x + \triangle x$, such that x is any non-constant function of t. In other words, for any value of t there must correspond a uniquely determinate and non-constant value of x.

(2) Everything is either resting or moving.

(3) A carried body is resting every time it is in a space equal to itself (Aristotle's definition).

(4) At time t, since the arrow is in a space equal to itself, its head being at the point x, it is not moving in its space.

(5) At time $t + \triangle t$, since the arrow is in a space equal to itself, its head being at the point $x + \triangle x$, it is not moving in its space.

(6) At time t, since the arrow is in a space equal to itself, its head being at the point x, it is not moving in the space $x + \triangle x$ where it is not.

(7) At time $t + \triangle t$, since the arrow is in a space equal to itself, its head being at the point $x + \triangle x$, it is not moving in the space x where it is not.

(8) Every moving of the arrow takes place either in the space where it is or in the space where it is not.

(9) Since it is not the case either that at time t or that at time $t + \triangle t$ the arrow is moving either in the space where it is or in the space where it is not (4–7), the arrow is never moving (8) and therefore it is always resting (2).

Let us complete the argument.

(10) However small the interval $\triangle t$ is chosen, the arrow is always resting.

(11) Since locomotion or local motion is regarded as that without which any other kind of motion (growth, alteration, genesis) would not be possible, everything is always resting.

This argument contains no fallacy. What it demonstrates is that at any instant the arrow is resting, i.e., exactly occupies the place where it is. This, as Russell saw,[47] amounts to expressing the simple truth that each possible value of a variable is a constant. No hypothesis is made about motion's continuity or discontinuity. Consequently the argument has been accepted (or independently formulated) by philosophers such as Diodorus Cronus, who held that time was composed of minimal parts.[48] A never-moving arrow, however, merely excludes any alleged dynamical 'state' of motion. As the first premise shows, a static universe of space–time values still allows a static definition of motion. As Diodorus rightly affirmed, from the arrow argument we can conclude that no dynamis ever actually exists, not that there has never been motion[49] (though the argument is in itself independent of the Diodorean hypothesis of indivisible lengths and durations). Between the empirical premise which would affirm, in agreement with Zeno's definition

(1), that there has been accomplished motion and the conclusion (10), there is thus no contradiction. In order to get a contradiction, another premise should have to be admitted, namely, that:

(12) If the arrow is never moving, then it has not undergone any accomplished motion.

Aristotle explicitly states this supplementary premise when he says that 'what has accomplished its change must have previously been in the process of changing'.[50] He believes that he demonstrates this premise by a *reductio ad absurdum* where he explicitly assumes time to be continuous and therefore indefinitely divisible. The accomplished motion is excluded as well in t_0 – the instant of starting motion – as in t_1 – the instant of the end of motion – since otherwise in both cases the head of the arrow should simultaneously coincide with two different points, x_0 and x_1. If the motion is instantaneously accomplished, it is then accomplished at an instant t' such that $t_0 < t' < t_1$. But for every instant t', the argument may be repeated: the accomplished motion cannot be done in the instant if the head of the arrow cannot be simultaneously at two different places. Therefore such a motion occurs in a finite lapse of time which is indefinitely divisible:

Hence, Aristotle concludes, since the change has occurred during a lapse of time and since every finite lapse of time is divisible, during the half of this time another change will have been accomplished, another one during the quarter and so on indefinitely; hence, when the change is accomplished, it must have been previously the process of what has been changing.[51]

It seems, then, that the growing spatial decomposition of the track left by motion would lose any dynamic character, should it not be given a supporting dynamis, namely, an ultimate process of changing.[52] But Aristotle's conclusion, grounded upon the impossibility of a sequence in the continuum – either of time or of space – only shows that the intervals of the covered space, which are the tracks and the marks of the accomplished motion, tend to a limit when the time intervals do. Points and instants are not parts or intervals of space and time and the continuum contains in itself, at least potentially, an infinite number of these limits. It is by no means proved that these limits have anything to do with processes of changing and moving, for they are static points like the corresponding instants of time. Therefore the premise (12), according to which an accomplished motion presupposes the past occurrence of a corresponding accomplishing motion must be regarded, contrary to Aristotle's wish, as an independent premise.

Let us sum up the four premises which lead to a contradiction:

(1) There is an accomplished motion.

(2) Everything is resting or moving.

(3) A carried body is resting every time it is in a space equal to itself.

(12) What has moved has been moving.

The arrow argument is directly rooted in mathematical axiomatics and leads into the labyrinth of the continuum. In order to escape the contradiction, we have to abandon one of the premises, though it is doubtful that intuition shows us the suspicious premise. As a deduction under hypotheses, the axiomatic method aims at universality and reaches it. But it results in turmoil and disagreement and it constrains us to abandon apparently self-evident principles and to choose between incompatible and rival ontologies.

(1) Nothing is better attested by our senses than motion, and motion bears witness to plurality which is itself the foundation of number. A disciple of Parmenides, Zeno probably removed the contradiction of the arrow by giving up its first premise. Motion and plurality are illusions. Being is one and it is resting.

(2) The second premise amounts to affirming that every magnitude is either finite or null. Now there have been ancient mathematicians who calculated areas and volumes by using a third kind of magnitude, the infinitesimal magnitudes. Eudoxus and Aristotle saw that the calculus appropriate to these magnitudes was incompatible with the standard calculus of the finite magnitudes. Hence they repudiated the infinitely smalls as pseudo-quantities between constants and variables.[53] It is probably that repudiation which Aristotle expresses when he rejects the arrow argument because it presupposes that 'time is made of instants'.[54] But we know today that we can accommodate the infinitesimals within a system to which finite magnitudes also belong, on the condition that a non-standard analysis should be built for this purpose. This will perhaps be the way which Leibniz will follow later.[55] Have there been Pythagoreans who tried to save their principles at the cost of such a reform, or at least by having an inkling of its requirements? The data we now have at our disposal do not allow us to answer the question.

(3) When we analyse the motion of the arrow into as many instantaneous situations in which, occupying the space where it is then, it happens to be immobilized, we divide the continuum indefinitely, and this division is permitted only if it occurs *in potentia*, not *in actu*, since the actualizations of the infinite would break motion into an infinity of stopping-places. According to Aristotle, Zeno's infinite is defective because it confuses potentiality with actuality. We must therefore completely abandon the set-theoretical representation of the straight-line and separate geometry and arithmetic, intervals and point-sets, things and numbers. The limits are merely potentially in the lengths as the instants are in the durations.

While Aristotle refuses to identify the one-dimensional continuum with a set of points, his distinction, within the continuum, between actual parts and potential point-elements announces the modern concept of the continuum, where these points are only defined in a correct way as limits.

Moreover, in principle, such a conception might or even should have helped, in dynamics, the introduction of instantaneous speed and accelera-tion as limits. That was not the case. For rest itself, according to Aristotle, is relevant to two properties. On the one hand it is the stopping-point which constitutes the last fragment of motion when our thought actualizes the infinite. On the other hand, it is the end towards which motion as such is tending, this state which is the contrary of its own and which from inside haunts and shakes the mobile and through which an incomplete being bears inscribed in itself the act of its incompleteness. When the Pythagoreans[56] oppose rest and motion as they opposed the limited and the unlimited, there is some rationale behind their classification, since its aoristic character allies motion to the unlimited. However, even if the process of motion is opposed to its being accomplished, motion remains distinguished from the unlimited by its full actuality. So the Pythagorean opposition is superseded by the modal opposition between act and potency. Everything which is movable is indeed imperfect, either because the perpetual motion of the eternal but sensible substances imitates through its periodical stability the immobility of God's reflection, or because the contrary motions of the perishable substances, of which we are, still imitate in a weaker disposition the kind of rest proper to the periodical motion of the heavens by making life, births, and deaths dependent on the cycle of the specific reproductions. Motion is then opposed to rest or to the perfection of God as the unique form of perfection which is appropriate to the imperfect. As perfection, motion will be an act; as perfection of an imperfection, it will be the act of a potency, and, since this imperfection is an essential, not a transitory feature, motion must be the act of a potency *qua* potency. By opening up an abyss between rest and motion, this celebrated definition[57] has for centuries subordinated dynamics to theology and hindered scientific development because it used obscure modal notions, and blocked analysis of instantaneous speed and acceleration.

(4) Finally, it is possible to deny that an accomplished motion presupposes the corresponding accomplishing motion. Motion is then reduced to a function of time. To the set of the 'points' which constitute a given lapse of time, the set of the 'points' which constitute a trajectory is made to correspond according to a law. The Megaric school conceived these static pluralities under the form of quanta of space, time and motion, a programme which until now has met insuperable difficulties. As to Cantor's solution,

which was to integrate dynamics into set theory, it leads into an analysis of the infinite which seems to have been entirely foreign to the spirit of Greek mathematics and philosophy.

This does not put an end to the list of possible ontologies. Indeed, it suffices to discover any questionable implicit premise in a *reductio ad absurdum* such as the arrow argument and to state a rival principle in connection with the other agreed premises in order to build a new ontology identical with the set of their possible consequences.

Greek philosophy, like any free philosophy, consists in stating puzzles (the task of eristic philosophy) and displaying the fan of their possible solutions (the task of proper philosophical systems).[58] We find the same method applied in every field of human knowledge. It even happens that the formulation of such a *reductio* delimits *a priori* – at least for a given philosophical school committed to accepting all the implicit premises in the argument – the number and the nature of the possible variants of a general ontology. A kind of structural history is then open to philosophy. This is the case for the Megarian–Stoic school with respect to what Leibniz called the second labyrinth of thought, the labyrinth of freedom in its relation to natural laws. For in his celebrated Master Argument, Diodorus Cronus is said[59] to have drawn a contradiction from the simultaneous positing of the three following rather 'natural principles':

1. Everything which is true and past is necessary.
2. From the possible the impossible does not follow.
3. There is a possible which is not the case and never will be the case.

Thus three possibilities were open to the common ontology of the school. Either the first or the second or the third premise had to be denied. Cleanthes, Chrysippus and Diodorus respectively chose these different solutions. It can be shown, besides, that the other philosophical schools did not fail to answer the challenge by questioning implicit premises contained in the Master Argument. In a debate to which Bayle and Leibniz are still active witnesses, even generally received principles such as the principle of the excluded middle and the principle prohibiting truth-value-gaps for statements were denied – and by no lesser figures than Epicurus (for the first principle) and Aristotle (for the second).[60]

Within the particular sciences, the methodological pluralism which is bound to the axiomatic method produces limited consequences. At a given time, only a few working methods are ripe and adopted in practice by all scientists along with their corresponding axiomatic systems. On the contrary, the premises with which philosophy deals are so general, numerous and complex that they resist any particular formal expression and perhaps even defy any particular historical expression, however thorough it is. Despite all the efforts of those who do not distinguish between science and philosophy, universally acceptable working standards have never been reached – and presumably never will be reached. Consequently, as applied to ontology, axiomatics inevitably produces pluralism and disagreement. Indeed, philosophical reason is born and lives in contest.

A third and final difference between the philosopher and his scientific companion results from the role of truth in their respective systems of signs. Genuine axiomatic systems may ideally be organized in such a way that historical improvements may be read as extensions which either preserve the truth of the previous systems or at least admit, so to speak, a point of truth-contact with them. Old truth is either absorbed or explained away by new science, so that in this field living knowledge does not need to refer to its own history as a pseudo-reality. When a rival system's claims challenge the present schemes of explanation, it is tacitly understood that further observational or experimental evidence will enable us to settle the question. The concept of appearance has therefore no place in ordinary axiomatics. Two exceptions are nevertheless worth mentioning. Firstly, certain geometrical techniques of the eighteenth century which were linked together by Lambert under the name of 'phenomenology', aim (1) at predicting for a given object how it would appear to a perceiving subject according to the place he occupies, and (2) at reconstructing the object from the appearances it underlies. Secondly, heliocentric astronomy calls the celestial motions that are perceived from our movable station of observation appearances. The real trajectory is inextricably distorted by our own motion and has to be disentangled from it. In both cases appearances result from confusing the subjective position or motion of the observer with objective position or motion.

Now, this is the ordinary situation met with by philosophers. The *reductiones ad absurdum* which axiomatics introduces into philosophy are accompanied by a feeling of wonder and uneasiness because they reveal an unexpected inconsistency among principles. If a philosophical system were to select some principles and reject others, the choice would lack any justification and the feeling of surprise would not be dispelled if it were not shown that the previous uncritical acceptance of premises now questioned expressed a mere illusion. Every system, even when reputed for its congeniality with common sense, is led to some conclusions which oppose common sense. Thus Diodorus is forced to refuse any role to disposition predicates. He only makes allowance for possibility *qua* that which is or will be. Aristotle, for his part, saves freedom (conceived of as the power of alternative choices) only at the price of accepting completely undetermined contingent futures and truth-valueless propositions. But from Aristotle's point of view the faultless actuality of the Megarian universe, which denies any sense to human deliberation, reduces this universe to mere appearance. The Megarians for their part would view the unlikely admissions of Aristotle as so many indications of the subjective prejudice built into a definition of freedom as an empire within nature.[61]

To sum up, philosophy results from the reorganization of the two dimensions of mythical signs. The mythical story gives way to the quest for true principles according to the standards of the axiomatic method. This was the first, foundational relevance of axiomatics to philosophy. At the same time, however, philosophy intends to reform and to restore mythical ontology dismissed by axiomatics. A determinate ontology takes the place of the equivocal reference to reality. The second connection of axiomatics with philosophy is through demonstration. But the requirement of consistency, which no material consideration comes to hinder in axiomatic method, has, in philosophy, to cope with ontology. Between self-evident principles equally recommended by common sense but mutually inconsistent, a choice is imposed on philosophy which explains its divisions. Finally, philosophy is like axiomatics in so far as both seek truth. But in contradistinction to scientific truth, its consideration of ontology makes philosophy generalize an opposition which is only of local and minor importance in science. Competing philosophical systems struggle for recognized, if not fixed, frontiers between appearance and reality.

4 | A CLASSIFICATION OF PHILOSOPHICAL SYSTEMS

There are many ways of subjecting myth to the axiomatic method and of answering the questions which determine a philosophy as a presumably consistent and systematic ontology. How are reality and appearance divided? What principles and what specific kind of demonstration are recognized as true and valid?

When the writings of a philosopher – or possibly some of his particular works[1] – are analysed in order to make explicit the principles and methods of proof according to which he draws the boundary between reality and appearance, the historian is naturally led to comparisons. By reconstructing in their individuality some of the systems which constitute the object of his discipline, he meets open discord as well as seeming agreements with other systems, and is obliged to trace their cause to differences regarding a given premise or a given set of premises. Partial, occasional and *a posteriori* classifications result from such comparisons.

We have met some cases of *reductiones ad absurdum* that seemed to delineate an *a priori* framework for the possible solutions which philosophical systems could give to a particular question. Nothing, however, hinted at a possible generalization. Moreover, the formal convergences which are suggested when a contradiction is analysed away threaten to conceal or to prejudge the genuine philosophical issues.

We shall first ask whether a general and truly *a priori* classification of philosophical systems is possible and on just what conditions that would be. The analysis of the elementary sentences given in chapter 2 will be shown to afford an appropriate principle for such a classification. The classification, or rather a sketch of it, will follow and six main classes of systems will be distinguished. Finally, the significance of the classification will be briefly examined with respect to philosophical truth.

I ON WHAT CONDITIONS IS AN *A PRIORI* CLASSIFICATION OF PHILOSOPHICAL SYSTEMS POSSIBLE?

At the end of chapter 2 is a complete table of elementary sentences or elementary forms of singular predication. By adding more and more verbal and subjective determinations to the predicative core of the nominal sentence and principally by examining the possible ways which give us access to the truth conditions, we distinguished six kinds of elementary sentences. These sentences convey the particular ontic claims that, without involving general ontological issues concerning what there is, correspond to the different types of predicative objectification by which language shapes the sensible world. The ontic distinctions thus displayed constitute the unquestioned objectual reference of myth, inasmuch as it encodes the world of common sense. The question is therefore: what transformations must determinate elementary sentences or combinations of such sentences undergo if, instead of referring according to the occasion once to this, then again to that portion of the world, they are to become ontological premises of a genuine philosophical system?

Systematic ontology requires that (1) a minimal set of undefinable concepts and of undemonstrable principles should be given from which the whole furniture of the world may be derived, (2) this derivation should proceed according to legitimated rules, and (3) rival ontologies should be explained away as mere appearances.

As to the first requirement, a given elementary sentence or combination of elementary sentences is transformed into an ontological principle if and only if every sentence which expresses an ontological claim receives the form of that elementary sentence or of that combination of elementary sentences. For example, to regard circumstantial predication as the unique ontological principle amounts to affirming that everything that exists happens. The local ontic claim of the sentence 'It is raining' thus becomes a philosophical principle. In order to be distinguished from subordinate principles connected with the particular articulation of the world, those principles will be called highest principles. Therefore a highest principle will be expressed in the form 'Everything which is is an X or a Y or ...', where $X, Y, ...$ stand for the names of the highest categories. Highest categories are simply what distinguish the elementary sentences from one another by exemplifying the type which instantiates the reference of the term occurring in argument position: Ideas are thus the highest category for nominal sentences, as substances are for substantial predication, accidents for accidental predication, events for circumstantial predication, constructions of the mind for judgments of method and subjective representations for judgments of appearance. Highest categories are not intended to divide the world into parts; they only name what there is in general.[2]

In order to determine what highest principles are possible, we must determine the possible minimal bases of elementary sentences by giving the corresponding complete list of highest categories. At first glance, it seems that we might transform the totality of elementary sentences into a highest, all-embracing principle, whose highest categories would be drawn from all elementary sentences. But nothing would guarantee the consistency of such a move. Moreover, if it were possible to build an ontology from a proper subset of elementary sentences, this more parsimonious ontology would be preferred not only for its elegance, but above all because the principle requiring a wider and more eclectic basis might very well lose its highest rank, and become a mere consequence, within the rival system. Here is a case where Ockham's razor has a constitutive and not only a regulative force. Consequently, we have simply to seek for the minimal ontological bases by determining the minimal number of elementary sentences which are necessary and sufficient for building a highest principle.

Now, two cases must be distinguished among elementary sentences. Although all of them enter into a general system of mutual relations and oppositions, within which and by which their particular meaning is determined, substantial and accidental predications are further characterized by their mutual correlation. Accidents are necessarily in their substances, and substances deprived of their accidents would reduce to nothing. A highest ontological principle would hence at least require a binary basis including the two terms of the correlation. On the other hand, since the totality of the world constitutes a particular, and since this particular, owing to the fact that it participates in space and time, is extraneous to the world of the Ideas, a highest principle based only upon the nominal sentence would run the risk of leaving the phenomena unexplained, if participation sentences were not associated with the basis. In both cases, when the basis is grounded on correlation or on association, two highest categories at least and consequently two elementary sentences are necessary to make a highest principle. If isolated elementary sentences furnish the whole basis, the corresponding highest principle admits only one category.

The second requirement concerns the specific rules of derivation and construction that an ontology may incorporate. But a particular circumstance singles out elementary sentences for the determination of these rules as soon as they are transformed into highest principles. Indeed, the major division within elementary sentences depends upon whether or not the predication involves a reference to the speaker's attitude towards predication. The possible ontologies then divide into two groups. There are the dogmatic systems, for which truth is defined by the correspondence with objective states of affairs; and there are the systems of examination, namely, those that rely on the subjective series of the elementary sentences and bind truth to the subjective process of knowledge. Therefore it is to be expected that, by transforming an elementary sentence or a combination thereof into a highest ontological principle, it is determined at once what kind of deductive or constructive moves are authorized. For example, when the basic elementary sentences lack subjective reference, the principle of the excluded middle is automatically accorded its full authority – an authority which is questioned when the basic elementary sentences belong to the subjective series.

The third and last requirement concerns the demarcation between reality and appearance. The highest principle for an ontology must allow us to interpret in its own terms the objects that language has placed within the scope of other elementary sentences which do not belong to the basis of this principle. Highest principles of rival ontologies, admitting these other elementary sentences as bases, will then be constructed and construed as appearances. Both perceptual organization and philosophical systems are crowned by simulation. While perceptual organization aims at planning action in the world, philosophical simulation aims at showing that the ground of competing systems is but apparent. For example, an ontology in which events constitute the highest category will have to construe substances and accidents as classes or as collections of events subject to particular conditions of connection, duration and place; constructions and opinions would require events of a special kind; ideas which would not be dismissed as mere illusions would probably be reduced to abstractive classes of events.

For brevity's sake and because of its paramount importance only the first requirement of the axiomatic method will be referred to in the sequel for classifying philosophical systems. This arbitrary decision may be somewhat justified by the following considerations. Contemporary logicians and philosophers have debated at length about the rules of derivation and construction to be admitted, and it has been one of the central features of analytic philosophy to elaborate methods for constructing within the modest means of a given and accepted language expressions simulating corresponding expressions which, in their original context, had a more demanding role. On the contrary, it does not seem that the pluralistic spirit of the axiomatic method has deeply penetrated contemporary philosophy.

2 SKETCH OF A CLASSIFICATION

A first class of philosophical systems is obtained when we start from nominal sentences. Ideas as objective and eternal entities are the highest category corresponding to the universals they admit in argument position. However, as has been said, some sort of existence must be recognized for particulars. Because the main use of the intelligible world is to 'save the phenomena', an extended basis is required. Nominal sentences must then be associated with participation sentences in order that the ideal world may 'inform' the sensible one. An important distinction arises here according to the way this 'information' is conceived.

An ontology which maintains the irreducibility of the supra-sensible but recognizes at the same time the existence of sensible individuals is not committed to the supposition that individual realizations fall short of the universals. Thus, for the Pythagoreans there is a structural and exact isomorphism between each regularity appearing in the sensible world and a given numerical ratio.[3] Moreover, the sensible becoming is not to be distinguished from the eternal generation of numbers. The borderline fades between nominal sentences and participation sentences so that not only 'the principles of the numbers are the elements of all beings and the whole heaven is harmony and number',[4] but numbers, which are primarily forms, afford at the same time the material and the efficient cause of the universe. The highest principle, 'Everything is number', leaves undecided whether numbers are Ideas or particulars. Theoretical physicists sometimes proceed in this way. They materialize the Ideas, so to speak, and give them an immediate sensible expression and power.

Because the first kind of realism does not distinguish between universals and particulars, it fails to distinguish particular realizations from structural universals that are common models for a whole set of realizations. Things which have a same number or a same equation in common become indiscernible,[5] and sensible substances, space, time and becoming itself are transformed into numbers or ratios. But there is a second, more roundabout way. When Ideas are realized in the sensible world, it is now supposed, these realizations are only approximations or 'imitations' of the Ideas, the Ideas in themselves being unconcerned with participation. Therefore, in order to constitute the phenomenal world, which Ideas have to 'save', a second highest category is explicitly needed besides Ideas. This is the field of space–time, or what Plato called the 'receptacle'. For such a genuinely dualist ontology, the highest principle states that everything is an Idea, or is a phenomenon, i.e., an imitation of an Idea. The ontology then fully qualifies as realist. If the word *res* (thing) designates any empirical manifestation in space–time, such a *res* can only express the descent of an Idea into the foreign sensible medium. The *res* then presupposes the previous separate existence of its Idea. According to a medieval expression, the universals are prior to the things: *universalia ante rem*.

Substantial predication differs from nominal sentences, in so far as the substances which support the defining properties are not to be construed as Ideas because of their intimate relation with a space–time no longer seen as a foreign medium. The several classes of philosophical systems that use substantial predication in their basis have in common the assumption that, if the existence of an unmovable, immaterial substance, unique in its kind and devoid of spatio-temporal ups and downs is to be granted, its existence cannot be grounded on the internal properties of an Idea, as might be allowed within realism. An ontological proof of God's existence will either not be admitted at all or it will be validated through the support of other proofs based on effects, i.e., drawn from substances or from attributes of substances, not from Ideas.[6]

Since substantial predication is correlated with accidental predication, the highest ontological principle, 'Everything is substance or belongs to substance', admits of a binary basis. Two classes of systems will be generated according to whether the correlation is established, as it must be, between elementary substantial predication and composite accidental predication, or between composite substantial predication and elementary accidental predication. For the first correlation a nominalist ontology will be shown to arise, the nominalism of things. The second correlation will furnish the basis of the conceptualist ontology. To respect the traditional ordering of the dogmatic systems, we shall first proceed to analyse the second correlation. However, a paradox must first be dispelled. It does indeed seem paradoxical that nominalism should correspond to a correlation in which, substantial predication being elementary, the universals are adequately instantiated by the individuals, whereas, when the universals are inadequately instantiated by the individuals, as happens when predication is composite, it is rather conceptualism that is obtained. For conceptualism grants some reality to the universals, according to our terminology, in contradistinction to nominalism.

The paradox vanishes as soon as we remind ourselves of what definition by abstraction is. In Peano's terms things are said to have a common abstract property if and only if an equivalence relation holds between them. Straight lines have the same direction if and only if they are parallel. Therefore, when a universal is adequately instantiated by individuals, as is the case with elementary substantial predication, the form which expresses the universal may be eliminated in favour of the equivalence relation between the particulars. We are thus not committed to the positing of the class or of the property. Those individuals exist alone which are equivalent *modulo* a relation of exact similarity. But suppose that, according to composite substantial predication, universals are inadequately instantiated by the individuals. At time t there exist Socrates, Callias, Timon, such-and-such horses, animals, natural things and artifacts. At a later time t' some of the individuals, and eventually all, will have disappeared and given way to new individuals like Mr Smith and Mr Jones. When we say that Socrates and Smith are men, we cannot imagine that the universal 'man' is in them as were their sittings and walkings. Otherwise being a man would inhere in Socrates and Smith, who would no longer get their being from being men and would therefore cease to be substances. This is why being a man is said of Socrates and Smith, without being in them. But for Socrates and Smith to have the relation of equivalence which defines them as men, the defining properties of the class must not have been altered between t and t'. This means that instances of man, dispersed in space and time, belong to their equivalence class without regard for their different spatio-temporal localizations. But this clause amounts to attributing to the species itself regarded as a 'secondary' substance the permanence which, when added to self-sufficiency, characterizes the 'primary' substances. In a Darwinian species, which merely brings together the variations of its individuals within a statistical whole, there are no longer any substances characterized by an immutable quiddity; the stability of forms gives way along with the distinction between substance and accident, specific definition and individual variation. On the contrary, if we maintain this distinction, as we do with the chosen basis, something more than Peano's definition is required. Since the universals are not adequately instantiated, the equivalence classes can no longer be merged with the individuals. The permanence of the forms deserves a special ontological foundation.

We may now consider that highest principle of conceptualism, 'Everything is substance or is in substance.' Individual substances are granted ontological priority. However, for sensible individuals to rank among substances, they must be 'informed' by actualizing their defining timeless universals. As a consequence of the inadequacy of this actualization, substances, or at least sensible substances, are composed of matter and form, though neither matter nor form has separate existence. Matter as subject is for a time animated by something eternal and quasi-substantial, which survives its ephemeral individuals. Sensible substances, as substances, need for their identification the authority of universals which constitute their essence. However, being sensible, they need accidents which inhere in the substance, according to elementary accidental predication.

Here is the ultimate foundation of change and motion. Individuals are restless because matter is never completely informed. In other terms, there is in every sensible substance a privation with respect to the form which this substance actualizes, and which it is potentially only. Between pure form or immutable actuality and pure matter or indeterminate potential, motion is the act of potential *qua* potential. The final cause is thus Nature's last word, uniting form, matter and privation.

The terms traditionally chosen to label this ontology are unfortunate but deeply entrenched. When universals are said to be in the things, *universalia in re*, we run the risk of understanding this in the sense of an accidental inherence. On the other side, conceptualism today suggests a connection with a subjective activity of our knowledge or of our will. Now, the species is precisely not in the individual: to qualify its permanent although inseparable existence, it would be more appropriate to say that the universals are with the things, *cum re*. Likewise, the species has a kind of reality that may be known, but certainly not produced by an abstractive operation: cosmic motion and life have nothing to do with the play of our representations.

I have borrowed the main features of conceptualism from Aristotle. Leibniz proposes a conceptualist system much closer to realism. He conceives the ultimate substances as indestructible, simple, spaceless, timeless. Moreover, in this extreme version, universals completely determine the individuals. But though a singular essence contains in its formula the whole phenomenal development of a monad, this formula, as far as it is subjected only to the principle of non-contradiction, remains a mere possible. For such a possible to become a real and complete individual substance, it has to be precipitated into the world of compossibles, which is ruled by the principle of the best. As among the infinite set of curves of a fixed length only the circle encloses a maximal area, among the set of possible worlds there exists – in the mathematical sense of the word – only one world which realizes a maximum of perfection or of being. Only the individuals belonging to the elected world are capable of activity and spontaneity. The tendency, which already haunts the inorganic world and makes the difference between abstract motion and *vis viva*, puts into life the machinery of a complete individual notion or idea, precisely because it subordinates all its disparate parts to a dynamical and synergistic principle: in other words, to a finality. The inadequacy of the individuals, which is here responsible for according a pseudo-substantiality to the universals, is no longer their falling short of timeless ideas but their abstractedness with respect to the system of their compossibles, that is, with respect to the principle of the best which makes them substances or elements of reality.

A new class of systems is obtained when elementary substantial predication is correlated with composite accidental predication. The highest corresponding principle bestows existence on substance or on modifications which result either from the aggregation of substances or from the division of substance. The same substances or perhaps the same substance eternally and actually constitute the world. The changes that the world undergoes or produces must then be grounded in the actual substantial reality through accidental aggregations or modal partitions which are and are known in the substances or in the substance. Now, accidents or modes do not express an inadequacy within the substance itself with respect to an alleged matter as potency. The causal chain which is needed in order to explain the actual determination of the aggregates of the substances or of the infinite or finite modes of the substance therefore obeys a strict necessity. Any other modality is *a priori* excluded and the imperfections that it would express concern the imaginative prejudices or ignorance of our inadequate knowledge, not things themselves. The highest principle of this present ontology requires not only that everything should be substance or in substance, but that what is substance or is in substance should be actual. The concepts of final cause and of hylemorphic dualism find no place here.

There are two consequences for the class of corresponding philosophical systems: mathematization and mechanism. Inasmuch as space is considered as an attribute of substance, all the benefits of geometrical analysis immediately apply. A clear and distinct, i.e., actual idea suits matter deprived of its former host of obscure tendencies. The systems of this class will then be amenable to a mathematical interpretation.[7] In the same way, motion, no longer subjected to final causes, is amenable to mechanical analysis. Dynamics no longer contains elements intractable to a purely mechanist interpretation.[8]

In the pluralist version of this ontology given by the older Atomists such as Leucippus and Democritus, the atoms fully and eternally actualize forms.[9] According to the definition by abstraction, such forms do not retain any existence beyond the existence of the same atoms eternally present in the universe. As to the meetings and aggregations of atoms that occur in order to produce visible bodies, they do not introduce any extra-existences into the world, since they only result from transitory atomic compositions.[10] The same remark applies to the unique substance of Spinoza and to its infinite as well as finite modes. As existence is completely and adequately captured by the individuals or by the all-encompassing individual, a thorough nominalism follows.

Universals are posterior to the things: *universalia post rem*. As the analysis of the next class of systems will show, it is important to emphasize that the concept of thing (*res*) has an essential occurrence in this statement. Then and only then do things indeed become eternal substances and eventually give way to a pantheistic God or to a panentheistic Nature. No analysis is therefore permitted to dissolve them into transient or finite things, according to the probable wish of most contemporary nominalists. In order to prevent confusions which could blur the whole classification, it is convenient to label the present ontology a *nominalism of things*.

The last among the dogmatic series, circumstantial predication, does not require substantial subjects; adverbs suffice. Universals are instantiated by events and events have an equalitarian ontological claim. Like citizens in democratic states, they are born with equal rights and develop very unequal powers, but no structural bondage limits their free competition. What they are is nothing but how they are, and their expansion is neither confined nor supported by the constraints of a more fundamental stuff. Therefore there is no correlation between a nature or essence and its accidents.[11] For a new class of philosophical systems to be built upon such a single basis, events must be chosen as the highest category. The highest principle states that everything which is is an event, whether the whole of the world or its parts. This is – with respect to universals – the minimal ontology among the dogmatic classes of systems since the only universals we require for distinguishing events are individualized by transitory determinations which exhaust their being and which are all parts of events. No permanence of universals has to be entertained. Therefore an extreme nominalism follows. If the universals may be said to be posterior to the things, it is only on the condition that the word *things* is given a Pickwickian meaning. In contrast to the nominalism of things, this *nominalism of events* agrees with contemporary tastes, as if it were natural and recommended by common sense. But this is an illusion. Despite their pervasive presence, events have properties of their own which are counter-intuitive. In particular – as the Stoic Posidonius remarked[12] – they may be superposed like the crests and the troughs of two waves in phase and raise physical quantities whose addition is equal to zero. Russell and others have shown the logical complexities and the distortions imposed on ordinary grammar that are involved when apparent substances must be explained away in terms of events. From the point of view of common sense, the nominalism of events enjoys no particular advantage within a philosophical classification. Witness the paradoxes of Stoic philosophy, one of the most perfect representatives of this class. The cosmic flow of Heraclitus finds its clearest expression in systems which give walking as an example of 'substance'[13] and conceive the world as Zeus' breath and each minutest part of the world as a particular vibration of this breath, more or less intense according to the phase of its vibrating with the other parts.

The dogmatic classes of systems have paid no regard to the speaker's subjectivity. The second part of the classification, which includes the systems of examination, will admit as its bases the elementary sentences belonging to the subjective series. Judgments of method and judgments of appearance belong to this series. They will be shown to correspond respectively to intuitionism and scepticism.

Judgments of method refer the existence of the object to the way in which it is known by the speaker. Thus every ontological posit is associated with a characteristic method of knowledge, without which it would make no sense. Let us call the possibility of referring the object to its appropriate method of knowledge the possibility of experience in general. The possibility of experience will become the unique highest category of an ontology, when, as highest principle, we admit that the existence of any object is contingent on the possibility of the experience by which it is given. Intuitionism is the ontology which is expressed by this principle.

From the intuitionist point of view, the whole dogmatic series of classes of systems that assume objective existence independently of any activity of the knower offers just so many illusions: a philosophical illusion being raised when the role of the subject is juggled away behind the veil of an object provided with an alleged autonomy. As soon as a philosopher abandons reflection and the possibility of experience, he gives in to illusions, which each intuitionist system describes in reference to the method it acknowledges as its standard. There are a number of different mechanisms of illusion involving different faculties of the mind: expectations over and above sensible representations; assertions made by a prejudiced and precipitated will, overreaching the passively received ideas of our finite understanding; the speculations of a reason overstepping the limits set by sensible intuition on the constructions of objects by the understanding. In all cases, however, illusions depend on the same excess of our infinite aspirations over our bounded power and on the same blind trust in the operations of logic conceived of as an organon of philosophy instead of being confined to the role of its canon. Doubt is to be recommended every time the object of knowledge does not meet the adequate procedures of construction.

The systems of this class differ according to the nature and the extension of the possibility of experience. Behind the question of whether the ultimate criterion of knowledge is empirical or rational hide the more involved decisions about what theoretical constructs may be admitted and how they can be justified. Epicurus contents himself with a loose requirement of non-falsification when he affirms the existence of the void with respect to the existence of motion.[14] Descartes's clarity and distinctness impose a more severe restriction on knowledge. But as ideas for him are representations of things, it may and does happen that an idea which clearly and distinctly bypasses all my powers of construction can be present to my mind and through its transcendence shows that what it represents exists. At the same time this particular idea is attributed the power of warranting the existence of the object represented by any idea whatsoever on the sole condition of its being clear and distinct. Such forms of intuitionism are thus compatible with strong theories like atomism or the geometrization of physics. Even when the possibility of the object of experience itself, instead of being merely posterior to the possibility of experience, is made identical with that possibility in conformity with the highest principle of transcendental idealism, the objectivity and universality of knowledge may still require theoretical constructs, though of more modest dimensions. The limitations that the structure of sensible intuition imposes on the categories of the understanding make possible a hierarchy of sciences which include the Newtonian world, though space and time lose their rank of *sensoria Dei* to become forms of our intuition. What such diverse realizations of intuitionism have in common is their assignment of limits to knowledge; their identification of objectivity with the boundaries of a subject's compass; and their rejection of all speculations which go beyond these boundaries, such speculations, according to their various pretensions, always aiming at a participation in the decrees of Providence.[15]

There is a close relation between intuitionism and scepticism. Both have recourse to doubt. Both belong to a subjective series. But sceptical doubt is an end in itself, whereas intuitionistic doubt is used as a method for reaching certainty. Within subjectivism, intuitionism and scepticism differ as the nominalism of things and the nominalism of events did within dogmatism. There the question was whether the subject of a dogmatic predication could do without a corresponding substance. Here the question is whether the subjectivity to which the predication is referred can do without an epistemological subject.

At first glance, the correspondence between scepticism and the last elementary sentence within the subjective series seems surprising. Judgments of appearance are certain inasmuch as they do not go beyond appearances. Now, sceptical doubt differs from intuitionistic doubt precisely in its prohibition of any ontologically committed relation, be it a subjective one or not, and is to be compared rather to fiction which neutralizes propositional attitudes to which doubt is relevant. The transition, however, is easily made. From the judgment of appearance, the sceptic retains that its content is only asserted as the object of a propositional attitude. This content is thus provisionally and tentatively given us as a fiction, in so far as fiction is a suspended assertion or rather an assertion where it is agreed that we suspend what the assertion is about. Make fictions the highest category, then. Admit as highest principle that every assertion conceals a fiction. You have defined scepticism: the philosophy of a suspended ontology. Sceptical doubt is very specific in that it leaves nothing behind it. Like rhubarb, it purges the subject from subjectivity.

Ancient scepticism is often divided into two stages. Arcesilaus' universal and systematic suspension of judgment is said to be a mere starting-point for Carneades, who, caring about positive action and knowledge, extended and perhaps from a historical point of view misinterpreted scepticism as probabilism.[16] This amounts to asking if a wise man who has rejected dogmatic or intuitionistic criteria of truth and therefore commits himself to the refusal of any alleged representation of reality is still justified in retaining opinions as mere conjectures for action. Now, it may be accepted by the most radical sceptic that we have personal preferences and that we face sets of uncertain alternatives in life, for preferences have nothing to do with truth and the probabilities we assign to uncertain, alternative events do not claim to represent anything other than subjective judgments reflecting our expectations. It is precisely because the expectations may fail to be confirmed that they enter into a sceptical programme. But from two assumptions, gambles and preferences, a conditional expected utility can be defined which expresses some form of internal consistency in our personal preferences.[17] Imagine a man having to choose between two politicians. The first one promises the moon and stars at the price of a part of the inheritance of his electors. The second one promises not to interfere with this patrimony at the price of leaving things nearly as they are. Is it possible to hesitate as to what the decision of a wise man should be, even if he is ready to admit that his preference is not shared by the majority of his fellow-citizens and that it is very uncertain that politicians can and will keep their promises? A sceptical rationality, seen as a quest for self-consistency, is thus possible. It requires no assent to representations accepted as true, or as probable in the objective sense of the word, and not even a belief that it should be accepted as a standard way of behaving.

To sum things up, we have described a hierarchy of classes of philosophical systems arranged according to the decreasing order of their ontological commitments. The following scheme draws the correlation between this hierarchy and the table of elementary sentences:

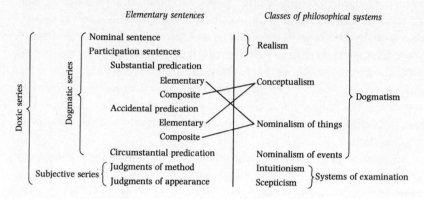

3 FINAL REMARKS

Three final remarks will aim at dissipating confusions which might arise about the relation between the proposed classification and, respectively, the history of philosophy, the philosophy of the history of philosophy and philosophy itself.

1. A classification does not deal with the individual systems of philosophy which constitute the genuine object of the history of philosophy. Nevertheless, particular constraints are imposed by the classification upon the historian. Thematics is to be subordinated to architectonics, so that a thematic coincidence never suffices to establish a systematic agreement.[18] Moreover, since philosophical systems are born and develop in conflict, an important part of their role is to give an image and a refutation of rival systems. When a philosopher 'translates' into his language a system which is distant from his own within the classification, it is not to be expected that either the meanings or the truth-values of the original statements will be preserved. Philosophical radical translations have indeed a strong claim to indeterminacy and the system rather than the term or even the statement is recognized by the classification as the unit amenable to philosophical comparison.[19]

A simple example will serve to show how the classification owing to the internal constraints of a system has or should have an important influence on the history of philosophy, how 'incivile est nisi tota lege inspecta judicare', as Leibniz said, and why any philosophy worthy of the name, not being simply a bag full of bits and pieces but an articulate cluster of parts, becomes intelligible only through the relation of its different philosophical themes to a highest principle. Interpreters wonder why Descartes, despite his full-blown conception of mathematical physics, came only – with the exception of geometrical optics – to build a mecanist, but purely descriptive, system of Nature from which all standard of scientific measurement was simply banished. (Indeed, as it stands by itself his system reads more like a novel than a treatise on physics.) How could a man who had at his disposal the two key concepts of generalized dimension and of matter reduced to extension and thus amenable to the mathematical method have failed so miserably? In order to explain this apparent internal inconsistency, it has been alleged that there is a tension between the realism of three-dimensional physical space and the idealism of many-dimensional geometrical space. But it must be remembered that Descartes never did reject the possibility of interpreting algebraic equations whose degree is ≤ 3 in a realist way. On the other hand, the bodies whose motions are studied in physics can only be measured with a space of three dimensions. The 'explanation' advanced is beside the point. In fact, the reason for his failure to carry out his programme of mathematical physics is to be sought in his over-narrow conception of geometrical functions as exact proportions, i.e., as algebraic curves. All transcendental curves, in so far as they can be developed into infinite series, are beyond the reach of our understanding as the power of clear and distinct ideas: they do not belong to *geometry*.

Descartes's identification of what physicists will call analytic curves – the curves which Nature is supposed to follow in her course – with algebraic curves has a direct effect upon the problem of differential equations with partial derivatives, which was the first problem of mathematical physics to be solved: namely, the problem of vibrating strings. Descartes certainly admits a legitimate usage of mechanical curves 'with a thread or a bent cord' (such as the gardener's ellipse) for constructing algebraic curves such as those met with in the *Dioptrics*. But he immediately adds that we must admit into geometry 'no lines similar to cords, i.e., that become now straight, now curved, because, the proportion which exists between straight and curved lines being not known and even, as I believe, being unable to be known among men, nothing could be concluded that would be exact and assured'.[20] Physics often leads to problems whose solution is impossible in terms of algebraic equations. This is the reason – well recognized by Leibniz – which prevented Cartesian physics from becoming mathematical.

But that is only part of the story! Descartes's letters show him constructing transcendental curves and solving problems of derivation and integration by means of mechanical curves that go beyond the compass of his *Geometry*. It was therefore a philosophical prejudice or, at least, a philosophical decision rather than a technical failure which was responsible for the divorce between Descartes's programme and his accomplishment. It is only when we seek further back to the origin of this decision that the divorce will be explained. Once it has been recognized that Descartes proceeds as an intuitionist, the explanation is at hand. In metaphysics, the linear *series* and the architectonic *nexus* of philosophical truths are relevant first of all only to our science of things. But after the demonstration of God's existence, they entail in turn the existence of the things themselves. These truths are introduced in an order reflecting their increasing distance from the simple subjective certitude which is confined to the clear and distinct idea of my thought. In his last *Meditation*, Descartes reached the consideration of sensation which is clearly and distinctly shown to be irreducible to a clear and distinct idea and to afford the minimum of objective reality which a subjective picture may claim.

His mathematics is not so compactly conceived. The algebraic curves are generated by a gliding set-square which is to his *Geometry* what compass and ruler were to Greek mathematics. Having solved these equations up to the fourth degree, he was confident that the method might be indefinitely extended – an illusion which was to be dashed with Lagrange, Abel and Galois. Furthermore, non-algebraic problems were solved by him to meet specific requirements *ad hoc*, as was usual at that time. But suppose that Descartes had been challenged to fit his own dispersed mathematical discoveries into a more correct and more general programme than his *Geometry*. Without doubt he would have tried firstly to distinguish between the algebraic functions which are solvable by square roots and those which are not, and secondly to classify the non-algebraic functions according to whether they were more and more distant from finite polynomials, because of involving higher and higher orders of infinity, for example. This exactly defines an intuitionistic programme, and it is because, in mathematics as well as in metaphysics, Descartes admits an intuitionistic highest principle that he stuck by such a narrow conception of what an analytic curve was and that consequently he could not construct a mathematical physics. Here is the significance of the system, without which there is no thematic explanation.[21]

2. Secondly, the classification entails no particular philosophy of the history of philosophy. Nevertheless, it does exclude a popular myth which identifies the True with the Totality, a presumably inconsistent concept. On the other hand, the proposed classification rejects as a subjective projection every classification which would order and rank the classes of philosophical systems according to their increasing proximity with respect to a given and assumed point of view.

3. Thirdly, the proposed classification does not answer the question '*Quod philosophiae sectabor iter?*' It is indeed tempting to imagine the choice between the classes of systems and even between the systems themselves on the pattern of the contemporary theory of decision-making or rather on an extremely simplified model of it: the Leibnizian conception of creation. The classes of philosophical systems would correspond to Leibniz's possible worlds. Since each possible world is correlated through its ontological capacity with a determinate degree of perfection, each class of systems would, through the way it satisfies the interests of reason, correspond to a determinate degree of philosophical perfection. As Leibniz's God necessarily chooses the best of these possible worlds, we should then choose the class of systems which offers the greatest philosophical perfection.

This is a misleading analogy. As grounded in the interests of reason, philosophical perfection involves a previous preference with respect to those interests. Is ontological wealth more valuable than security or simplicity? Conflicting interests do not submit to the linear ordering of Leibnizian perfections. In order to assign them their relative weights, we must already have adopted a particular class of philosophical systems. If classical theodicy may be of some help in understanding the classes of philosophical systems in terms of rational decisions, the God of Malebranche is to be preferred to the God of Leibniz. At each more and more demanding hierarchical level of His creation, considered as nature and as grace, He has to compose, to compensate and to adjust the conflicting maxims which He follows in his decrees by honouring the majesty of the worker, the splendour of the work and the simplicity of the way. Supreme rationality results in the abysses of Providence.[22]

Leibniz's linear order of perfections guarantees *a priori* that all possible worlds are mutually comparable with respect to their perfections. On the contrary, possible worlds in Malebranche's sense, which would have obtained had God mixed in a different way His competing maxims, are incomparable among themselves, since no previous objective rule assigns the relative weights of these maxims in His decision. Indeed, we cannot expect to get a principle of decision from a comparison between classes of philosophical systems whose mutual translations are indeterminate.

This indeterminacy is the warrant for the relative independence of philosophy. Certainly, according to the common origin of axiomatics and philosophy, there is a give and take between the positive scientific laws and the corresponding philosophical conceptions of laws. It is not by mere chance that sceptical empiricism is a philosophy of physicians, while nobody was permitted to enter Plato's Academy who was not skilled in geometry. A philosophy that is no longer nourished by science declines and fades into scholasticism. Nevertheless, scientific laws never uniquely determine philosophical concepts. Philosophical systems and *a fortiori* classes of philosophical systems are never directly confronted with scientific laws as with crucial experiments. Consequently, no scientific discovery is by itself able to force a philosophical decision.

Two consequences result from the relative independence of philosophy.

Firstly, philosophical systems and classes of systems are never definitely refuted by scientific actuality. When classical mechanics gained its authority, Leibniz made fun of 'le bonhomme Epicure'. Atomism was then defended only under the respectable form of its classical versions as given by Leucippus and Democritus, according to whom 'every kind of atomic size and every kind of atomic shape exists in nature'.[23] Quantum mechanics produced a revulsion in favour of the *clinamen* and it is indeed hardly imaginable that, before it, an interpreter could have written, and written in praise of Epicurus, that 'atoms are so constituted that variations in atomic lengths occur only on integral multiples of the smallest atomic length'.[24] This shows how scientific discoveries may revive worn-out philosophical concepts and how new theories influence the interpretation of philosophical systems.[25]

The second consequence results from the philosophical concepts' retaining their specificity and their relative autonomy in spite of their sensitiveness to the occasional influence of scientific events. Scientific situations are clear especially for people who contemplate them from outside. It is therefore always or frequently the case that a scientific idea, when inspiring a philosopher, carries along accidental elements, impurities, distortions and overdeterminations that encumber philosophical systems. A critical analysis then ought to separate what genuinely follows from the highest principles of a system or of a class of systems from the consequences that are due to contingent and historical circumstances. In Kant's system, for example, the identity between the possibility of experience and the possibility of the object of experience is interpreted as implying the complete determination of sensible intuitions by the categories of pure reason. This interpretation, which entails over-narrow concepts of pure intuition, categories and principles, is questionable and emendations may be proposed for the *Critique of Pure Reason* as for the *Critique of Practical Reason* that purify the highest transcendental principle from its incidental trappings.[26] Philosophies are thus alive because they may be indefinitely rewritten.

What has been said for positive scientific laws might be extended to scientific theories and, more generally, to all institutions and events produced by human history. A classification which warrants the relative independence of philosophy is bound to maintain the pluralism of the classes of systems in the face of any pressure from the facts. At the same time, because new facts never cease challenging philosophy, old systems are given new life and new systems are expected to arise.

Our choice, of course, can only be one; but the proposed classification tells us neither which is the best choice nor even what it might look like. Still, the ultimate pluralism to which we are led expresses the condition of our finite reason, operating within any of the several classes of philosophical systems. A philosophical decision, if honest, necessarily supposes that the maxim it follows is universally valid. A philosophical classification, if useful, throws light upon our situation in relation to others, by reminding us that it must be recognized that they too have good reasons for choosing according to a maxim which is not ours.

Is such a choice *a priori* confined within the bounds of the proposed classification, and, if it is, in what sense? In other words is, or in what sense is, this classification complete?

The great systems of rationalism and classical philosophy have been organized according to simple ontologies, even if realism generally required the dualism of the ideas and the phenomena, not to speak of the third reality of the soul, or if some version of conceptualism distributed the beings over a continuum of perfections, or if an intuitionistic system in conformity to the subordination of ontology to method first opposed thought and extension to reunite them into a third substance, the compositum of mind and body. All these variations and differences remain compatible with a certain sense of ontological simplicity and unity. On the contrary, it may be asked if contemporary pluralistic pragmatism fits into this scheme, tolerant as it is of different ontologies. A celebrated philosopher, for example, vindicates sets, things and perhaps events as the furniture of his world, regretting in other respects that he is not able to eliminate from the universe the extensional tracks of the ideas. The same philosopher, in morals, grants himself leave to build a more parsimonious construction since the ideas, reduced to sets, work in the theory of science but are idle in the theory of action. Such a system borrows one of its components from realism – but from an impoverished realism –, the other or the others from nominalism. Now, even were its highest principle, 'Being is being a set or a thing', recognized as a necessary and sufficient condition to account for the whole of experience, it would, owing to its eclectic basis, reveal a kind of internal instability. On the one hand the philosopher's own unsuccessful efforts to do without sets have been taken over by the partisans of a meagre and simpler ontology, who constructed calculi and tricks to simulate sets within the bounds of nominalism. On the other hand the extensionalist amputation of realism is criticized and intensions try to find their way back through the sets. These complementary moves at least show the regulative, if not the constitutive, force of the present classification.

There are, however, more serious objections coming from quantum physics which has shaken the whole conception we had of participation sentences. Is there an ultimate distinction between the analysis into things and properties and the analysis into events? Are dogmatic propositions and subjective judgments really separable? How must highest categories and principles be redefined in order to cope with the requirements of microphysics? Those are questions for the future, upon which scientists and philosophers are still working in the dark. There is but one certainty in all this: whatever the issue of this further inquiry may be, future classifications will merge into the present one once they come back to describing our ordinary, macroscopic experience.

NOTES

I PERCEPTUAL ORGANIZATION

1 D. Hume, *Enquiries Concerning the Human Understanding and Concerning the Principles of Morals*, Oxford, Clarendon Press, 1951, 2nd edn, section V, part II, p. 52.
2 Hume, *Enquiries*, section VII, part II, p. 76.
3 The higher level is shown in the logical complexity of the *Definiens*: x causes $y =_{Df} x$ is immediately followed by y. (z) $[z$ is similar to $x \supset (\exists v)$ z is immediately followed by v. v is similar to $y]$.
4 J. Vuillemin, *Physique et métaphysique kantiennes*, Paris, PUF, 1955, pp. 19–25, pp. 334–9.
5 In contradistinction to Kant's transcendental highest principle, Hume's identity between experience and object assigns, in principle, no determinate structure to our experience. Is it then by experience that Hume knew that for example 'there be no such thing as *Chance* in the world' (Hume, *Enquiries*, section VI, p. 59)? On the need to amend Hume in order to build a modern theory of causality, see P. Suppes, *A Probabilistic Theory of Causality*, Amsterdam, North Holland, 1970, pp. 9–10.
6 This is the theme developed by Konrad Lorenz in all his work. See, for example, 'Der Kumpan in der Umwelt des Vogels' (1935), in *Über tierisches und menschliches Verhalten, Gesammelte Abhandlungen*, München, Piper, Bd 1, pp. 139–48.
7 Hume, *Enquiries*, section III, p. 24.
8 Hume, *Enquiries*, section III, p. 24.
9 Hume, *Enquiries*, section III, p. 24, n. 4.
10 The argument says that:

Night contrasts with day $=_{Df}$ Nightfall causes obscurity and obscurity is similar to the negation of day.

Then we have to replace in this definiens the expression 'causes' through its *definiens*.
11 Experiments made on the compound eye of the horseshoe crab show evidence of an additive and distance-dependent inhibition:

This is a device to ... *enhance contrast* at the edges of objects, because if a part of the scene is light and a part is black, then the ommatidia (= the single cells of a compound eye) in the lighted area give impulses that are inhibited by all the other light in the neighbourhood, so it is relatively weak. On the other hand, an ommatidium at the boundary which is given a 'white' impulse is also inhibited by others in the neighbourhood, but there are not as many of them, since some are black; the net signal is therefore stronger.
(R. P. Feynman, R. B. Leighton and M. Sands, *The Feynman Lectures on Physics*, Reading, Mass., Addison-Wesley, vol. 1, 1963, ch. 36 pp. 10–11)

135

The inhibition is much stronger in the first two classes of contiguity ((a) and (b)) than in the third one (c). As frequently happens, what is surprising is the mechanism which physiology discovers behind appearances.

12 P. Bouguer, *Essai sur la gradation optique de la lumière* (1729 and 1760); Vuillemin, *Physique*, pp. 130–1.

13 The second reservation is not to deny the legitimacy of psychophysics. Many criticisms of phenomenologists against psychophysics rely on a confusion. The logarithmic scaling proposed by Weber and Fechner can be looked upon as the first 'major attempt to add nonbasic psychological variables to the existing structure of physical quantities' (David H. Krantz, R. Duncan Luce, Patrick Suppes and Amos Tversky, *Foundations of Measurement*, New York–London, Academic Press, vol. 1, 1971, p. 519). Were we to impose on our statements a phenomenological interpretation, such a statement would subvert the phenomenological method, which requires basic and pure psychological variables. Phenomenology is limited to finite weak orders. We can immediately, that is, without further hypothesis, decide whether one illumination is greater or smaller than the other or indiscernible from it. We cannot count units, because we cannot identify which element of the structure is the sum of two others. An additional feature is necessary for counting units. For example, the set A on which the relation 'to be greater than or equal to' is defined must factorize into a Cartesian product: $A = A_1 \times A_2$ (Krantz *et al.*, *Foundations*, p. 17). This happens with Bouguer's law $E = I/_{r^2}$ (where E, I and r respectively designate the illumination on the surface, the intensity of the source and their distance, the light being supposed to fall normally on the element of the surface). The variables I and r are hypothetical physical quantities, not phenomenological data. In the case of Fechner's law, we argue on the functional logarithmic relation between two Cartesian products $A \times A$ and $B \times B$, where A is the set of the intensities of perceived sensations and B is the set of the corresponding stimuli. Fechner's postulate, which may be questioned, is the phenomenological existence of equal felt differences between pairs of immediate successive intensities. But as soon as this postulate is abandoned for a weaker assumption according to which the equality of differences is indirectly inferred from such-and-such behavioural properties, psychophysics is no longer objectionable. It is like other sciences. Its hypothetical deductive argument does not depend on direct phenomenological appearances, even if its conclusion runs against any pretension of phenomenology to give an undistorted picture of reality.

14 Feynman *et al.*, *The Feynman Lectures*, vol. 1, ch. 35 p. 6 (see also ch. 35 p. 4). The whole theory of the anticipations of perception ('intensive qualities') in Kant's *Critique of Pure Reason* relies on the same method (Vuillemin, *Physique*, pp. 129–46).

15 Some psychologists say there are four apparent colours (blue, yellow, green and red); white then does not 'feel' like blue or red. Analysing these psychological assertions critically, Feynman rightly observes: 'It is clear that we have such feelings, *but it is very difficult to obtain much information about them*' (vol. 1, ch. 36 p. 3).

16 B. Russell, *Principles of Mathematics*, 2nd edn, London, Allen & Unwin, 1937, p. 166. I replaced the word *is* in Russell's text by the expressions in square brackets. In order to justify this change two remarks are necessary.

(1) Russell distinguishes between Peano's *definition* by abstraction and his own *principle* of abstraction. Russell's principle analyses an equivalence relation between two objects *a* and *b* into a relation between these objects and a new 'absolute' entity, *c*: if a straight line *a* is parallel to a straight line *b*, then *a* and *b* have the same direction *c*, or: if an event *a* is simultaneous with an event *b*, then *a* and *b* occur at the same time *c*, or: if a set *a* is equipotent with a set *b*, then *a* and *b* have the same cardinal number *c*. Peano's definition is read the other way round: when two 'concrete' objects *a* and *b* have a common property *c*, this property may be explained away in favour of the corresponding equivalence relation between the objects themselves. At the time that he published the *Principles* (1903), Russell made his option for a Platonic interpretation of mathematics (J. Vuillemin, 'Platonism in Russell's Early Philosophy and the Principle of Abstraction', in *Bertrand Russell: A Collection of Critical Essays*, ed. D.F. Pears, New York, Anchor, 1972, pp. 305–24).

(2) Even once the advantages of a nominalist attitude are recognized for the economy of ontology, Russell's principle keeps its phenomenological appeal, which is the reason for the change which I introduced into Russell's text.

17 On the vision of the frog, see Feynman *et al.*, *The Feynman Lectures*, vol. i, ch. 36 p. 11.

18 H. Helmholtz, *Handbuch der physiologischen Optik*, 3te Aufl., Hamburg and Leipzig, Voss, Bd. i, 1909, pp 139–48; *Die Tatsachen der Wahrnehmung*, Schriften zur Erkenntnistheorie, hrsg. von Hertz und Schlick, Berlin, Springer, 1921, p. 126.

19 Helmholtz, *Handbuch*, Bd ii, 1911, p. 101; *Die Tatsachen*, pp. 113–14. This difference is surprising (Feynman *et al.*, *The Feynman Lectures*, vol. i, ch. 36 p. 2).

20 J. Nicod, (*La Géométrie dans le Monde sensible*, ière éd., Paris, Alcan, 1923, préface de Russell) is still worth reading. His first geometrical structure is built upon two relations given on musical impressions: a total precedence and a global (perfect) similarity (pp. 81–92). On the essential limitations of such 'geometries', see J. Vuillemin, *La Logique et le monde sensible*, Paris, Flammarion, 1971, pp. 226–47.

21 Our assertion is limited to signals of position. Methods of cross-modality matching are known (Krantz *et al.*, *Foundations*, vol. i, p. 164), and establish an equivalence relation on the set of all pairs

$$\bigcup_{i=1}^{m} A_i \times A_i$$

where $A_1, \ldots, A_m$ are different sensory continua (different modalities, or submodalities).

22 For instance, Aristotle, who speaks of κοινὴ αἴσθησις (πρῶτον αἰσθητικόν) in Περὶ αἰσθήσεως καὶ αἰσθητῶν (450ª10–12).

23 On Poincaré's construction, see J. Vuillemin, 'La Théorie kantienne de l'espace à la lumière des groupes de transformations', *The Monist*, vol. li, no. 3, July 1967; 'Poincaré's Philosophy of Space', *Synthese*, Dordrecht, Reidel, 1972, 161–79; 'Conventionalisme géométrique', *Archives de l'Institut des Sciences Théoriques*, Bruxelles, OFFILIB, n° 20, 65–105. The group of rigid motions is undetermined since it corresponds to any constant value of space's curvature – a zero as well as a positive or a negative value. Consequently Poincaré concluded that since the three

geometries made rigid motions possible and since rigid motions were the only requirement imposed by experience, our choice between these geometries was only conventional and ruled by considerations of convenience. The application of group–theory to the analysis of geometric invariants originates with Helmholtz.

24 The 'dynamic' character of *Gestalt* qualities of position often depends intuitively on the relation between several correlated laws of order. In the simple illusion of Müller-Lyer, two equal segments of a straight line, A and B, appear as unequal when closed by oppositely oriented extremities:

```
A   ←—————————→
B   >—————————<
```

The form A is closed, while the form B is open, which means that by bringing together respectively the two extremities of A and B we should obtain a lozenge or a St Andrew's cross. This dynamical character implies two observable consequences: (1) the illusion is stronger the shorter the equal segments and the greater their extremities, (2) an intermediary form, C, will be produced by adding the extremities of A and B:

```
C   ×—————————×
```

25 K. Lorenz, 'Psychologie und Stammesgeschichte', in *Gesammelte Abhandlungen*, München, Piper, 1967, Bd II, pp. 230–31.

26 K. Lorenz, 'Gestaltwahrnehmung als Quelle wissenschaftlicher Erkenntnis', in *Gesammelte Abhandlungen*, Bd II, pp. 274–6 (with on p. 276 a short description of the physiological mechanisms imagined by von Holst); on an 'existentialist' interpretation of these illusions, see M. Merleau-Ponty, *Phénoménologie de la Perception*, Paris, NRF, 1945, pp. 320–4.

27 H. Poincaré, *La Science et l'Hypothèse* (1902), réédition avec préface de J. Vuillemin, Paris, Flammarion, 1968, p. 104.

28 *Ibid.*, p. 101.

29 See how Poincaré builds the unity of space and its three-dimensionality in *La Valeur de la Science* (1905), réédition avec préface de J. Vuillemin, Paris, Flammarion, 1970, pp. 77–100 (and pp. 10–12).

30 H. Weyl, *Philosophy of Mathematics and Natural Science*, Princeton University Press, 1949, pp. 78–84.

31 Poincaré, *La Science*, p. 83.

32 I. Kant, *Kritik der reinen Vernunft*, B 39.

33 This is a fundamental difference in distinguishing species in a genus, in a group or a family or an order of animals (Lorenz, 'Psychologie', pp. 224–31; 'Gestaltwahrnehmung', p. 268). But while the intuitiveness of the centrally represented space seems to be implied by the authors, it is nowhere clearly analysed.

34 Aristotle, *Physics*, IV, 4, 212b20.

35 Weyl, *Philosophy of Mathematics*, p. 75.

36 'It is impossible to imagine absolute space. When I want to imagine objects and myself simultaneously in motion in absolute space, I indeed imagine myself motionless and looking at the motion around me of several objects and of a man who is external to me, but whom I call by convention myself' (Poincaré, *La Valeur*, p. 67).

37 Aristotle denies the subjectivity of space, because places have different potencies: '"down" is not any chance direction but where what has weight and what is made of earth are carried' (*Physics*, IV, 1, 209a20). The theory of natural places goes beyond phenomenology, at least beyond the phenomenology of images. (For phenomenological descriptions of spatiality at the level of representations, see Merleau-Ponty, *Phénoménologie*, pp. 162ff.)

The fundamental difference between Kant and Leibniz with respect to the principle of indiscernibles consists not in the principle itself, but in its application to identifying things. Imagine a possible world made of an infinite and homegeneous draughtboard where, in both directions, the same patterns periodically recur. Once a determinate pattern has been chosen, every same pattern has asymmetrical relations of position with respect to it and the principle thus applies. But try to individuate a determinate pattern describing its qualities without using its position as given by a demonstrative! On this point, see P. Strawson, *Individuals*, London, Methuen, 1959, p. 119 and 125.

38 Malebranche, though his occasionalism makes him deny any communication of forces, does approvingly quote Aristotle who asserts it. Only, Malebranche says, this assertion uncritically follows the testimony of the senses. On this point, see A. Michotte, *La Perception de la causalité*, Louvain, Publ. de l'Univ. de Louvain, 2ème éd., 1954, p. 6. According to Michotte (p. 19), we have a direct and living experience of the generation of motion.

39 On these 'forms', see *ibid.*, pp. 83f., pp. 160f. A certain invariant of similarity between the spatio-temporal and kinematical properties of the two motions is required for an impression of causality to arise (p. 123). If one of the objects is motionless, no impression of causality is obtained. (There is no impression of attraction nor of repulsion. The case is the same when the squares move in very different directions (p. 216).)

40 *Ibid.*, pp. 214–15. 'By ampliation of motion is understood the birth, the extension of the pre-existing motion of an object to another object, of which this motion realizes the displacement' (p. 139). On the question whether such *Gestalt* formations are innate or learned, see M.D. Vernon, 'Perception and Perceptual Learning', in E.A. Lunzer and J.F. Morris, eds., *Development in Learning Behaviour: Learning: Education* (II), *Development in Human Learning*, London, Staple Press, 1968, ch. 1, p. 45.

41 Descartes, *Principes*, I, 62, in *Oeuvres de Descartes*, éd. Charles Adam et Paul Tannery, Paris, Cerf, 1897–1913, vol. IX, 2, p. 53.

42 Descartes, *Méditations*, in *Oeuvres*, vol. IX, p. 26.

43 According to Michotte, *La Perception*, 'the causal impression is foreign to the pure qualitative modifications and is in fact limited to combinations of motions or of changes of form'. What Michotte demonstrates is that *as Gestalt*, causality is reduced to mechanical or, more exactly, to kinematical causality. Other types of causality are possible, but belong to the domain of concept.

44 Lorenz, 'Gestaltwahrnehmung', p. 277:

> The mechanism of perception first surveys the whole field of vision and notices the wavelengths reflected by it on the average. If the wavelength of a given spectral colour dominates, the mechanism supposes that the source of light emits it more than it does wavelengths of other colours. The mechanism thus operates on the supposition, not completely sure, but merely probable, that the objects which fill the field of vision reflect

on the average equally well all spectral colours, without favouring any one of them. If this hypothesis is false, i.e., if among the things seen there is one which dominates in such a way that, for example, red should be preferentially reflected, the mechanism of constancy then jumps to the conclusion that the colour of the lighting contains much red and it thus attributed (correctly from the standpoint of formal logic, but necessarily mistakenly since the premises are wrong) to the visual things which reflect little red the property of reflecting red less than other wavelengths, i.e., of preferentially reflecting the latter.

On the mechanism itself, see *ibid.*, pp. 273–4.

45 W. Jaeger, *The Theology of the Early Greek Philosophers*, (1947), London, Oxford University Press, 1967, p. 239. This is the question answered by Anaxagoras' theory of *homoeomeries*.

46 The word *simulating* is at least ambiguous and may denote either the simple subjective, passive synthesis obeying the peripheral control of trials and errors, or the subjective and active regulation of this synthesis. It is highly debatable then whether two nervous activities belong or not to the same level of behaviour integration (J. Vuillemin, 'Concetto', *Enciclopedia*, III: *Citta-Cosmologie*, Torino, Einaudi, 1978, p. 714). The framework of these chapters has prevented the author from taking such distinctions, however important, into consideration.

47 Lorenz, 'Der Kumpan', pp. 205 and 267.

48 *Ibid.*, pp. 122, 161.

49 K. Lorenz, 'Induktive und teleologische Psychologie' (1942), *Ges. Abh.*, I, p. 398; 'Der Kumpan', p. 151.

50 Lorenz, 'Der Kumpan'.

51 On the specificity of imprint, see Lorenz, 'Der Kumpan', pp. 171, 270, and 'Ueber die Bildung des Instinktbegriffes', *Gesammelte Abhandlungen*, Bd I, p. 330. This conception is criticized by W.H. Thorpe, *Learning and Instincts in Animals*, London, Methuen, 1962.

52 Let us suppose that two or several instincts must tend to the same thing as object, if their biological meaning is to be preserved. Then there are two possibilities for assuring the unity of the treatment of the object. One of them consists in grasping the object objectively as a thing that appears in the environment of the subject as the same in all functional circles. The second possibility ... lies in the ... connection of the different instincts established *from the object's* point of view, without this object being experienced as a unity in the environment of the subject.

(Lorenz, 'Der Kumpan', p. 120; also p. 269)

53 For baby's smiling response and other reflexes, see R. Ahrens, 'Beitrag zur Entwicklung des Physiognomie – und Mimikerkennens', *Zeit. f. Exper. u. Angew. Psychol. II*, 1954, 412 and 599; R. Spitz and K. Wolf, 'The Smiling Response', *Genet. Psychol. Monogr.*, XXXIV, 1946, 57–125; E.A. Salzen, 'Visual Stimuli Eliciting a Smiling Response in the Human Infant', *J. Genet. Psychol.*, CII, 1963, 51–4.

54 Lorenz, 'Der Kumpan', p. 122.

55 Many psychologists and anthropologists insist that neoteny is an important feature of human evolution. Some go so far as to deny authentic human instincts because of the open and learning-like character of human drives.

56 According to J. Bowlby, 'The Nature of the Child's tie to his Mother', *Internat. J. Psycho.-Anal.*, XXXIX, 1958, 350–73, the relation of the child to its mother depends

on five instinctual forms of behaviour: smiling, crying, sucking, clinging, and following. At first independent, these forms of behaviour are integrated at the proper time into a unique mother-pattern. The social relation, therefore, is not a secondary product which results from the satisfaction of other more primitive drives. It is primary, inasmuch as the child is given, at birth, a behavioural pattern, whose biological meaning is the acquisition and requirement of a narrow connection with the mother. The child learns that one and the same person is the object of all these behavioural elements which in the beginning are separated.

57 Vernon, 'Perception and Perceptual Learning', ch. 1, pp. 27-8.

58 H. Keller, *The Story of my Life*, New York, Doubleday; E. Cassirer, *Philosophie der symbolischen Formen*, III, Phänomenologie der Erkenntnis, 2nd edn, Oxford, Cassirer, 1954, p. 131.

59 In the beginning of the *Handbuch der psychophysiologischen Optik*, 3te Aufl., Hamburg and Leipzig, Voss, Bd III, 1910, p. 10.

60 J. Vuillemin, 'Poincaré's Philosophy of Space', in *Space, Time and Geometry*, ed. P. Suppes, Dordrecht, Reidel, 1973, pp. 159-77. Objections could be drawn from linguistics which seem to show that the expression of time presupposes the expression of space, since it almost always uses it. But nothing obliges us to admit that linguistic priority entails perceptual priority.

61   A typical example of this process is the colour perception function which distributes the wavelength continuum in an altogether arbitrary manner along the discontinuous colour spectrum. This is done for the sole purpose of organizing this information in such a way that the colours neutralize one another in pairs and form a colour 'white' expressly created to this end: a qualitatively homogeneous form of experience to which there corresponds absolutely nothing simple in reality. Since there is no actually existent wavelength contrary to the middle of the spectrum which could be used to extinguish it by compensation, the complementary colour 'purple' is also invented, like the 'white', and buckles the colour series in a ring. The performance serving the conservation of the species in this whole process is simply that of compensating for the aleatory differences in the colour of the lighting and thus extracting, as contraries, the reflective properties adhering to objects. . . It makes no difference to the bee . . . to know what reality is lurking behind the phenomenon 'light'. What a bee must be able to do is to recognize a flower by the reflective properties constantly adhering to it, independently of the fact that it is exposed to a bluer or redder light. (Lorenz, 'Gestaltwahrnehmung', pp. 260-1)

62 F. de Saussure, *Cours de linguistique générale*, édition critique préparée par Tullio de Mauro, Paris, Payot, 1978, pp. 306-12. Even the grammatical proceedings which once passed for the best expression of a collective mentality result from morphological, as well as from phonological, accidents. For instance, it has been said that the 'constructed state' of the *determined* placed before the *determining* was characteristic of the Semitic mentality ('The constructed and emphatic state of the substantives, the numerous forms of the verb, the absence of determined tenses, the expression of mood by means altogether foreign to Indo-European languages, the absence of procedures for forming compound words and verbs preceded by prepositions, are important characteristics which obviously assign the Semitic grammar a place apart', E. Renan, *Histoire générale des langues sémitiques*, *Oeuvres complètes*, éd. Psichari, Paris, Calmann-Lévy, 1958, t. VIII, p. 546). But Old French used an analogous construction, clearly induced by chance (Saussure, *Cours*, p. 311). Renan, from his speculations about language-form (understood in

Humboldt's sense), drew conclusions bringing together linguistics and biology. According to Geoffroy Saint-Hilaire, an organ highly developed in one species continuously diminishes in neighbouring species, in such a way that in the end it will disappear from the scale of beings (law of type degradation). Similarly, 'grammatical procedures have their linguistic area and from one language to another they disappear by successive degradations' (Renan, *Histoire*, p. 515). Since all these characters are associated to constitute an organism, they constitute a form, and a language can never go beyond its predetermined form:

> Hand, the instrument of prehension for man, becomes foot for quadrupeds, wing for chiroptera, while for birds and fish, it is much diminished or is defigured; arm, on the contrary, becomes wing for birds, fin for fish. With respect to languages, functions often undergo equally bizarre inversions. Thus the *forms* of a Semitic verb, which seem analogous to the *voices* of the verb in Greek and Latin, do not really correspond to them, but are indeed procedures that in Indo-European languages have only secondary importance, as iterative, factitive, etc. The expression of tenses and moods, which is so explicit in Aryan languages, is made only indirectly in Semitic languages – made by way of two aorists and by the final endings of the second aorist, (Renan, *Histoire*, pp. 514–15).

An important distinction must be drawn between the concept of form which is used by Humboldt and the concept of form which is used by Saussure. Humboldt's form is still a Lamarckian concept: language is supposed to be an organism, its different parts obey functions subordinated to a same *Weltanschauung*, its evolution is confined within a general and improving law of adaptation to circumstances. Saussure's form is a Darwinian concept: the structure of language is synchronically defined, and diachronic evolution results from the casual selection of innovations eventually organized by the constant, but always casual, pressure of the circumstances. The first conception entails a strong radical thesis of untranslatability between languages expressing different world-views, a thesis completely foreign to the second conception.

63 B. Berlin and P. Kay, *Basic Color Terms: Their Universality and Evolution*, Los Angeles, University of California Press, 1969, make improper use of arguments which from the presence of so-called basic colour terms conclude to their previous basic nature in a given language as well as of arguments which from the absence of such terms conclude to the actual absence of the corresponding basic concepts (see S. Tornay, ed., *Voir et nommer les couleurs*, Laboratoire d'Ethnologie et de Sociologie comparative de Nanterre, 1978).

64 De Saussure, *Cours*, p. 155.

65 Mauro's note (n. 227), *ibid.*, pp. 463–4. On the relations between Saussure and Cassirer's culturalism, see *ibid.*, p. 379.

66 See n. 16.

2 LANGUAGE AND THE SENSIBLE WORLD

1 E. Benveniste, *Problèmes de linguistique générale*, Paris, Gallimard, 1966, vol. 1, p. 223: 'The sign has always and only a generic and conceptual value. Therefore it does not admit of any particular or occasional signified; everything which is individual is excluded; situations, circumstances are to be taken as irrelevant'.

2 F. de Saussure, *Cours de linguistique générale*, édition critique préparée par Tullio de Mauro, Paris, Payot, 1978, pp. 99–100.

3 On the distinction between monemes and words, see A. Martinet, *Eléments de linguistique générale*, Paris, A. Colin, 3ème éd., 1963, p. 99 (Remember Voltaire, challenged by someone to find a sentence shorter than 'Eo rus' ('I go to the country'), and answering 'I!' ('Go!'): L. Wittgenstein, *Tractatus logico-philosophicus*, 4.032.) On the utility of 'words' and even on their necessity, see Benveniste, *Problèmes*, vol. I, p. 123.

4 The psychology of thought has shown that verbal thought, as opposed to perceptual thought, does not use 'images' in the sense of individual instantiations of the concepts.

5 De Saussure, *Cours*, p. 169. The word *form* is not used here in the sense of Humboldt or Cassirer, for whom language is supposed to express a collective soul. It means only that a sign of a given language is primarily defined not through its association with the external or psychical objects it designates, but through the conceptual system of paradigmatic and syntagmatic substitutions, differences and oppositions which it admits in relation to the other signs.

6 De Saussure, *Cours*, p. 182.

7 This new dimension of analysis would be insufficiently characterized if it were described as syntagmatic or reckoned as belonging to what Saussure calls language's axis of actual 'successivities', in contrast to its axis of 'simultaneities'. There are indeed many syntagmatic determinations in this sense – such as word composition – which still depend on the code of language and do not require for their existence the concurrence of the words within the unit of a sentence. Here is the real point at which Saussure's analysis is defective. His opposition between language and speech has generally conduced to relegating from the realm of language in that of speech, considered as the sum of the individual performances of a speaker, the referential determinations that words receive as sentence constituents.

The meaning, through which the reference of the words is delimited, lies in the system of oppositions (*Cours*, p. 107), that is, in the pure relations these signs have with the other signs. Now, these relations are relevant to two possible orders. When they occur inside a sentence's linear chain and are given *in praesentia*, they are called syntagms. They are called paradigms when only one of their terms appears in the actual chain, its correlate being called forth *in absentia* by a memory association (*Cours*, pp. 170–5). While syntagmatic relations have but few terms by definition, the number of the terms in the case of lexical associations may become indefinite, although it is strictly limited with respect to morphology. A language proceeds to classify its elements in the same way a naturalist does when analysing the body of an animal into its parts or organs, comparable to syntagms, while each of them is associated with its homologous paradigms in the other species.

But this function is still proper to the code of language. Syntax as resulting from using the signs in effective sentences depicting the world is something else. To illustrate this point let us consider creation by analogy, the linguistic creation *par excellence* for de Saussure, and let us then try to apply the procedure to the creation of sentences. In Latin, in consequence of a phonetic change, instead of saying *honōs: honōsem*, people said *honōs: honōrem*. A resemblance then arises between *ōrātōrem* and *honōrem* because of the formal identity of the terminal part of the words: *ōrem*. The flexion scheme *ōrātōrem: ōrātor* had already been fixed. Analogy would then be brought to bear. The x such that *ōrātōrem: ōrātor = honōrem: x* was sought. It yielded $x = honor$ (*Cours*, p. 222). Or, in German, *Gast*: *Gäste*, *Balg*: *Bälge* being phonetically given, analogy created *Kranz*: *Kränze* (formerly *Kranze*). *Tag*: *Tage*, *Salz*: *Salze*, and so on were nevertheless retained.

Now imagine that we constructed with this same elementary, matter-conditioned model a syntactical theory of sentences. When we recognize that 'Peter runs' and 'Agnes bleats' have the same sentence form, no material identity is supposed. What we need is an abstract analogy between the functional role of the elements. The role which 'Peter' plays has to the role which 'runs' plays the same relation as the role of 'Agnes' has to the role of 'bleats'. Thus the question is how to extract f and g such that

$$\frac{f(a)}{g(b)} = \frac{f(c)}{g(d)}$$

where only a, b, c, d are materially given.

Here a recursive theory seems to be unavoidable and the structural framework of de Saussure's linguistic theory is definitely too narrow. De Saussure contrasts speech with language and he entrusts sentences to speech. But the move does not live up to its promise. Although it is false to say that 'rule governed creativity' has been ignored by de Saussure, nevertheless speech (in contrast to language) seems to retain a mere rule-changing creativity, as is shown by the role played by analogy. (See, however, the note in *Cours*, pp. 400–1.)

Two final remarks may be ventured to mitigate or at least to specify the criticism of de Saussure.

First, there are the puzzling rules of selection which are needed to stop the recursive machine. Encroachments which are not felt as illicit also run against the abstract rules of transformation. Ernest Renan already noticed that when the Psalmist (12:1–13:1) asked: 'Until when, Jehovah, wilt Thou forget me forever', he used two different grammatical constructions which encroached upon one another:

(1) Until when   Jehovah, wilt Thou forget me
(2)   Jehovah, wilt Thou forget me   for ever?
(*Histoire générale des langues sémitiques*, in *Oeuvres complètes*, éd. Psichari, Paris, Calmann-Lévy, 1958, t. VII p. 261; the King James version says: 'How long wilt Thou forget me, O Lord? for ever' adapting the original to English grammar).
Some mechanism of analogy in de Saussure's sense is perhaps at work in this case.

Secondly, two aspects of de Saussure's linguistics need revision. In the first place, he reduced syntax to morphology. In this regard, there is, however, nothing in his fundamental conception to prevent a structural study of syntax. The first person to have rediscovered the internal creative form of language was a student of de Saussure's, Charles Bally (*Précis de stylistique*, Genève, 1905). Just as for Lucien Tesnière (*Eléments de syntaxe structurale*, Paris, Klincksieck, 1952, p. 17, n. 1), he does not fail to remind us of the importance of de Saussure's second principle: the linear character of the signifier (*Cours*, p. 103). As to the second defect of the theory, the ignoring of semantics, it is clear that, by allotting to speech all functions inappropriate to language and structure, de Saussure confounded semantics with pragmatics. This confusion, which was common not only among linguists but also among logicians (see, for instance, B. Russell when he was writing the *Principles of Mathematics*, or R. Carnap at the time of the *Logical Syntax of Language*) has been one of the main obstacles to be removed by those who criticized psychologism. Is this the right place to recall in vindication of de Saussure the proverb 'Solatium miseris, socios habuisse malorum'?

8 To use Wittgenstein's expression (*Tractatus*, 4.0311).

9 Benveniste, *Problèmes*, vol. I, p. 129. The illusion that several complete, i.e., asserted sentences may be parts of the same asserted sentence is removed as soon as it is remarked that (1) subordinated 'sentences' are not asserted sentences, (2) neither are coordinated sentences, since, for instance, when we assert that $p = q$, we only assert that p and q have the same truth-value without precisely stating what this truth-value is.

10 A. Arnauld and P. Nicole, *La Logique ou l'art de penser*, (1662), éd. par P. Clair et F. Gribal, Paris, PUF, 1965. (The expressions 'runs', 'is-wise', 'is-a-man' will be equally considered as predicates or verbs in the atomic sentences that are formed when they are appended to the singular term 'Socrates'.)

11 B. Russell, 'On Denoting', (1905) in *Logic and Knowledge, Essays 1901–1950*, ed. R.C. Marsh, London, Allen & Unwin, 1956, pp. 41–56.

12 W.V.O. Quine, *Word and Object*, Cambridge, Mass., MIT Press, 1960, p. 161.

13 On the systematic as well as many-levelled character of Aristotle's table of categories – in contrast to the alleged 'rhapsodic' enumeration to which it has been reduced by Kant and by the general opinion of philosophers – cf. J. Vuillemin, *De la logique à la théologie, cinq études sur Aristote*, Paris, Flammarion, 1967, ch. 2, § 4, pp. 75–84.

14 Henceforth I shall use the word *deduction* in the context 'deduction of categories' in Kant's sense. Kant borrowed the word from the jurists, who are said to deduce a concept when they leave the *quaestio facti* to put the *quaestio juris*. A deduction, in the philosophical sense, requires the same move. The linguistic arguments here afforded may be compared to the part of the juridical inquiry which is relevant to the *quaestio facti*. The solution of the *quaestio juris* requires a principle according to which a concept is legitimated.

15 Quine, *Word and Object*, p. 122. Latin would express 'Humility is rare' by an explicit copula, 'humilitas rara est', because it is a mere fact, not an essential or defining property of humility to be rare. Such a sentence clearly does not belong to the class of pure predication. In the same way, in the sentence 'Humanity has more members than donkeyhood', only empirical considerations can decide whether or not as a matter of fact there are more men than donkeys. A little reflection, however, shows that these forms are not atomic. They abbreviate in a perverse and not truly natural way molecular sentences built with names of particulars in the argument positions. Since most universals that correspond to natural kinds are not determined with respect to the number of their instances, and since speaking of these instances entails speaking about spatio-temporal things, every time we use 'more' or 'rare', that is, verbal universals as apparently applied to nominal universals, we have to paraphrase our speech into a sentence which is about nominal particulars. 'Humble persons are rare' and 'There are more men than donkeys' must therefore be considered as the genuine sentences of natural language. The required paraphrase may not be near at hand. Prima facie predicates such as 'more' or 'rare' admit only classes as arguments. Indirect

devices must then be introduced to effect the paraphrase. For instance, we may use Goodman's calculus of individuals. 'There are more men than donkeys' will then be translated into:

$(x)\ \{(y)\ (My\ V\ Dy\ .\supset Pt\ y,\ x)\} \supset Hx$'

which will read as: 'Everything of which every man and every monkey is a part has more men than donkeys as parts' (N. Goodman, *The Structure of Appearance*, Indianapolis, Bobbs-Merrill, 1951, p. 42). A new one-place predicate thus must be introduced: Hx, which means 'x has more men than donkeys as parts'.

Those who will protest against this translation because it seems artificial are reminded that, with regard to counting, natural language (as a rule) refers its operations not to sets or classes (which, being universals, are not in space and time) but to collective individuals or groups which may be found here and there and which are further characterized by their collective behaviour (E. Cassirer, *Philosophie der symbolischen Formen*, Oxford, Cassirer, 1954, vol. I, pp. 190–5, 202). Note the difficulties that mathematicians encountered before they had clearly distinguished between sets and individual collections. Now, if the collections of natural languages are individuals, the individuals of the 'calculus of individuals' are the right paraphrases for them. Indeed, when we compare the numbers of men and donkeys, we imagine more or less large companies and herds to which the predicate 'x has more men than donkeys as parts' significantly applies.

As to the sentence 'Humble persons are rare', the paraphrase gives rise to an additional difficulty, for the predicate 'is rare' hides a two-term relation. Here a first approximation would read:

$(x)\ \{(y)\ (My\ V\ (M.H)y\ .\supset Pt\ y,\ x\} \supset Jx$'

where $(M.H)y$ means that y is a man and y is humble and Jx means that x has, as parts, more men than humble men. A difficulty arises because humble men are rare only if we could in the previous formula replace Jx by Kx, where Kx means that x has, as parts, many more men than humble men. Another solution would consist in writing:

$(x)\ \{(y)\ (M.\sim H)y\ V\ (M.H)y\ .\supset Pt\ y,\ x\} \supset J'x$'

and interpreting $J'x$ as meaning that x has, as parts, more non-humble men than humble men (the occurrence of M being non-essential).

16 See the example given by Lévy-Bruhl and reused by Cassirer (who draws from it conclusions different from ours). The name for *five* means, in the language described by Cassirer, that the hand on which the operation of counting was made is closed, while the name for *six* prescribes leaping from one hand to the other: *Philosophie*, vol. III, p. 399.

17 Quine, *Word and Object*, pp. 119–20.

18 When Osthoff insisted upon the importance of the suppletive formations in Indo-European languages for marking the system of flexion or word-construction (as applied to the cases of nouns, as well as to the tenses of verbs or to the degrees of adjectives), he concluded that the 'grouping' conception which is met with in classical Greek or Latin, where one word, for example, is used to express the several kinds of walking, was preceded by a more individualizing stage, where the

slightest shade of walking was expressed by a different root (H. Osthoff, *Vom Suppletivwesen der indogermanischen Sprachen*, Heidelberg, 1899):

> Just as it is always the objects the nearest in space that man perceives the most distinctly, so the eyes of the soul, of which language is the mirror, grasp all the more clearly and distinctly the objects of the world of representations as these objects are closer to the sensibility and thought of the speaker, as they thus exercise a more intense and vivacious hold on his mind, as they excite the psychical interest of a being – be it an individual or a people. (Quotation in Cassirer, *Philosophie*, vol. 1, p. 265)

This psychological theory of verbal suppletism – inadequate if suppletism has grammatical foundations inasmuch as it combines aspectual and lexical oppositions – is nicely expressed by Osthoff, who quotes the German proverb 'Liebe Kinder haben viele Namen.' The resulting priority of the concrete over the abstract, while fitting an empiricist scheme all too well, was admitted also by thinkers inclined to rationalism, like Cassirer (*Philosophie*, vol. 1, p. 211). Osthoff himself is a good example of this general tendency. He wanted to explain how the Germanic word *Treue* (trust) had, in addition to its moral and ideal sense, a companion root meaning *tree*, as the English word testifies (Gothic *true*) (H. Osthoff, 'Eiche und Treue', *Etymologica Parerga*, 1901). He placed at the beginning of the whole morphological and semantic development the Indo-European word represented by the Greek *drūs* (oak), from which the moral values implied in *Treue* and *truste* would have resulted. According to Osthoff, this is a typical pattern for a concrete designation evolving into a moral notion. 'A social institution would have arisen from a plant symbolism' (Benveniste, *Problèmes*, vol. 1, p. 299).

But Benveniste has shown that there is no name for oak in Indo-European and that the formal basis which must be given the abstract sense of 'being firm, strong, healthy' was subsequently employed to designate the tree and more specifically the oak. 'The name **drū* of the tree has nothing "primitive"; it is a qualification which, once attached to its object, became its designation and happened to be separated from its semantic family; hence the coexistence of two morphemes turned distinct, such as *true* and *tree* in English' (Benveniste, *Problèmes*, vol. 1, p. 301).

19 An unexpressed element may have a real linguistic occurrence, if language is Form, not substance; because a system of oppositions, which exhausts the reality of the words, may contain a 'degree zero'.

20 A. Meillet, *Mémoires de la Société de Linguistique de Paris*, tome XIV, 1907, p. 16.

21 Examples: πάντων μέτρον ἄνθρωπος ('man is the measure of all things' (cited by Tesnière, *Eléments*, p. 156)); *triste lupus stabulis* ('the wolf is an ill thing for stalls'); ἔργον δ' οὐδὲν ὄνειδος, ἀεργίη δέ τ' ὄνειδος ('working is not a disgrace; it is idleness which is a disgrace' (Hesiod, quoted by Benveniste, *Problèmes*, vol. 1, p. 163)). As catalogued by linguists, nominal sentences extend far beyond the class of atomic predicative sentences. In the first place, they contain molecular predicative sentences, where definite descriptions and deep structures are often hidden: 'Omnia praeclara rara'; 'Summum jus summa injuria'; 'Testis unus testis nullus.' In the second place, linguists have not seldom been drawn into confusion between predication and identity. In their lists we therefore find predicative identity statements: 'trois fois quatre douze' ('three times four is twelve', Tesnière, *Eléments*, p. 157); 'tvám Várunah' ('Thou art Varuna', absolute homology put

between Agni who is addressed and Varuna with whom he is identified, Benveniste, *Problèmes*, vol. I, p. 165). Were the confusion removed between *is* and *is(are) identical with*, the nominal sentence would have to express the particular predicate *is(are) identical with* by a noun (identity with).

22 What I have called a participation sentence.

23 Benveniste, *Problèmes*, vol. I, p. 159.

24 *Ibid.*, p. 160

25 *Ibid.*, p. 165.

26 In both cases, although there is a logical and real chasm between nominal sentence and substantial predication, one must not be surprised to see linguists and languages themselves rather confused about them. A few alleged examples of nominal sentences have proper names as subjects (see n. 21 or ὁ γὰρ [Ζεύς] κάρτιστος ἁπάντων ('For Zeus is the master of all things' (Homer, quoted by Benveniste, *Problèmes*, vol. I, p. 164)). In many examples, a common name occurs in such a way as to denote individuals: τό δὲ νέαις ἀλόχοις ἔχθιστον ἀμπλάκιον ('This crime is the most frightful for young brides' (Pindar, quoted in *ibid.*, p. 162)); οὔπω πάντες ὅμοιοι ἄνδρες ἐν πολέμῳ ('Not all men are similar in war' (Homer, quoted in *ibid.*, p. 164)). In all these examples, the confusion seems to be not with substantial but with accidental predication. But qualitative degrees of qualities and circumstantial relative comparisons have here a merely apparent occurrence. His superlative power defines Zeus ('id quo nihil maius cogitari potest'), as its superlative frightfulness defines this crime. As to the inequality of men in war, it is indeed a defining property of ἄνδρες (= *Männer*) as opposed to ἄνθρωποι (= *Menschen*).

27 The substantive verb *is* is existential, not only classificatory. 'When an historian wants to say that "Crete is an island", he will not write ἡ Κρήτη νῆσος; ἡ Κρήτη νῆσός ἐστι is suitable' (Benveniste, *Problèmes*, vol. I, p. 164), because the historian is supposed to describe a contingent state of affairs, not to classify things under permanent types.

28 Aspect is probably the most resistant stuff of the verb. See Cassirer, *Philosophie*, vol. I, pp. 182, 220.

29 In French, for example, aorist, imperfect, pluperfect and prospective tenses appear in accidental predication, while the other tenses – present, perfect, simple and compounded future – are excluded (Benveniste, *Problèmes*, vol. I, p. 245).

30 D. Wiggins, *Sameness and Substance*, Oxford, Blackwell, 1980, § 4.

31 Cl. Lévi-Strauss, *La Pensée sauvage*, Paris, Plon, 1962.

32 A. Gardiner, *The Theory of Proper Names: A Controversial Essay*, London, 2nd edn, 1954.

33 On the difference between the primary and the secondary occurrence of expressions, see Russell, 'On Denoting', p. 52; on proper names in general, see J. Vuillemin, 'Qu'est-ce qu'un nom propre?', in *Fundamenta Scientiae*, Oxford, Pergamon Press, 1980, vol. I, pp. 261–74. 'The Moon' and 'the Sun' may be regarded as proper names just as Saturn, Mercury and Venus are.

34 Aristotle, *Categories*, 2. 1a20 – 1b9.

35 On related but different views about the relations between modality, proper names and predication, see S. Kripke, *Naming and Necessity*, Oxford, Blackwell, 1980, and D. Wiggins, *Sameness and Substance*.

36 Cassirer, *Philosophie*, vol. I, p. 142.
37 Were we to admit universals such as 'socratizes', the distinction would be blurred between universals whose instantiations exclude and universals whose instantiations involve corresponding realizations. Now when instantiations involve corresponding realizations, there is no possible lawlike determination of their extension. These determinations cannot then be issued except by decrees and conventions, a procedure characteristic of proper names that, in an ordinary lexicon, cannot be transferred to the domain of universals.
38 Contrary to common prejudice, the 'third' person, which was eventually admitted into substantial or accidental sentences as a pronoun standing for a substance, is not a person at all. Two different correlations must be distinguished. The correlation of personality opposes the non-person (he, she), namely, the absent, to the person (I, you) which occurs only in dialogue and therefore in circumstantial predication. Within circumstantial predication, the correlation of speakership opposes the partners exchanging the roles of speaker and hearer, for there is always only one possible speaker addressing a plurality of hearers (Benveniste, *Problèmes*, vol. I, pp. 225–36; Tesnière, *Eléments*, p. 117. I prefer the expression 'correlation of speakership' to Benveniste's expression 'correlation of subjectivity', because a speaker is certainly a subject in the dialogue, but his designation as speaker is given in a completely objective way).
39 Tesnière, *Eléments*, p. 238.
40 When a verb's action is referred to substances, remarkably enough it gives way to adverbial constructions only when it is understood in such a way that the verbal universal which was considered as a one-place predicate becomes interpreted as a two-place relation. One place has to be filled by a substance term, the other by a term standing for what would be an instance of the universal. Thus understood, action verbs have one foot in accidental inherence, the other in adverbial location. This interpretation has been urged by D. Davidson, ('The Logical Form of Action Sentences', in N. Rescher, ed., *The Logic of Decision and Action*, University of Pittsburg Press, 1967); by the same author in 'On Event and Event Descriptions', in J. Margolis, ed., *Fact and Existence*, Proceedings of the University of Western Ontario Philosophy Colloquium, 1966, pp. 64–74; and in his 'Events as Particulars', *Nous*, vol. IV, 1970, 25–32; see also D. Wiggins, *A Note on Action Sentences and Adverbs*. Davidson's theory may be considered as a formally extensional interpretation of Aristotle's *inesse*. Its extensionality is the reason why the attribution of an action to a person is treated as the localization of an event.
41 This is the case for Benveniste, *Problèmes*, vol. I, pp. 263–268.
42 Many linguists seem to agree in recognizing three fundamental moods: indicative, interrogative and imperative. These are said to express three fundamental types of behaviour: informing, asking and commanding. This classification, however, fails to cover two further cases: (1) the optative, and in particular, the subjunctive, that grammarians count as moods because of the corresponding classes of formal expressions and (2) the performative, which, although it obeys some formal constraints, is determined by the social context. I do not see how to reconcile Benveniste's discussion of the three fundamental moods (*Problèmes*, vol. I, p. 130) with his own discovery of the performative (*Problèmes*, vol. I, pp. 265 and 267–76). The present deduction deals only with subjectivity within assertion.

43 Aristotle, *Posterior Analytics*, 1.4.73b32 – 74a3.
44 On this question, see J. Vuillemin, *Mathématiques et métaphysique chez Descartes*, Paris, PUF, 1960, pp. 42–51; J. Vuillemin, 'Définition et raison, le paradigme des mathématiques grecques', *Proceedings of the Third International Humanistic Symposium at Athens and Pelion* (1975), Athens, 1977, pp. 275–78.
45 Benveniste, *Problèmes*, vol. 1, p. 61.
46 Significantly, logicians have interpreted propositional attitudes in two different ways.

Some logicians (Frege, Carnap) analyse a sentence such as 'John believes that Jesus is God' into the two-place predicate 'believes' and the two arguments 'John' and the proposition 'that Jesus is God'. Whereas in ordinary or extensional contexts the occurrence of sentences is truth-functional, propositional attitudes introduce non-extensional contexts in which we have to use propositions – i.e., meanings or intentions – or intensional structures of sentences. Because propositions delimit the system of the logical consequences of a sentence (or the part of the system which is, for example, accessible to the knowledge of the subject), the interpreting of 'John believes that Jesus is God' by referring John's belief to the proposition that Jesus is God essentially amounts to *understanding* John's belief.

By contrast, a second group of logicians (Wittgenstein, Russell, Quine) disclaim all propositions in order to make belief an indirect way of relating John to the sentence 'Jesus is God' mentioned in *suppositio materialis* or to transform it into a psychological or behavioural property of John. John's state of belief is then identified with a distribution of stimulations that results from a causal chain of events and has in principle nothing to do with Jesus's being God. This second interpretation aims at *explaining* John's belief and may completely disregard any understanding of it.

Both interpretations have well-known difficulties. Meanings resist identification, because synonymy is independently definable only if the selection and grouping which articulate the speaker's sensible world are already present as such in perceptual organization. (This reason is weaker than Quine's (*From a Logical Point of View*, Cambridge, Mass., Harvard University Press, 2nd edn, 1961, p. 61). Quine accepts Cassirer's and Whorf's culturalism according to which there is no perceptual organization independent of language.) As for identifying a belief without resorting to its object by scrutinizing a form of behaviour, such an identification would require a knowledge that is more than human.

In any case, neither interpretation is tied to the speaker's subjectivity – not, at least, as long as what is being described and asserted is *someone else's* propositional attitude. Such descriptions belong, by right, to the dogmatic series, and they include every propositional attitude that is not expressed in the present time and in the first person – for instance, not only John's belief but also my own previous beliefs. Those dogmatic assertions, however, have something peculiar about them. What decides their interpretation is the current content of the beliefs of the group. When I say: 'Neville Chamberlain believed that gentlemen's agreements could be entered into with Hitler', I turn my hearer's attention to understanding Chamberlain's attitude. Even if I consider Chamberlain as a weak and naive politician, my statement is at least prima facie about the object of his belief. On the contrary, when I say: 'Neville Chamberlain believed in Father Christmas', 'Father Christmas' has no essential occurrence in my statement, so that I may substitute for it 'Santa Claus' or 'everyone' *salva significatione*. In other words, my sentence then amounts only to saying that Chamberlain believed all manner of things. Thus my hearer is warned to give heed to a behaviour that has no relation to Father Christmas. I want him to explain, not to understand. Now, experience shows that many propositional-attitude sentences leave us hesitating between understanding and explaining, and laughter may be provoked by making use of such situations.

47 The confusion between the correlation of subjectivity and the correlation of speakership spoils Russell's theory about objectivity and expression. Unfortunately, his justified insistence on distinguishing expression from indication is interpreted in a psychological way. He starts from so-called 'object-words', i.e., from circumstantial predication restricted to the present and to the first person, 'where the fact indicated is a state of myself and is the very state that I express'. This starting-point blurs expressing a psychological state ('I am hot') and performing a linguistic act ('I see a red patch'). For linguistic analysis, however, expressing a psychological state is as dogmatic as any circumstantial predication. By putting the sentences 'I am hot' and 'I see a red patch' on the same level, Russell (B. Russell, *An Inquiry into Meaning and Truth*, London, Allen & Unwin, 1976, p. 206) wanted to define the 'significance' of propositions by reference to the speaker's state. When the indication of a fact coincides with the expression of this state, empirical evidence is complete, and no falsehood is possible. At the same time, we cannot expect that our fellow-men are hot when we are or that they see the red patch as we see it. Communication, in the full sense of the word, grows out of the distinction between indication and expression.

There is an ambiguity in Russell's conception of expression. When I say 'I am hot', I express two different states: firstly, a psycho-physiological one, and secondly, a mood as the implicit state that is bound to the linguistic act of assertion. Russell (*ibid.*, p. 203) considers 'I see a red patch' to be logically simpler than 'I see a red flower' or 'There is a red flower', because in the second case I expect others to see the object, while presumably in the first case I weaken these expectations so as to restrict my assertion to my own impressions. But how can expressing a state weaken the indication of a fact? 'I see a red patch' answers an implicit question: how do you know that there is a red patch? Stating that I see a red patch amounts to stating my grounds for asserting that there is a red patch. Therefore, expressing my seeing has a relation to asserting which expressing my being hot does not have. We must therefore distinguish two kinds of expression in a sentence. A particular sentence may express the psycho-physiological state of the speaker. (It expresses it very often by describing it.) However, this expression has nothing to do with the linguistic correlation of subjectivity. The latter kind of expression bears on the way we express the mood of assertion which is generally left implicit, as happens in the dogmatic series.

48 Benveniste, *Problèmes*, vol. I, p. 264. The phrase 'I have the feeling that. .' is itself ambiguous and may be employed to express, as well as to describe, my propositional attitude. The French phrase 'Je sens que le temps va changer' is more definitely used to express something.

49 Cassirer, *Philosophie*, vol. I, p. 225:

> The essence of the I consists in being a subject, while in thought or speech every concept of the actually thinking subject becomes an object. This opposition can only be mediated and solved by the fact that the same relation that we have previously observed inside nominal and verbal expression repeats itself at a higher level. Also in the circle of pronominal expressions an acute designation of the I can only be found if it opposes itself to the designation of its objectification on the one hand, but on the other hand goes through this objectification (*durch sie hindurchgeht*).

50 Benveniste, *Problèmes*, vol. I, p. 265.

51 J.L. Austin, *How to Do Things With Words*, Oxford, Clarendon Press, 1962.

52 Self-pledging explains why, in judgments of appearance, its expression is sometimes changed or even omitted, as also happens with genuine performatives. The president of a session is licensed to say 'I declare that the session is open' or 'The session is open.' The expression of the reflexive predication may vary in the same way. In given circumstances the sentences 'I doubt that the sky is blue' and 'Is the sky blue?' are synonymous.

The importance of self-pledging pragmatics cannot be overstated. There are languages admitting several theoretical moods called 'dubitative' and 'quotative' by the grammarians according to whether the reported state of affairs is dubious or only known through another's testimony. A proper suffix, when added to the predicate, may allow us to decide how the subject is acquainted with what he is speaking about. Is he, for example, acquainted with it by seeing or hearing? Or does he know it only by description? Is it something from a dream or from the waking state (Cassirer, *Philosophie*, vol. I, pp. 221–2)? Imagine, then, a language where every nuance that is meant by our lexically determined predicates of propositional attitudes was expressed morphologically. Assume that the concerned morphemes are distributed over a system S of oppositions. Then every predicate could be regarded as resulting from the addition of an ordinary predicate plus a morpheme of S, this morpheme of S belonging to the degree zero if the predicate belongs to the dogmatic series. Suppose, for example, that the morpheme a means that a state of affairs is believed (in the sense of 'conjectured according to sensible signs'). Then the predicate contained in the sentence 'It will rain' (= is an instance of raining) and the predicate 'is believed to be an instance of raining' will be respectively expressed by the forms '$\emptyset f(x)$' and '$af(x)$'. A difficulty that we already met with in connection with verbs of action arises when we want to identify the author of the propositional attitude. In such a case we must split the predicate into a two-term relation '$af(x, y)$', where the variable x ranges over the set of instances of rain, while the variable y ranges over the set of men. In such an analysis it makes no difference whether y is replaced by 'John' or by 'I'; and therefore such an analysis is insensitive to the contrast between describing an operation and expressing an attitude. Everything is in the self-pledging; and self-pledging itself, if it is attached to the first person and to the present tense, develops its consequences from the staging of a propositional attitude. That is why the sentence 'I believe it will rain' may be shortened into the sentence 'it might well rain', although it is impossible to omit 'I' in the circumstantial predication 'I know you.'

53 E. Husserl, *Ideen zu einer reinen Phänomenologie und phänomenologischen Philosophie*, 1913, quoted from the third edition (Niemeyer, Halle, 1928), pp. 225–6.

54 *Ibid.*, p. 226.
55 *Ibid.*, p. 232.
56 *Ibid.*, p. 227.
57 This is Sartre's interpretation both in *L'Imaginaire* and in *L'Etre et le néant*.
58 Montaigne, *Essais*, livre II, ch. 12. The text is immediately followed by the celebrated motto 'Que sais-je?' The comparison with rhubarb is drawn from Diogenes Laertius, IX.76c.
59 Two French scholars have recently revived mythology: G. Dumézil in the field of Indo-European, Cl. Lévi-Strauss in the field of general mythology. According to Dumézil, Indo-European myths refer to the structural division of Indo-European society into three classes. According to Lévi-Strauss, the deep reference of myth is not reality itself as represented by the doxic series, but the human mind's architecture, that is, the universal, anonymous, and objective structure of oppositions and transformations which make all thought and language possible. The deep or hidden sense made manifest by myths is said to be nothing but a second-level code, by which the rules of the first-order, doxic code are fixed.

3 AXIOMATICS, ONTOLOGIES, PHILOSOPHIES

1 L. Lévy-Bruhl, *Les Carnets de Lucien Lévy-Bruhl*, préface de M. Leenhardt, Paris, PUF, 1949, p. 48:

> I would no longer place the two fundamental characteristics of the primitive mentality, the prelogical and the mystical, at practically the same level, as I did in 'Mental Functions in Inferior Societies'. It now appears that there is but one fundamental characteristic, that is, the mystical; the other, the prelogical one, which I thought it necessary to put on a par with the first as no less essential, now seems to be but another aspect, or rather a consequence of the first.

Ernst Cassirer, quoting only from Lévy-Bruhl's *La Mentalité primitive*, Paris, Alcan, 1922, was not acquainted with this amendment.
2 E. Cassirer, *Philosophie der symbolischen Formen*, Oxford, Cassirer, 1954, vol. III, p. v.
3 Cassirer, *Philosophie*, vol. III, p. vi.
4 'Dingzeichen'/'Ordnungszeichen', *Philosophie*, vol. III, p. 389.
5 *Philosophie*, vol. II, p. 51. J.E. Smith, 'Some Comments on Cassirer's Interpretation of Religion', *Revue Internationale de Philosophie*, cx, 28ème année, 1974, fasc. 4, has rightly insisted on what distinguished myth and religion in Cassirer's sense from the standpoint of a spectator or observer (p. 477): 'the crucial point for the understanding of religion as a generic trait of human existence is the marking off of what is unusual, wonderful, terrifying, marvelous in its bearing on the meaning of human life from the neutral territory of the familiar and mundane' (p. 478). This aspect of the question is kept in the background, if not neglected, in Claude Lévi-Strauss's picture of myth.
6 Cl. Lévi-Strauss, *La Pensée sauvage*, Paris, Plon, 1962, p. 22.
7 Lévi-Strauss, *La Pensée sauvage*, p. 14.
8 Such is the methodological theme developed by Claude Lévi-Strauss in his *Mythologiques*, Paris, Plon, vol. I, 1964, vol. II, 1966, vol. III, 1968, and vol. IV, 1971.

9 Lévi-Strauss, *La Pensée sauvage*, p. 25.

10 Lévi-Strauss, *La Pensée sauvage*, *passim*.

11 Lévi-Strauss, *La Pensée sauvage*, pp. 26–33. Ernst Cassirer (*Philosophie*, vol. III, p. 393) compares language to a river which does not find its bed already made but has to dig it again and again at every place and consequently always produces new forms. Claude Lévi-Strauss's comparison inspired the biologist François Jacob in his account of how evolution works ('Evolution and Tinkering', in *Science*, 1977, no. 196, pp. 1161–6).

12 External resemblance, analogy, contiguity, contrariety, sameness in relative position and even psychoanalytic identification are called into play.

13 Lévi-Strauss, *La Pensée sauvage*.

14 Cassirer, *Philosophie*, vol. II, p. 50; Lévi-Strauss, *La Pensée sauvage*, pp. 48ff.

15 Cassirer, *Philosophie*, vol. III, p. 393: 'For the same content a same sign must always be chosen.'

16 Cassirer, *Philosophie*: 'Every new concept which is introduced into scientific thought is *a priori* related to the whole of this thought, to the whole of possible concept formations.'

17 τὴν περὶ αὐτὴν φιλοσοφίαν.

18 ἄνωθεν (Lit. 'by regressing').

19 νοερῶς.

20 Quoted by I. Thomas, *Euclid's Elements*, vol. I, pp. 149 and 147.

21 'A unit is that in virtue of which each of the things that exist (ἕκαστον τῶν ὄντων) is called one' (*Euclid's Elements*, book VII).

22 'A point is that which has no part' (*Euclid's Elements*, book I).

23 'A line is length without breadth' (*Euclid's Elements*, book I).

24 'A number that is divisible into two equal parts' (*Euclid's Elements*, p. 67).

25 'Rectilinear figures are those contained by straight lines' (*Euclid's Elements*, p. 411).

26 αἰτήματα / κοιναὶ ἔννοιαι.

27 Magnitudes are said to be in the same ratio the first to the second and the third to the fourth, when, if any equimultiples whatever be taken of the first and the third, and any equimultiples whatever of the second and the fourth, the former equimultiples alike exceed, are alike equal to, or alike fall short of the latter equimultiples respectively taken in corresponding order. (Thomas, *Euclid's Elements*, pp. 446–7)

One can express the definition in the following way:

$$\frac{a}{b}=\frac{c}{d}=Df\,(m)\,(n)\,\{m,\,n\,\epsilon\,N\supset(ma\gtreqless nb\supset mc\gtreqless nd)\}.$$

28 J. Vuillemin, 'Définition et raison: Le paradigme des mathématiques grecques', *Proceedings of the Third Int. Humanistic Symposium*, 1977, 273–82.

29 J. Vuillemin, *Mathématiques et métaphysique chez Descartes*, Paris, PUF, 1960, pp. 77–9, 85–8, 148–54; J. Vuillemin, *La Philosophie de l'algèbre*, Paris, PUF, 1962, t. I, pp. 160–73, pp. 540–2.

30 Aristotle, *Metaphysics* Γ, 7.1011b23–1012a28.

31 Diels–Krantz, *Die Fragmente der Vorsokratiker*, 8th edn, Berlin, Weidmann, 1959, vol. II, fr. 3, p. 33 and fr. 6, p. 35. H. Weyl, *Philosophy of Mathematics and Natural Sciences*, New York, Princeton University Press, 1963, p. 41.

32 H. Bergson, *Les Deux Sources de la morale et de la religion*, Paris, Alcan, 1932, 3ème éd., pp. 142-4.
33 Vuillemin, 'Definition et raison'.
34 J. Vuillemin, 'Résumé des cours et travaux', *Annuaire du Collège de France*, 78ème année, 1977-8, 427-42.
35 P. Duhem, *Le Système du monde*, 10 vols., Paris, Hermann, 1913-59, t. I, pp. 303-6.
36 *Almagest* XII.1.
37 According to Cassirer (*Philosophie*, vol. III, p. 390), scientific languages use the 'activity of the sign', in the full sense of the word.
38 W. Jaeger, *The Theology of the Early Greek Philosophers*, Oxford University Press, 1967, p. 28.
39 Jaeger, *Theology*, 1967, p. 19.
40 Plato, *Theaetetus*, 203a – 204a.
41   The theory of magnitudes is treated without any particular consideration of lengths, areas, volumes, durations, etc. The magnitudes of a same kind are characterized by the fact that they can be compared, added, subtracted and that they satisfy Archimedes' axiom. The system is provided with a law of internal composition (addition) and with a law of external composition (multiplication). This last law has as operators the proportions on which Eudoxos defines multiplication.
   (N. Bourbaki, *Eléments d'histoire des mathématiques*, Paris, Hermann, 1960, pp. 157-8)
42 Aristotle, *Metaphysics* Γ, 3.1005b24-5.
43 B 94 (quoted in Jaeger, *Theology*, p. 116).
44 This argument is expressed before Aristotle gives his celebrated list (*Physics*, Z.9.239b5-9). It is then considered again within the list as the third argument (*ibid.*, 239b29-33).
45 Diogenis Laertii *Vitae philosophorum*, Paris, Firmin Didot, 1850, IX.72 (B 4).
46 Aristotle, *Physics*, Z,239b5-9. I use for τὴν φερομένην οἰστόν the translation which Carteron gives for the second occurrence of these words (239b30). Surprisingly, he neglects here the sense of process.
47 B. Russell, *The Principles of Mathematics*, London, Allen & Unwin, 1937, 2nd edn, 1956, § 332, pp. 350-1.
48 K. Döring, *Die Megariker – Kommentierte Sammlung der Testimonien*, Amsterdam, Grüner, 1972, fr. 124 (Sextus Empiricus, PH.III.71), p. 36.
49 Döring, *Die Megariker*, fr. 123 (Sextus Empiricus, M.x.85-101), pp. 35-6.
50 Aristotle, *Physics* Z, 6.237a18-19.
51 Aristotle, *Physics* Z, 6.237a28.
52 Bergson's first work (1899) was a Latin dissertation, 'Quid Aristoteles de loco senserit', in which he elucidated with acumen and sympathy Aristotle's theory of place. Despite all that separates him from Aristotle's analysis of time, his conception of the process of changing which supports his whole theory of intuition is clearly inspired by Aristotle. The following extract, from *Durée et simultanéité* (1924), is one of many passages in which Bergson discussed and rejected Einstein's theory of special relativity. It illustrates, by referring to our subjective experience, what happens in motion in Aristotle's sense:

   Mais si notre science n'atteint ainsi que de l'espace, il est aisé de voir pourquoi la dimension d'espace qui est venue remplacer le temps s'appelle encore du temps. C'est que notre conscience est là. Elle réinsuffle de la durée vivante au temps desséché en espace. Notre pensée, interprétant le temps mathématique, refait en sens inverse le chemin qu'elle a parcouru pour l'obtenir. De la durée intérieure elle avait passé à un certain mouvement indivisé qui y était encore étroitement lié et qui était devenu le mouvement modèle, générateur ou compteur du Temps; de ce qu'il y a de mobilité pure dans ce mouvement, et qui est le trait d'union du mouvement avec la durée, elle a passé à la trajectoire du mouvement, qui est pur espace; divisant la trajectoire en parties égales, elle a passé des points de division de cette trajectoire aux points de division correspondants ou 'simultanés' de la trajectoire de tout autre mouvement: la durée de ce dernier mouvement se trouve ainsi mesurée; on a un nombre déterminé de simultanéités; ce sera la mesure du temps, ce sera désormais le temps lui-même. Mais ce n'est là du temps que parce qu'on peut se reporter à ce qu'on a fait. Des simultanéités qui jalonnent la continuité des mouvements on est toujours prêt à remonter aux mouvements eux-mêmes, et par eux à la durée intérieure qui en est contemporaine, substituant ainsi à une série de simultanéités dans l'instant, que l'on compte mais qui ne sont plus du temps, la simultanéité de flux qui nous ramène à la durée interne, à la durée réelle.

(H. Bergson, *Mélanges*, Paris, PUF, 1972, ch. 3, pp. 113–14, 'Le temps déroulé')
On p. 115, Bergson approvingly quotes A.N. Whitehead, whose concept of an advance of Nature is analogous to Bergson's view about the process of changing.

53 Russell, *Principles*, § 324, p. 345 and § 333, p. 351.

54 Aristotle, *Physics Z*, 9.239b31–2.

55 See, e.g., G. Granger, 'Philosophie et mathématiques leibniziennes', in *Revue de Métaphysique et de Morale*, 1, 1981, 27, with a reference to A. Robinson's non-standard analysis.

56 Aristotle, *Metaphysics* A,5.986a24ff.

57 Aristotle, *Physics Γ*, 2.201b28.

58 Compare with Russell's dictum: 'A logical theory may be tested by its capacity for dealing with puzzles, and it is a wholesome plan, in thinking about logic, to stock the mind with as many puzzles as possible, since these serve much the same purpose as is served by experiments in physical science' ('On denoting', in *Logic and Knowledge*, ed. R.C. Marsh, London, Allen & Unwin, 1956, p. 47).

59 Epictetus, *Dissertationes*, II.29.1–5 (Döring, *Die Megariker*, fr. 131, p. 39).

60 In my book *Nécessité ou contingence? L'Aporie de Diodore et les systèmes philosophiques* (Paris, Editions de Minuit, 1984), I have analysed the Master Argument as a principle organizing Greek philosophy and, more generally, moral philosophy.

61 We are used to characterizing formal axiomatics – in contradistinction to material axiomatics – (1) by the procedure of implicit definitions, and (2) by the meta-mathematical method, in which the demonstrations move from things to signs. Now, the first characterization may go without the second one. This is always the case when philosophy itself proceeds in an axiomatic way and this is the reason why, despite the occurrence of implicit definitions in philosophy, only material axiomatics has been said to be relevant to philosophy (see pp. 101, 104–5 above).

4 A CLASSIFICATION OF PHILOSOPHICAL SYSTEMS

1 This distinction is introduced in order to account for the opposition – fundamental for some philosophical systems – between the analytical order of reasons and the synthetical order of science. Thus, the analysis of the *Metaphysical Meditations* of

Descartes obeys particular constraints which do not bind other works such as his *Principles of Philosophy* (M. Gueroult, *Descartes selon l'ordre des raisons*, Paris, Aubier, 1968).

2 In the Aristotelian system, the categories of substance and of accident would correspond to these highest categories, while the sub-categorization of the accident into nine categories would concern the division of the world into different parts. In the same way, we should have to consider as the highest Kantian category the phenomenon, all the Kantian categories proper being concerned with the business of world division.

3 Consider the three tones of the scale produced by a vibrating string of unit length, namely the fourth, the fifth and the octave, the three corresponding lengths of the vibrating string, the three radii of the spheres to which are attached the Moon, the planets and the fixed stars – the radius of the sphere of the Sun being given as unit length. To all of them correspond the ratios 4:3, 3:2, 2:1 (Aristotle, *Metaphysics* A, 5.985b32–986a3).

4 Aristotle, *Metaphysics* A, 5.986a1–3.

5 Criticizing the Pythagoreans, Aristotle says: 'were the same number common to several beings, these beings, which have the same number form, would be identical. For example, there would be identity between the Sun and the Moon', (Aristotle, *Metaphysics* N, 6.1093a10–13). Aristotle probably means that if the periods of movement of Sun and Moon have the same numbers nothing will prevent the identification of the things themselves (W.D. Ross, *Aristotle's Metaphysics*, A Revised Text with Introduction and Commentary, Oxford, Clarendon Press, 1958, vol. II, p. 496). Physicists yield to the same temptation when, from the fact that phenomena belonging to different parts of physics obey the same differential equation, they draw ontological consequences regarding the 'underlying unity' of Nature (R.P. Feynman, R.B. Leighton and M. Sands, *The Feynman Lectures on Physics*, Reading, Mass., Addison-Wesley, vol. II, 1964, pp. 12–17).

6 As for Spinoza's demonstration of God's existence, it results from the consideration of the *causa sui* which itself follows from the concept of substance (what needs nothing else to exist and to be known) when fully exploited in its extreme consequences. This demonstration is not an ontological proof.

It is true that Leibniz acknowledges the value of the ontological proof reduced to itself. But he discovers a gap in it. A previous demonstration is required that the concept of the *ens perfectissimum* is not contradictory (*Meditationes, Opera philosophica quae extant latina, gallica, germanica, omnia* ed. J.E. Erdmann, Berlin, 1840, 80 a/b; *Die philosophischen Schriften* von G.W. Leibniz, herausgegeben von C.I. Gerhardt, Berlin, 1875–90, vol. IV, 624). Because of his repeated and vain attempts to achieve the proof (*Meditationes* of 1684, *loc. cit.*; Letter to Huyghens, 10 March 1690, *Leibnizens mathematische Schriften*, herausgegeben von C.I. Gerhardt, Berlin, 1849–63, vol. II, 51; Letter to Oldenburg, 28 December 1675, *Sämtliche Schriften und Briefe*, herausgegeben von der Akademie der Wissenschaften der DDR, Dritte Reihe, Bd I, Berlin, Akademie-Verlag, 1976, p. 331), Leibniz must have considered that he did not and perhaps that he could not fill the gap. His own specific proof through the possibles, to which we are thus referred back, belongs typically to the proofs by effects.

7 Descartes's geometrization of extension is relevant to the Spinozist as an attribute

of God. As for the indivisibility of the Democritean atoms, a distinction is required. Democritus is said (68 A 43) to have admitted the existence of very large atoms having the magnitude of stars; but he saved his theory of the indivisibility of atoms by distinguishing the atomic physical indivisibility from the mathematical indefinite divisibility of any geometrical magnitude (Aristotle, *De generatione et corruptione* A, 2.316a10–12).

8 Ancient atomism (but not Epicurean atomism) entails mechanism. Spinoza adopts Huyghens' mechanism as his own.

9 Diels–Kranz, *Die Fragmente der Vorsokratiker*, 8th edn, Weidmann, 1959, vol. II, 68 B 141, B 167, A 57. Proper forms, magnitudes, spatial orientation and relative situation count among these forms (Aristotle, *Metaphysics*, A, 4.985b13–16).

10 The void must be considered as a being not only because it makes motion possible, but also because it is needed for localizing the atoms. A double difficulty arises for atomism. What kind of being is the void? If atoms are in the void, are they not in another thing, contrary to the requirement of the definition of true substances? Whatever the solutions be that atomism may give to these questions, the existence of the void occurring among the conditions of the existence of the atoms themselves, it remains true to say that their meetings and aggregations do not introduce any extra-existence.

11 The Stoic table of categories follows a progress towards more and more precision in individuation; it does not dispose them at different degrees of ontological depth (V. Goldschmidt, *Le Système stoïcien et l'idée du temps*, 4ème éd., Paris, Vrin, 1979, pp. 20–5). Where walking is a substance, there is no question of determining an essence by its accidents.

12 Strabonis *Geographica*, ed. C. Müllerus et P. Dübnerus, Paris, Firmin-Didot, 3 vols., 1853–80, t. I livre 3, ch. 5, para. 8, p. 144; P. Duhem, *Le Système du monde*, 2ème éd., 10 vols., Paris, Hermann, 1974, t. II, pp. 281–2.

13 Seneca, *Ep.*, 113, 23 (*Stoicorum Veterum Fragmenta*, ed. J. von Arnim, 1903–24, vol. II, 836); Goldschmidt, *Le Système*, p. 23.

14 Sextus Empiricus, *C. Dogm.*, 1.2.11.

15 J. Vuillemin, 'Trois philosophes intuitionnistes; Epicure, Descartes, Kant', *Dialectica*, XXXV, nos. 1–2 (1981), 21–41.

16 On this point see for instance Cicero, *Academica Priora*, XXXI.

17 David H. Krantz, R. Duncan Luce, Parick Suppes and Amos Tversky, *Foundations of Measurement*, New York–London, Academic Press, vol. I, 1971, pp. 369ff. For a particularly clear and vigorous expression of contemporary probabilism, see P. Suppes, *Probabilistic Metaphysics*, Oxford, Blackwell, 1984.

18 That a philosopher admits proofs of God's existence is an important theme. More important, however, is the consideration of his methods of proof and even of the order of their presentation. Compare, for instance, St Thomas, who does not accept the ontological argument at its face value and Descartes, who makes it dependent in the *Meditations* as truth of the thing (*veritas rei*) on the proof by effects, as truth of my science (*veritas rationum*); on this see Gueroult, *Descartes*, t. I, pp. 339–46, 357–62). Since all the five Thomist ways are proofs by effects (*Summa theologica*, I, Q.2, Art. 3), and since Descartes, besides the proof of God as efficient cause of the idea of the perfect in my mind, uses a second proof by effects where God, considered in himself as *causa sui*, is posited as the creator of my substance, it is tempting to

NOTES TO PAGES 128–31 | 159

class both philosophers among conceptualists and, as some interpreters did, to minimize the revolution of thought accomplished by a Descartes replaced in the scholastic tradition. However, as soon as we fill in some detail, the confusion vanishes. Thomas starts from sensible certitude, Descartes from methodical doubt. They give different senses to those effects upon which the burden of the proofs lies. For Thomas, they are data of the sensible world as perceived by our sensible knowledge, namely, motions, efficient cause, contingency, grades of perfection in qualities, and final causes. For Descartes, in the first proof by effects, the effect consists in the objective reality of the idea of the perfect. A Thomist would certainly question whether this is a genuine effect. As to the second proof by effects, Descartes starts from my existence as a finite *ego* having the idea of the perfect, and this may be considered as a given effect. But to go from this effect to its cause, Descartes needs *a priori* elements, in particular some positive representation of the cause which by producing us produces in us the idea of the perfect (Gueroult, *Descartes*, vol. I, pp. 265–70). This again is beyond the sensible effects in the Aristotelian or Thomistic sense. Cartesian effects are characteristic of intuitionism, while sensible effects are relevant to conceptualism.

19 The distortion imposed by translation may often give a measure of the distance between systems. It is often symptomatic within a given class. Within intuitionism, Kant tends to forget that the intellectual intuition of the Cartesian *cogito*, though uncontrolled by spatial and temporal conditions, is not for all that a creative power. He therefore misses that limitative bearing which the criterion of clarity and distinction has. Nevertheless, even if the *cogito* lacks the exact kind of substantiality which Kant's criticism would require, it is still a treasury of representative ideas and not at all a pure activity of synthesis, so that, distorted as it is, the opposition between the two conceptions of the 'I think' still remains objectively grounded. But now consider what image Kant gives of realism. In their theoretical use the Kantian ideas receive a regulative legitimation, while, inasmuch as they are constitutively interpreted, they give rise to unavoidable dialectical illusions. But as they are defined according to the norms of intuitionistic criticism by the complete set of the conditions of possible experience, they paradoxically invade every dogmatic system, even conceptualism and nominalism as if the completness of experience amounted to the transcendence of an idea on the pretence that both of them were beyond the possibility of experience. According to this interpretation conceptualism and nominalism bend under the discipline of realism, as is evidenced when all rational theology is said to depend for its validity on the ontological proof. In practical philosophy Kant seems to draw nearer to Plato. Like him, he withdraws morality from the realm of experience. But the cosmic Idea of the Good remains poles apart from the Kantian duty, which is content with translating the Idea of the Good within the bounds of a subjective and sinful consciousness.

20 Descartes, *Oeuvres*, éd. Charles Adam et Paul Tannery, Paris, Cerf, 1897–1913, t. VI, p. 412; *Geometry*, text and translation by D.E. Smith and M.L. Latham, New York, Dover Books, 1954, p. 340 (Moritz Cantor, *Vorlesungen über Geschichte der Mathematik*, Leipzig, Teubner, 1898, pp. 794, 807, and 778).

21 On these questions, see J. Vuillemin, *Mathématiques et métaphysique chez Descartes*, Paris, PUF, 1960, pp. 93–8; *La Philosophie de l'algèbre*, t. I, Paris, PUF, 1962, pp. 5–28.

22 See M. Gueroult, *Malebranche*, t. III: *Les Cinq Abîmes de la Providence*, Paris, Aubier, 1959.

23 G. Vlastos, 'Minimal Parts in Epicurean Atomism', *Isis*, LVI, 1965, 2, no. 184, 139.

24 Vlastos, 'Minimal Parts', 198.

25 The influence may be more creative when a philosopher deliberately builds a system whose concepts are to harmonize with a given scientific theory. This seems to have been the case for the positivism of Auguste Comte. In his *Analytical Theory of Heat*, Fourier had established the heat diffusion equation. According to this equation, the time rate of change of temperature is proportional to the second derivative of temperature's spatial dependence. The equation of gravitation still referred, to use the Schoolmen's terminology, to an obscure quality, namely, to a force mysteriously acting at a distance. In Fourier's equation, no term is directly accountable to a hypothesis for its explanation, since conduction deals only with temperatures, their changes and change of changes in time and space and with experimental coefficients. Newton, who declared that he had 'not been able to discover the cause of [the] properties of gravity from phenomena', refrained from framing hypotheses, i.e., explanations 'not derived from phenomena' (*Mathematical Principles of Natural Philosophy*, book III, General Scholium). However, the cause of gravitation, as deduced from phenomena, remained the crux of the matter. Fourier's heat theory was completely analytical, free from hypotheses and nevertheless leaving no unexplained remainder. It was true and self-contained, whatever the fortune may have been of the kinetical speculations. Comte's positivism is born from generalizing Fourier's model: a radical form of intuitionism became possible, according to which science never speaks of causes and is to be reduced to the analytical complete theory of phenomena (on this see J. Vuillemin, '*Résumé des cours et travaux*', Annuaire du Collège de France, 80ème année, 1979–80, 424–47).

26 J. Vuillemin, 'Kant aujourd'hui', *Actes du Congrès d'Ottawa sur Kant dans les traditions anglo-américaine et continentale tenu du 10 au 14 octobre 1974*, éd. P. Laberge, F. Duchesneau, B.E. Morrisey, Ottawa, The University of Ottawa Press, 1976, pp. 17–35; 'Les Lois de la raison pure et la supposition de leur détermination complète', *200 Jahre Kritik der reinen Vernunft*, ed. W. Marx and J. Kopper, Hildesheim, Gerstenberg, 1981, pp. 363–84.

INDEX

Educational Linguistics/TESOL/ICC
Graduate School of Education
University of Pennsylvania
3700 Walnut Street/Cl
Philadelphia, PA 19104